The Saint Paul & Pacific Railroad

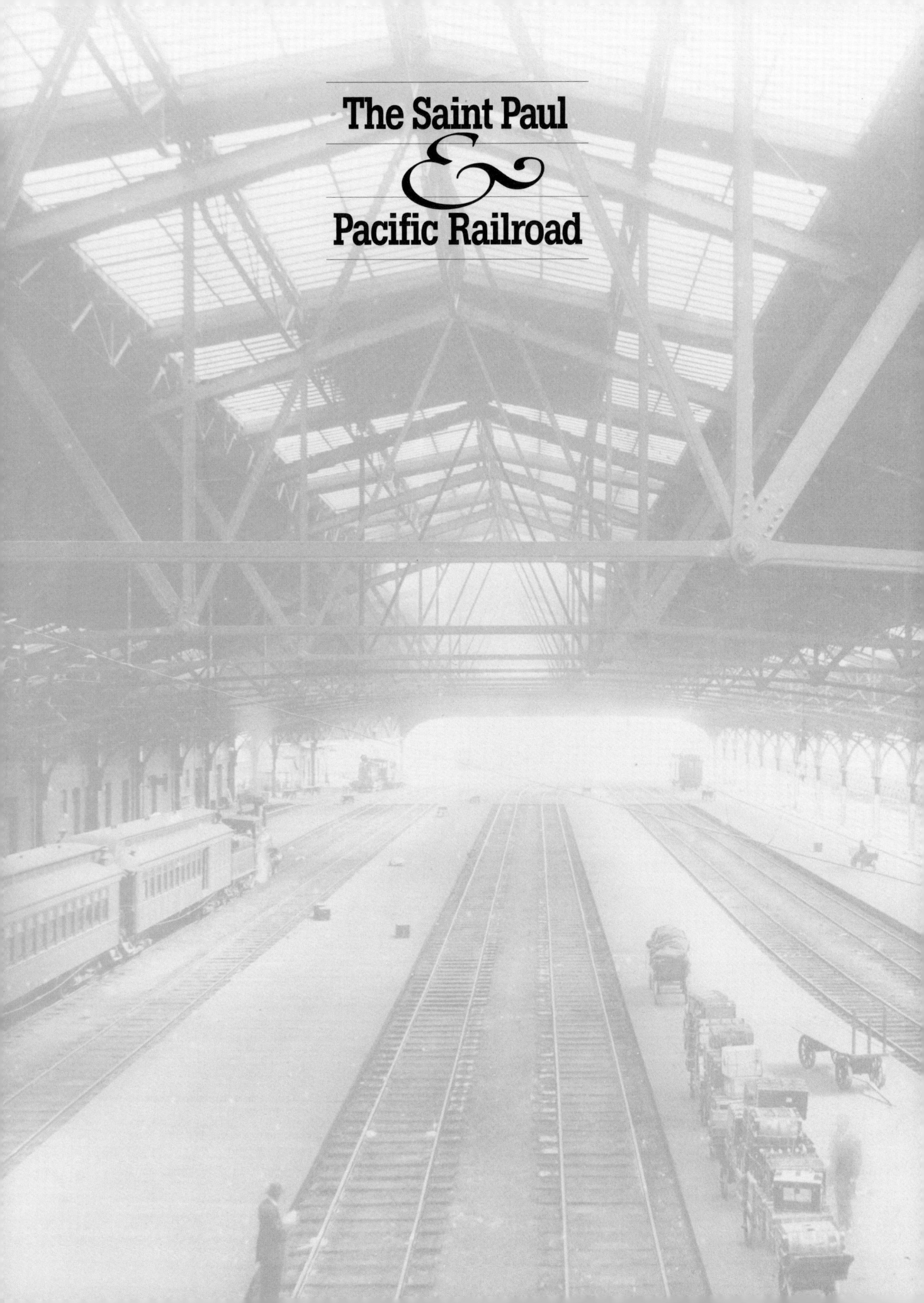

The Saint Paul & Pacific Railroad

An Empire in the Making, 1862–1879

Augustus J. Veenendaal, Jr.

NORTHERN

ILLINOIS

UNIVERSITY

PRESS

1999

Published by the Northern Illinois University Press,
DeKalb, Illinois   60115
Manufactured in the United States
using acid-free paper

Design by Julia Fauci

Three maps have been reprinted by permission of
Harvard Business School Press. From *The Great
Northern Railway: A History,* by Ralph W. Hidy, Muriel
E. Hidy, Roy V. Scott, and Don L. Hofsommer.
Boston, MA 1988, pp. 2, 7, & 35. Copyright © 1988
by the President and Fellows of Harvard College, all
rights reserved.

Credits for uncaptioned illustrations:
p. i—J. R. H. Cruikshank, West Vancouver, B.C.,
Minnesota Historical Society
p. iii—ALCO Historic Photos
p. vi—Railway & Locomotive Historical Society
p. 1—W. H. Illingworth, Minnesota Historical Society

Library of Congress Cataloging-in-Publication Data
Veenendaal, A. J.
The Saint Paul & Pacific Railroad : an empire in the
making, 1862–1879 / A. J. Veenendaal Jr.
        p.   cm.
Includes bibliographical references (p.   ).
ISBN 0-87580-252-4 (hardcover : alk. paper)
1. Chicago, Milwaukee, St. Paul and Pacific Railroad
Company—History—19th century.
I. Title.
HE2791.C67V46   1999
385'.0973—DC21   99-24980
                          CIP

Contents

· ST PAUL · MINNEAPOLIS · & MANITOBA · R'Y ·

Red River Valley Line

RY & LOCO
HIST. SOC.

Red River Valley Line

RY & LOCO
HIST. SOC.

S.P.M.&M.Ry.
Double Track Stone Arch Bridge
Minneapolis, Minn.

· THROUGH THE PARK REGION TO THE NEW NORTHWEST ·

W. S. ALEXANDER, GENERAL TRAFFIC MANAGER.
C. H. WARREN, GENERAL PASSENGER AGENT.
ST. PAUL, MINN.
S. L. WARREN, N. Y. & New Eng. Pass'r Ag't, 495 Broadway, Albany, N. Y.

JAS. J. HILL, PRESIDENT.   A. MANVEL, GENERAL MANAGER.
ST. PAUL, MINN.

A complete in-depth history of the Saint Paul & Pacific Railroad seemed long overdue, despite the recent excellent history of the Great Northern Railway by Ralph and Muriel Hidy. While writing my earlier book *Slow Train to Paradise: How Dutch Investment Helped Build American Railroads,* I became deeply interested in a particular 'Dutch' railroad, the Saint Paul & Pacific, into which millions of Dutch guilders had been sunk. Although I was not at that time able to devote more than one chapter to that early Minnesota line, I never lost it completely out of view. As soon as *Slow Train to Paradise* had been published, I turned my attention again to the Saint Paul & Pacific and to the early development of Minnesota.

A generous grant from the James Jerome Hill Library in St. Paul in 1996 made it possible for me to delve into the treasure trove of the vast holdings of the J. J. Hill Papers. Curator Thomas White and his assistant Eileen McCormack were most helpful in guiding me through the Hill correspondence and other related material and never tired of answering my questions. The Great Northern Railway Records, now preserved by the Minnesota Historical Society at St. Paul, proved to be another fertile source for material on the Great Northern's early predecessor. The staff of the MHS was always courteous and helpful, made me acquainted with the cataloging system used, and always brought out the many boxes I requested without complaints. A third source of information was the John Walker Barriger III Library, then in the care of the Mercantile Library of St. Louis. During my visits there the curator, Charles E. Brown, and his staff were always helpful and supportive.

Donald Haks, director, and the Board of my Institute of Netherlands History at The Hague granted me a four-months leave of absence in the fall of 1997 to do more research and start the writing of the book. Those four months were spent at St. Louis, where Richard W. Davis, director of the Center for the History of Freedom of Washington University, and his wife, Elisabeth, made me feel at home and kindly offered me the use of an office, computer, and other facilities. I owe them a great deal. As I had been there before, back in 1989, when working with them on another project, I did indeed feel at home again in my old office. The staff of the Olin Library of Washington University was always ready to answer my questions and calls for help.

My good friend H. Roger Grant, now at Clemson University, South Carolina, encouraged me whenever we met and talked, and he was kind enough to read several consecutive versions of the manuscript critically. His comments were much needed, and they helped me a lot and have certainly improved the text. James A. Ward, of the University of Tennessee at Chattanooga, also read the manuscript more than once and commented on it. His remarks were always to the point, and I have used them wherever I could. Ethan Miller, then sophomore at Washington University at St. Louis, did research on the fur trade in early Minnesota and wrote a paper for me on the subject. His findings have helped me cover this early, but important, part of Minnesota history.

Mary Lincoln, director of Northern Illinois University Press at DeKalb, and Susan Bean, managing editor of that Press, took care of my manuscript, guided me through the editing process, and helped me in many ways. Julia Fauci was responsible for the layout and illustrations and did a marvelous job with the material that I supplied, which was sometimes of rather poor quality.

Illustrations came from the vast holdings of both the Minnesota Historical Society at St. Paul and the James Jerome Hill Library in that same city. Don L. Hofsommer, of St. Cloud State University, St. Cloud, Minnesota, supplied copies of some old photographs, and the ALCO Historic Photos produced another good photograph. Jacqueline Pryor, archivist of the Railway and Locomotive Historical Society, found some splendid illustrations in the collections of the R&LHS. I thank them all for their kind cooperation and help.

Of all persons involved in this project I owe most to my wife, Jannie. As in the case of my earlier expeditions into the wilds of America for other projects, she accompanied me gladly to St. Paul, took care of the logistics, drove with me along the lines of the old Saint Paul & Pacific into the Minnesota prairies, visited railroad museums, and enjoyed herself most of the time. She never tired of hearing my—sometimes undoubtedly tedious—stories about Jim Hill, Johan Carp, and others, listened patiently to my tales of rails, steam, and dollars, and stimulated me in every respect. I dedicate this book to her.

Pijnacker, the Netherlands

The Saint Paul & Pacific Railroad

Most railroad historians will immediately recognize the railroad when the name Saint Paul & Pacific is mentioned, yet the company's corporate history is relatively unknown. Most will know about the famous first steam engine in Minnesota—the *Wm. Crooks,* now in the Railroad Museum in Duluth—but exactly where and when it ran will be less-common knowledge. The Saint Paul & Pacific Railroad itself had a short history, lasting only from 1862 to 1879, but it was the direct ancestor of the Saint Paul, Minneapolis & Manitoba Railroad, which in turn became the giant Great Northern Railway. The latter, together with the Northern Pacific and the Chicago, Burlington & Quincy, came under control of one management at the beginning of the twentieth century; much later they were formally merged into the Burlington Northern, which in turn became an essential part of the Burlington Northern Santa Fe, a current mega railroad system. So the tiny Saint Paul & Pacific was to be the nucleus from which would grow one of today's giant railroads.

The Saint Paul & Pacific was considered one of the Granger railroads, just like its bigger and older neighbors the Chicago & North Western, the Chicago, Milwaukee & Saint Paul, or the Chicago, Rock Island & Pacific. But unlike these it never during its lifetime measured its mileage in the thousands, rather only in the hundreds. At the very end of its corporate existence it had climbed, although barely, into the select group of railroads with a staff of one thousand or more,

well on its way to becoming a major carrier in the Northwest. After reorganization as the Saint Paul, Minneapolis & Manitoba Railroad, and under the vigorous leadership of that supreme railroader James Jerome Hill, it became one of the best-managed and most profitable of American railroads, its securities much sought after on the stock exchanges of America and Europe, and its technical and commercial astuteness an example to others. After the Manitoba was renamed the Great Northern Railway, it finally did reach the Pacific, unlike so many other roads with Pacific in their names. James Hill's later familiar nickname was the Empire Builder, hence the subtitle of this book. The Saint Paul & Pacific Railroad, after all, formed the beginning of his railroad empire.

♦ ♦ ♦

The short and relatively sad history of the Saint Paul & Pacific Railroad ended with the start of the Saint Paul, Minneapolis & Manitoba Railroad Company in May 1879. While the Saint Paul & Pacific was begun with high hopes and a lot of optimism by a regional group of businessmen and helped by the State of Minnesota, it soon passed out of their control. Outside, and in this case even foreign, capital had to be sought when local funds dried up. Bad financial management, possibly even outright fraud here and there, prevented the line from being built as quickly as envisaged. Outside causes—the Civil War, the grasshopper plague, and the general crisis of 1873—aggravated an already hopeless situation and led to the bankruptcy of the road in 1873. Conflicts of interest between shareholders and bondholders and the continuing jealousy of a larger neighbor, the Northern Pacific, prevented any swift solution to the railroad's problems. The process of reorganization was slow, and it took five years to reach an understanding with all parties concerned. The Dutch investors, who had been the principal bondholders of the railroad and therefore the only ones to put up actual capital for construction, lost on the immediate deal, but they were happy to get out of the morass with at least something saved. Their patience and faith in the future of the line was later to be amply rewarded by their investment in the successor company.

Despite its shaky finances, its disinterested personnel, its wheezing engines and decrepit rolling stock running over flimsy wooden bridges and on old, bent, iron rails, the great potential of the railroad was recognized by most people concerned, including the Dutch bankers who had put up the capital for its construction. After all it did run along old, established trails and trade routes to the West and the North and its traffic was growing almost every year after the effects of the 1873 crisis wore off. Immigrants were pouring in by the thousands to people the fertile prairies and raise bumper crops of wheat that were hauled away by the railroad. Minneapolis had started on its meteoric career as the milling capital of the world, thanks to the existence of the railroads of Minnesota, including the Saint Paul & Pacific.

One of those who clearly saw the potential of the railroad was James Jerome Hill, still relatively unknown outside St. Paul. An astute businessman, a tireless worker, and somewhat of a visionary, he followed the operations of the Saint Paul & Pacific from close by and he had noticed the possibilities of getting the bankrupt road on its feet again. Slowly the idea formed in his head that he should be the one to get hold of the railroad and bring it to new life. It took him some years to convince others, of more financial strength than he could muster himself, that this railroad—in good hands— could have a brilliant future, but he succeeded. In his dealing with the represen-

tatives of the Dutch bondholders he drove a hard bargain, as was only to be expected. The Dutch did the same, in their turn, and the result was a compromise that was acceptable to all parties. The Dutch lost on their initial investment, but by giving Hill and his associates the benefit of the doubt and accepting securities of the new company instead of cash, they made a fortune in the end. Hill got the railroad cheap, in not too good a shape, and he had to invest a lot of money to get it in reasonable condition again. Much of this new capital was provided by the same Dutch investors, a sure sign of their confidence in James Hill and his abilities as a railroad man.

James Hill indeed proved to be a giant in the field of railroading. By personal attention to the smallest detail, close supervision of his subordinates, shrewd dealings with other parties, parsimony, and untiring energy, he managed to turn the fortunes of the Saint Paul & Pacific—and its successor road, the Saint Paul, Minneapolis & Manitoba— around in the course of two years. The new company became a model for others, its finances were in the best shape, and its securities commanded high prices on American and European stock exchanges. It never defaulted, it never passed a dividend, and its stocks were seen as a blue chip investment. Its train service became dependable as never before and its traffic grew enormously with the filling up of the vast empty prairies. When Hill saw the potentially lucrative Canadian market closed by the building of an all-Canadian line, he ended his personal interest in this Canadian Pacific Railway and headed west with his own railroad. In doing so he became a formidable competitor to both the older Northern Pacific and the new Canadian Pacific.

◆ ◆ ◆

In the 1850s and 1860s railroads were seen as the best vehicle for the development of the vast American Midwest. The fertile prairies beckoned the immigrant, but the crops he raised could be marketed only when transportation became available. Away from the rivers, roads were nonexistent and no freight could be carried far. Railroads promised to be the solution to this transportation problem, but railroads cost money, lots of it, and money was always scarce. Some states, such as Indiana and Michigan, had ruined themselves with ill-conceived internal improvement schemes; they were almost broke. Illinois too had poured much capital into the canal connecting the Illinois River with Lake Michigan, among other schemes, and was financially exhausted.

But in Illinois for the first time a new way was developed for financing a railroad in an undeveloped region. After much pressure from Western states and after long and sometimes acrimonious discussions, Congress in Washington in 1850 finally approved the donation of public land to two planned railroads, the Illinois Central and the Mobile & Ohio, which together were to constitute a North-to-South railroad from Chicago to New Orleans. Secured by a mortgage on this land grant, bonds could be issued to finance construction, and as this was considered very safe, investors took up this loan at par. In contrast, earlier construction bonds—not secured by the land grant—had been sold at only 86 percent of par, indicating the lack of confidence on the part of the investors.[1]

Other railroads were also provided with a congressional land grant, generally with the same financial organization as in the case of the Illinois Central, with one major exception. The share capital of this road was fully paid up, whereas later companies used their shares to limit control to an inner circle of promoters and capitalists, and as an incentive to raise loans, but never expected the owners to pay the nominal value of the shares. Actual construction of the lines was to be financed by loans secured by a mortgage on the property and on the land grant, which was considered safe enough. After the lines had actually been built and the allotted sections transferred to the company, the land could be sold to farmers and the proceeds used to redeem the bonds.[2] The Saint Paul & Pacific was one of these land grant roads.

Not all Midwestern railroads were provided with land grants, however, and quite a few managed to construct their lines without this Federal help. Early lines such as the Chicago, Burlington & Quincy (1856), Chicago & Northwestern (1864), Chicago, Rock Island & Pacific (1866), and the Chicago, Milwaukee & Saint Paul (1873) were all started as fairly conservative and well-managed regional companies, which slowly grew from their small beginnings. Only the last named ever reached the Pacific over its own metals, but all others did stretch their networks well into the Rockies. Their financial framework reflected the conservative policies of their incorporators. Shares were issued and generally fully paid up in installments. When more construction capital was needed, which was usually quite soon, bonded loans were issued, secured by a mortgage on the property. And as these railroads had an excellent financial performance, they had no trouble in floating these loans and selling their stock on the market, where their securities commanded high prices, quite often well above par. None of these companies was forced to default during crises such as the ones of 1873 or 1893, and their dividends generally continued even in those troubled years.

Opposition to squandering away so much of the public domain, already present right from the beginning, grew in strength over the years. Scandals connected with the sale of lands, fraudulent activities of land speculators, and complaints from homesteaders and veterans did the rest. The policy of giving out Federal land grants to railroads was discontinued in 1871. Later railroads had to fend for themselves.

The first promoters of local or regional railroads were businessmen from the area, and as such, they had easy access to the local sources of capital. They canvassed among their friends, relatives, and business associates and generally had little trouble in obtaining the necessary funds. But out west such funds usually were very limited, and outside help had soon to be sought.

Boston merchants such as John M. Forbes and James F. Joy took over and played an important role in the setting up of Western lines. These two, after having pioneered regional lines such as the Boston & Albany, shifted their operations to the West, where they took over the Michigan Central from the state of Michigan. The Chicago, Burlington & Quincy was also originated by them and developed into one of the best-run and most profitable lines in the country.[3]

Another Massachusetts merchant, David A. Neal, played an important role in the organization of the Illinois Central, and it was Neal who first interested European investors in this railroad. Through his former activities as a merchant in British India and the Dutch East Indies, he had built up a network of contacts that he now could use to advantage for this new venture.[4] Boston banking firms such as Kidder, Peabody & Company and Lee, Higginson & Company continued to play an active role in American railroad finance, even after New York's Wall Street in the 1850s developed into the most important source of capital for railroad construction and development in the United States.

The amount of capital needed to construct the fast-growing railroad network was staggering and could not be found in the United States alone. English, Dutch, and other European investors had already invested a lot of capital in early internal improvement schemes and were now switching over to railroads on a large scale. They were generally not interested in running the railroads they owned, neither in part nor completely. As long as the company in question honored its financial obligations and paid interest and dividends regularly, the

foreign investors did not much care what happened in America. They did have their representatives on the boards, however, and the American directors of these companies were wise enough to keep in close touch with their European shareholders and bond-holders. The Illinois Central, for instance, was one of the roads with a very large foreign interest. In the 1870s, 54 percent of its stock was held in England and 26 percent in Holland; its president, William H. Osborn, took good care to keep the English and the Dutch owners of his company in a friendly mood.[5] The Saint Paul & Pacific was another such railroad, owned almost completely by Dutch investors, who shrank from running the road themselves when it went broke.

The total amount of foreign capital invested in American railroads is hard to establish, as contemporary estimates vary wildly. A U.S. Treasury report of 1853, before the big boom in railroad building really started, gave totals of 3 percent of the stock and 26 percent of the bonds of the 244 American railroad companies then in existence as being in foreign hands. In 1873 the total of foreign-held railroad securities was given as 20 percent, a figure that was to grow to 33 percent by 1890.[6] However undependable and incomplete these figures may be, it is abundantly clear that foreign capital did play an important role in the financing of the American railroad network, especially in the boom years between 1865 and 1873. And because most of the Midwestern roads were relatively late in building, the foreign share in their capital was generally larger than in the case of their earlier Eastern counterparts. Again, neither the Saint Paul & Pacific nor its successor the Saint Paul, Minneapolis & Manitoba were exceptions to this rule.

As other states before, Minnesota did its best to attract railroads to its territory. But as the young state was not in a position to give straight subsidies to railroads (which moreover was expressly forbidden in its constitution), it had resource to the issuing of state bonds in support of the railroads, including the Saint Paul & Pacific. Even this measure of support was considered by many to be of doubtful legality, but it was sanctioned nevertheless. In the end it did not help Minnesota very much to obtain the desired railroads; instead, it saddled the state with a long-running debt. To the state's everlasting credit it must be stated that the state honored its obligations to the bondholders down to the last cent. Only the Federal land grant helped the railroads, again including the Saint Paul & Pacific, to finance their early construction before receipts from traffic were enough to cover expenses.

Apart from the financial problems, Midwestern roads were troubled with labor problems also. Labor was always scarce, and although immigrants came in by the thousands, most of them were in search of land and were not much interested in the hard and dangerous work on the railroads. Unskilled laborers drifted from one place to another, wherever the pay, the food, or the weather promised to be good, and the lure of quick riches in the gold mines of the Far West made many a man anxious to reach this Eldorado before others did so. Minnesota, a remote frontier region in the early 1860s, had little to attract settlers other than its land and timber. Its climate was said to be extremely healthy for all kinds of respiratory ailments, but winters were long and severe. Skilled personnel was always hard to get there and even harder to keep, as the labor history of the Saint Paul & Pacific will show.

The locomotives used on the first railroad in Minnesota were pretty much standard products from Eastern manufacturers. The pioneer railroad was in no position to ask for special favors and was interested only in a low price and in timely delivery. The first engines were on the small side, no problem with the relatively flat terrain and light traffic of the first years. But after the takeover by Hill, stronger machines were soon needed to haul the heavier trains. Rolling stock was spartan but solid, and only later in its existence did the Saint Paul indulge in the luxury of having sleeping cars of its own, when traffic to Winnipeg, Manitoba, grew to dimensions that warranted this extravagance. The impecunious road could not afford to try costly experiments but always bought standard off-the-shelf freight cars and coaches. James J. Hill himself invented a center-dump car for ballasting new track and had it built by Eastern firms. All rolling stock was manufactured at the established factories, although some freight cars were built at the company's St. Paul shops during slack times.

When the first railroads were mooted in Minnesota in the late 1850s and early 1860s, the Midwest was still fairly virgin territory. Around Chicago, already linked to the East and the South, a real network had developed with feelers stretching out into Wisconsin and Iowa. Wisconsin had a railroad center of its own at Milwaukee. From there in 1857 lines were run to the Mississippi River at Prairie du Chien, and the next year lines from Milwaukee reached La Crosse, Wisconsin, also on the Mississippi River but still some 130 miles downstream from St. Paul and the closest railhead available. The first railroads in Minnesota thus were isolated lines in almost virgin country, with no railroad connection at all. All equipment, rails, and other supplies had to be brought in by boat, and only firewood for the locomotives and ties for the track could be locally had. Logistics were therefore important in those first years, as river traffic was closed by ice for many months every year. St. Paul was then virtually cut off from the outside world. Despite these adversities a railroad was opened in 1862 between St. Paul and St. Anthony, opposite Minneapolis, a small line out of which was to grow the giant Great Northern system.

An early view of St. Paul from the Mississippi River. (From Oliphant, *Minnesota and the Far West*)

Early Minnesota

At the beginning of the nineteenth century, the land now called Minnesota was hardly known at all; even its name did not yet exist. Although the area had come into the possession of the United States with the Louisiana Purchase of 1803, nobody in Washington fully understood what had actually been acquired from French emperor Napoleon I. President Thomas Jefferson had sent out Meriwether Lewis and George Clark's 1804–1806 expedition, but while it was a great success, it had not really touched the northern area, having stayed to its south and west.

What was known about the Northwest before the Lewis and Clark expedition came mostly by way of French Canada. Two French explorers—Pierre Radisson and Médard Chouart, sieur des Grosseilliers—had left Montreal and traveled westward in the 1650s and 1660s; they may even have reached the Mississippi River at some point. Later French voyageurs and missionaries Louis Joliet and Jacques Marquette did indeed reach that great river in 1673 and floated down all the way to the mouth of the Arkansas River. Another Frenchman—Daniel Greysolon, sieur Duluth (also spelled Du Luth)—planted the arms of his king on the western shore of Lake Superior on July 2, 1679. Present-day Duluth, on Lake Superior, was named after him.[1]

The next year saw another Frenchman, Robert Cavelier, sieur de La Salle, and the Belgian Franciscan priest Father Louis Hennepin, with a large party of Sioux, landing at a place in Minnesota where a small creek, now known as Phalen Creek, fell into the Mississippi River. This was the first time a European traveler had set foot at the place that was to become the city of St. Paul. Father Hennepin is also the discoverer of the Falls of St. Anthony in the Mississippi River near what is now Minneapolis, and he named the falls after his patron saint.[2]

Although these French explorers and traders had established contacts with the Native American tribes of the region, hardly any permanent settlement on Minnesota soil had been founded as yet. A profitable trade in furs and peltries with the local tribes was carried on by French and half-breed trappers, traders, coureurs de bois, and voyageurs in their birch canoes and light boats. These hardy men knew the many lakes, rivers, and streams as no one else. They had useful contacts with the Native Americans of the region, but they were interested only in trade, not in permanent settlement.[3]

The French dominion of Lower Canada came to an end with the Treaty of Paris of 1763. Great Britain, already strongly established in the Hudson Bay area, in Upper

Canada in the north and west, and in the Hudson and Ohio River valleys in the south, took over. Although then under British sovereignty, the trappers and traders remained the same, however, and the French patois spoken by these fellows remained the most common language. Then the American War of Independence meant another change of sovereignty. All lands east of the Mississippi were ceded by Great Britain to the United States, although the northern frontier was still ill-defined. The area south and west of the Great Lakes became American, and the Canadian fur traders were slowly excluded from this region, which had formerly been their almost exclusive haunt, although a fairly large number of Canadian-born traders and merchants remained in that part of the country.

The Fur Trade

Furs were much sought after in Europe for the making of hats and clothing, and pelts of beaver, otter, and other animals became important trade goods. These animals were abundant in North America, and consequently the European settlements on that continent became the primary source of pelts. English, French, and Dutch colonists traded pelts for European goods with the Native Americans of the area. The Dutch West India Company made Beverwijk—now Albany—on the Hudson River its most important entrepôt for pelts; the French were strong in Lower Canada; and the English traded both from Virginia and the New England colonies. No one managed to establish a complete monopoly, however.

The English Hudson's Bay Company, which was to play a certain role in the development of the Minnesota area later, was incorporated in 1670 and obtained, in its charter, not only the exclusive right to trade in British Canada but also the jurisdiction over a large but as yet undefined tract of land called Prince Rupert's Land.[4] For a long

time its monopoly was challenged by the French. It was only after the Peace of Utrecht of 1713 that the Hudson's Bay Company was actually strong enough to exclude its European competitors. Competition was great. In 1783 Montreal traders formed a loose partnership, called the North West Company. It was a flexible and aggressive business venture and it soon managed to acquire the greater share of the fur trade.[5] The Hudson's Bay Company did recover in time, and in 1821 the North West Company was taken over.

A great competitor to the two British Canadian companies was founded in 1806 by John Jacob Astor of New York City. His American Fur Company managed to establish itself as the foremost trading company in the whole Northwest, including Minnesota. Headquarters for this part of the American Fur Company were established at Mackinaw Island, between Lakes Huron and Michigan. Astor, having accumulated an enormous fortune and of advanced age, retired from the business in 1834. The Northern Department, which retained the name of the American Fur Company, was then sold to Ramsay Crooks, who had already been directing this part of the business for years.[6] Ramsay Crooks was born in Scotland in 1787 and died in New York in 1859. After coming to Canada in 1803, he was active in the fur trade before entering the service of J. J. Astor in 1817. He was related by marriage to the influential Chouteau family of St. Louis. His son William Crooks was to be the first engineer in chief of the Saint Paul & Pacific Railroad, thus continuing the link between the Crooks family and Minnesota.

Political History of the Minnesota Area

Originally it was not the U.S. government that claimed the Northwest from Britain at the end of the War of Independence, but the state of Virginia. In its original colonial charter Virginia was said to consist of the territory from its Atlantic seashore "as far west as the sea." And although these boundaries were ill-defined, they were taken seriously. Only in 1784 was the whole area, which included Illinois and Wisconsin, transferred to the United States and organized as the Northwest Territory.[7]

In 1800 things changed fundamentally. At a hint from Napoleon Bonaparte, at that time still only first consul of the French Republic but on his way to imperial dignity, the Spanish government transferred Louisiana to the French. This treaty of San Ildefonso was meant to be kept secret, but soon its provisions leaked out, giving rise to strong protests from the United States. An American envoy, Robert R. Livingston, was sent to Paris to protest officially and also to offer a certain sum for the purchase of New Orleans and Florida. To Livingston's surprise Napoleon not only was willing to consider the sale of New Orleans but offered the whole of Louisiana to the astonished American. Livingston and James Monroe, the new American minister to France who had just at that moment arrived, did not hesitate long to accept the French offer. On April 30, 1803, French Louisiana changed hands for $15 million. Of this sum $11,250,000 was to be paid in U.S. government bonds bearing 6 percent interest. And as Napoleon greatly preferred cash over bonds, he was only too happy to accept an offer from the London banking house of Francis Baring & Company to take these bonds off his hands—at a discount, of course. Baring and his Amsterdam connection Hope & Company bought the bonds at a price of 78.5 percent of par, just before hostilities erupted again between Great Britain and France. They had little trouble in selling them to English and Dutch investors, and so these American "sixes" ended up at the London and Amsterdam Stock Exchanges, where they soon commanded prices around par. At St. Louis, on

The Red River cart, a heavy two-wheeled vehicle made without a single piece of iron. This cart was the most common means of transportation before the coming of the railroad. (From Beadle, *The Undeveloped West*)

March 10, 1804, the French tricolor was struck and the American Stars and Stripes hoisted in its place, and the northwestern part of Louisiana was officially transferred to the United States.[8]

The northern frontier between British Canada and Minnesota, which was still not clearly marked, was only fixed definitely at the Treaty of Ghent (Belgium) of 1813, which ended the War of 1812 between Great Britain and the United States. From Grand Portage on the northern shore of Lake Superior the frontier was to run along the Pigeon and Rainy Rivers to the Lake of the Woods and from there to the west along the forty-ninth parallel, which became the border between British North America and the United States in that area.[9]

Establishing the exact position of this forty-ninth parallel in the unknown terrain proved no easy task. In 1823 Major Stephen H. Long of the U.S. Army established the true location of the crossing of the Red River of the North and the forty-ninth parallel. It turned out that the Hudson's Bay Company trading post at Pembina on the Red River, formerly owned by the Northwest

Company, was actually south of the line, in America. It was duly moved north in that year. Altogether all but one house of the (Canadian) Pembina settlement was on American soil. Shortly after 1857 the U.S. Army erected a fort at (American) Pembina, on the west bank of the Red River.[10]

Long's reckoning was confirmed in 1850, but when the new British-American boundary commission of 1872 started its work to establish the exact location of the forty-ninth parallel in the terrain, it turned out that Long's post marking the parallel had been placed 250 yards to the south of the true line. The Hudson's Bay Company store was indeed just north of the true line, but the Canadian customhouse was south of it. North Pembina, the Canadian counterpart of American Pembina, was later renamed Dufferin.[11]

Native Americans in Minnesota

When the first European explorers crossed the area of what is now Minnesota, they found the land in possession of a large tribe of Siouan stock, at that time generally called the Dakota, and later known as the Sioux. They lived in more or less permanent villages around the lakes in central Minnesota. Wild rice, which grew in abundance in the lakes, was one of their staple foods. Their existence was threatened by an invasion of Chippewa, around the end of the seventeenth century. The Chippewa, of Algonquian stock, were originally settled on the St. Lawrence River in Canada, but they were driven into Minnesota and soon clashed with the Dakota-Sioux. The latter were armed still with Stone Age weapons, and the Chippewa were armed with steel knives and even firearms obtained from Europeans, so the Dakota-Sioux were gradually driven to the Southwest. Bloody warfare between the two nations continued for decades, and clashes continued even after the white man had already settled in Minnesota.

In the nineteenth century, through trade with Europeans, all came into possession of iron and steel tools, and the flintlock musket gradually replaced the traditional bow and arrow. Roman Catholic and Protestant missionaries were established here and there, and they did a lot of good, but their beneficial work was all too often offset by the debilitating influence of strong liquor. Unscrupulous European traders knew the value of whiskey in their negotiations with the native tribes, and they did not hesitate to sell it to them, in spite of many official prohibitions. Contagious illnesses such as smallpox and measles were also introduced by white traders and these epidemics found the Native American population wholly unprepared. Sometimes whole villages were wiped out by epidemics in the course of a couple of weeks.

American Explorations and Regional Organization

After 1804 interest in Minnesota was slowly growing and knowledge of the newly acquired territory was judged of great importance. Exploratory parties were sent out by the Washington government after 1805, also for purposes of negotiating with the Native Americans for ceding parts of their land.[12] Good relations had to be established, and a first treaty was signed with the Sioux at Portage des Sioux, near St. Louis, in 1815.

Treaties alone were not considered enough, however, and Colonel Henry Leavenworth was ordered in 1819 to proceed north and establish a post at the confluence of the Mississippi with the St. Peter's River (now called Minnesota River). A temporary wooden structure soon gave way to a more substantial stone building, which was named Fort Snelling after Leavenworth's successor, Colonel Josiah Snelling. For many years Fort Snelling was to remain the farthest outpost of American civilization in the wilderness of Minnesota. The military reservation around the fort was large; it encompassed also the Falls of St. Anthony in the Mississippi River. Waterpower of the falls was soon used to drive a mill to saw logs for the construction of the fort. In 1821 Snelling also built a gristmill on the falls, and soon civilians joined the military in using the waterpower, thus starting the later phenomenal industrial development of Minneapolis–St. Anthony. For the time being, however, the area remained part of the military reservation.[13]

Apart from the Fort Snelling area, all of Minnesota was "Indian country" and off-limits to white settlers until 1837. In that year representatives of the United States and the Chippewa and Sioux Nations agreed that the tract of land between the St. Croix and Mississippi Rivers was to be given over to the white man in return for annuities, trade goods, and provisions. In 1838 the U.S. Senate ratified the treaties.[14]

For many years the only settlement of any importance in the area, apart from Fort Snelling, was just across the border with British North America. The Scottish nobleman and philanthropist Thomas Douglas, earl of Selkirk and a major shareholder of the Hudson's Bay Company, had acquired from his company a large tract of land in what is now the Canadian province of Manitoba. Selkirk, appalled at the fate of the poor crofters evicted by the clearances in the Scottish Highlands, wanted to establish them here. Settlements were started—Fort Douglas on the confluence of the Assiniboine and Red Rivers and Fort Garry farther north—and between 1811 and 1814 several hundreds of Scottish peasants were brought in. Later, Swiss and Italians were induced to settle in Selkirk's colonies as well, but with few permanent results. Most colonists drifted up the Red River and ended up at Fort Snelling, until they were evicted from the military reservation in 1840. Some of them then settled a few miles downriver in what was to become St. Paul. In 1849 the Selkirk settlement still numbered about five thousand people in all, most of them catering in some capacity or other to the then still important fur trade. Fort Garry, later called Winnipeg, became the most important center of their activities.[15]

Pierre Parrant—a former Canadian voyageur, nicknamed Pig's Eye because of his one squinting eye—was the first white settler at St.-Paul-to-be. He was evicted from Fort Snelling in 1840 and then set up a grog shop at a convenient point close by, which became known under the same name as its proprietor.[16] Most of the first inhabitants were French-speaking colonists from the Selkirk settlements. Father Lucien Galtier, one of the few Roman Catholic priests in the area, built a crude chapel at Pig's Eye in 1841 and dedicated it to Saint Paul. From then on the locality became known as St. Paul's Landing or simply St. Paul. It quickly attracted new, English-speaking settlers, as it was the last convenient landing place for ships on the Mississippi River before the Falls of St. Anthony made navigation upriver impossible. A post office was established in 1846, and schools and more churches soon followed. The site was surveyed and platted in 1847, and the land on which the town was built was offered for sale by the U.S. Land Office in St. Croix the next year.

Territorial Organization

Most of Minnesota had been part of Wisconsin Territory since 1836, but when Wisconsin became a state in 1848, the area west of the St. Croix River was left out and became a kind of no-man's-land with a most unclear status. After some wrangling over technicalities, Congress in Washington in 1849 decided to set up the Territory of Minnesota, which stretched from Duluth on Lake Superior down the St. Croix and Mississippi Rivers to the border of Iowa (admitted as a state in 1846). In the west the Missouri River was taken as the border, and

The steamboat landing at St. Paul in 1859, lined with the steamers *Grey Eagle, Frank Steele, Jeannette Roberts,* and *Time and Tide.* (Minnesota Historical Society)

large portions of the later states of North and South Dakota were accordingly part of Minnesota Territory. Total white population of the vast new territory in 1849 was 4,057 souls.[17] Most of these lived in the few "towns"—Stillwater, a lumbering town on the St. Croix River northeast of St. Paul, St. Paul itself, and St. Anthony, a few miles upstream. The Native American population was estimated at some twenty-five thousand, give or take a few thousand.

In 1849 Alexander Ramsey of Pennsylvania was named the first governor. Arriving in his capital, St. Paul, he found some twelve frame houses and ten log buildings in addition to tents and other temporary dwellings. Total population was estimated at between 250 and 400 at most. But soon a

tidal wave of immigrants was going to change all this.[18]

One big problem faced Governor Ramsey: what to do with the vast territory west of the Mississippi River, which was still officially closed to white settlement. Many different groups put pressure on the territorial government in St. Paul and on Congress in Washington for the acquisition of the "Suland," as it was colloquially known. Congress was in no hurry, however. Only in 1851 did formal negotiations with several bands of the Sioux Nation begin at Traverse des Sioux on the Minnesota River. After a month of haggling over terms, the Sioux consented to vacate all their land in Iowa and Minnesota, roughly east of the Red River, in return for cash, blankets, and other goods. Other bands of Sioux followed suit and signed also. In February 1852 Congress finally endorsed the treaties with the Sioux, making them operative. How much the Native Americans were tricked into signing away their lands for a pittance is hard to establish. Private interests of traders and Indian agents did play a conspicuous and negative role, and it is not certain that everything went above board. A later observer said about these treaties: "They were as fair as any Indian treaties."[19]

The Chippewa meanwhile remained in possession of their vast lands in the North. Governor Ramsey had concluded a treaty with them in 1851, but the Senate in Washington had thrown it out, as the government was not interested in acquiring lands in a region so remote and inaccessible. Only in 1854 and 1855 were new treaties signed and ratified at the request of mining and lumbering interests, whereby the Chippewa ceded large parts of their land. They kept the most northerly areas for themselves. The area west and northwest of Lake Superior with its—then still largely unknown—iron ore deposits and enormous tracts of the most beautiful timber were thrown open to the white man.

Unrest caused by the Native Americans who felt cheated or who had broken loose from the authority of their chiefs continued to trouble the settlers on the frontier, however. The so-called Sioux War of 1862 was a direct result of the way the treaties had been executed by the government, and a last attempt on the part of the Native Americans to recover their lost ground. Trouble was largely over after 1862 (see "The Sioux Uprising" in Chapter 4).[20]

A steady stream of immigrants was filling up the lands vacated by the Native Americans, new townships sprang up everywhere, and agriculture and industry were growing in importance every year. The population of established towns almost exploded in these years. St. Paul grew from 400 souls in 1849 to 840 the next year and 5,000 by 1855, and the population doubled again in the next five years. A movement toward statehood gained force quickly. The total population of the territory was optimistically estimated at almost 250,000, enough to apply for statehood. Afterward, when a more precise count was made, not more than some 150,000 souls could be found. Great advantages such as the power to borrow money and the fact of being represented in Washington were seen in statehood, and in 1857 the territorial assembly applied for admission to the Union. Despite opposition from the Southern states, who did not favor admission of another free, nonslavery state, Minnesota in 1858 was admitted to the Union as the thirty-second state. The western border was established at the Red River, and the territory to the west of that river was set up as Dakota Territory. The 1860 U.S. census gave the total number of white inhabitants as 172,022. Of these more than 112,000 were American-born, mostly from New England, New York, and Pennsylvania; there were 17,000 Germans, 13,000 Irish, 12,000 Scandinavians, 8,000 Canadians, and 419 Dutchmen.[21]

Early Transportation in Minnesota

Since time immemorial the principal mode of travel in the Minnesota area had been the Native American birch canoe. The many rivers and thousands of lakes made every other kind of vehicle unnecessary. The light canoes were able to hold a sizable cargo or a fair number of passengers but could easily be carried around obstacles such as logjams, shallows, or portages between different rivers. Roads were virtually nonexistent; they were not necessary as almost everything was moved by water. The Selkirk colonies around Fort Garry, although on British soil, were heavily dependent on the transportation route through Minnesota. The area north of Lake Superior was considered completely inaccessible, hence all supplies and furs went by way of the Red River valley and further south along the Mississippi valley. The main route ran from Fort Garry south along the Red River to the border at Pembina, where a trading post was set up in 1843 by Norman Kittson, agent of Pierre Chouteau & Company of St. Louis, the successors to Astor's American Fur Company.[22] From Pembina it was about 450 miles overland to St. Paul. Two routes were available: one, the most used route, ran via the Red River valley as far as modern Moorhead and from there southeast to St. Cloud on the Mississippi River. The other route followed the Red River further south to what is now Breckenridge and from there in a southeasterly direction to St. Anthony and St. Paul.

Norman Wolfred Kittson was born in Sorel, Canada, in 1814 and came to Minnesota in 1834 as fur trader and manager for the American Fur Company in Northern Minnesota, with headquarters in Pembina. From 1851 to 1855 he was a member of the Minnesota territorial legislature for this northern district. In 1858 he was mayor of St. Paul. A future partner of James Jerome Hill, he was like Hill interested in the transportation business in Minnesota in general. He died on a train to St. Paul in 1888.

Kittson set up a transportation firm, Forbes & Kittson, in 1854 and opened a regular line from Pembina to St. Paul. There was no road to speak of, just an Indian trail that avoided the lowest places and softest ground. The vehicle used was the Red River cart, a heavy two-wheeled cart drawn by a single ox, with broad wheels so as not to bog down in soggy soil. It was constructed solely of wood, without a single piece of iron, and it creaked so loudly that it could be heard for miles around. It cost about $15 to build and carried 600–700 pounds of freight. The average journey took from thirty to forty days. And traffic was hefty, helped by the fact that the Hudson's Bay Company, which had taken back the government of the Selkirk settlements in 1834,

transported most of its goods by way of St. Paul and Pembina. In 1851 102 carts were employed in this annual trip; six years later this number had grown to 500; and in 1858 600 carts made the trip. As proof that civilization proceeded even on the frontier, it was remarked with some pride that pianos were a regular freight from St. Paul north to Pembina and Winnipeg.[23]

These annual journeys were the big event in Pembina and St. Paul. Streets were thronged with carts, oxen, and their colorful drivers, mostly French-speaking mixed-bloods, and quiet returned only after they had left, with axles creaking, drivers shouting, and animals bellowing. In winter, traffic came to a virtual standstill, and dog sleighs were the only means of communication in case of necessity. After the introduction of the first steamboat on the Red River (about which more later), the number of carts declined quickly; when the railroad reached St. Cloud and stayed there for a time, that town became the railhead and the carts disappeared from the streets of St. Paul for good.

River traffic had its limitations and was, moreover, impossible in winter, and the call for all-weather roads became louder as populations and trade increased. A stage and wagon line opened between St. Paul and St. Anthony in 1849 and extended all the way down to Prairie du Chien, Wisconsin, in the next year. This was the "Red Line" of Messrs. Willoughby & Powers, operated with two-horse, red-painted Concord coaches obtained from the factory in New Hampshire in 1851. A competitor for the St. Paul–St. Anthony traffic was the "Yellow Line" of Messrs. Patterson & Benson, who put four-horse coaches in service.[24] But these stages continued to use mostly ungraded trails, as roads were still not made. Minnesota's territorial representative in Washington tried to persuade Congress to give subsidies for road building in 1848–1849, and with some success, but funds soon ran out.

A stage line was opened between St. Paul and Lake Superior in 1856, and another one between Superior, Wisconsin, and St. Cloud by way of Little Falls. The Northwestern Express Company was founded in 1854 and was followed in 1859 by the Minnesota Stage Company, which gradually took over most of the existing stage companies in Minnesota. Roads remained primitive, however, and the financial and economic crisis of 1857 effectively put an end to all further road building for many years.[25]

Only almost a decade later, between 1866 and 1869, was the road between St. Paul and St. Anthony and on to Fort Ridgely on the Minnesota River really graded and crudely paved. It entered St. Paul from the west along what is now Third Street and abutted on Jackson Street, the principal street leading down to the steamboat landing.[26] A ferry across the Mississippi to West St. Paul had already been opened in 1852, and in 1856 a bridge for vehicular traffic was started by a private company, with Geo. L. Becker as director and J. S. Sewall as engineer. When the company ran out of funds, as it soon did, the city loaned money to finish the work, and the city eventually took over the bridge. It was a high bridge on very tall piers; it began at Wabasha Street, was 1,311 feet long, and was of mixed iron and wood construction, with a total cost of $116,855.11. Apparently construction was not very solid, for it had to be extensively rebuilt in 1870.[27]

This Mississippi bridge at St. Paul was not the first one, however, across the father of waters. St. Anthony, further upstream, had experienced a rapid development because of the cheap waterpower available at the falls, and just across the river, a new town sprang up, also as a result of the availability of this cheap power. Sawmills had been established at the falls back in 1838 by the military of Fort Snelling and by civilians, and Eastern capitalists soon noted the importance of the cheap power. A grist and flour mill was

An advertisement of William F. Davidson's Northwestern Union Packet Company from the 1870s. (Author's Collection)

opened in St. Anthony in 1851, and it was
soon followed by others. The Washburn and
Pillsbury families selected the falls for the
establishment of their flour mills and they
soon gained great influence in Minnesota.
St. Anthony was incorporated as a city in
1855, and its cross-river neighbor one year
later.[28] When the problem of naming the
new town on the west bank arose, some
people suggested All-Saints as a suitable
name. Others were repulsed by this idea:

> It is bad enough to have had the rivers, woods
> and villages of this Territory so thoroughly be-
> sainted by the Canadian voyageurs who first
> discovered this land of promise. But that at
> this day the saintly calendar should be [used]
> . . . to christen a thriving young city is past be-
> lief, especially in the prodigality of beautiful
> and expressive Indian appellations still unap-
> propriated.[29]

Someone then coined the name Minneapolis, and Minneapolis it became.

Of the two islands in the Mississippi between St. Anthony and Minneapolis, Nicollet Island had already been connected to the
mainland at the St. Anthony side. Then, in
1854–1855, a wire suspension bridge with
wooden towers was built over the main
channel of the river; this was the first bridge
across the Mississippi anywhere in America.
T. M. Griffiths was the engineer of this wonder of the day, and he used four cables, each
of five hundred strands of iron wire, to carry
the deck. The last beam was laid in December 1854 and on January 23, 1855, the
bridge was opened for vehicular traffic.
Some months later during a severe storm
the bridge deck was forced loose from the
cables and heavy repairs were necessary,
which were speedily effected.[30] For such a
young community this was an achievement
to be proud of. After all, Minneapolis and
St. Anthony together cannot then have
numbered more than some eight thousand
souls at the most.

Immigration was booming during these
years, and the future seemed full of possibilities. A veritable real estate mania developed
after 1855 and prices of town lots everywhere skyrocketed.[31] St. Paul opened a city
gas works, hotels were built, banks and
shops were organized. Then, suddenly, the
bubble burst with the failure of the Ohio Life
Insurance and Trust Company in August
1857. Many other financial institutions followed, banks suspended specie payments,
trade came to a virtual standstill, settlers
stayed away or went elsewhere, and St. Paul's
population fell by an estimated 50 percent.

River Navigation

Navigation on the Western rivers had
long been a predominantly downstream affair. Working a boat upstream was not impossible, but it was hard and laborious
work. A trip from New Orleans to Louisville
could take from three to four months.[32]
Steam power was to change that for good.

The first experiments with steamboats on
the Mississippi River were held in
1811–1812, and soon more or less regular
steam-packet services were established between New Orleans and St. Louis and other
towns upriver. Navigation on the Upper Mississippi above St. Louis was hindered by the
rapids near the confluence with the Des
Moines River and at Rock Island, but in 1823
the first steamboat managed to negotiate
these rapids successfully and proceed to
Galena, Illinois, the center of the important
lead trade. In the same year the small steamboat *Virginia* (109 tons) continued all the
way upstream to St. Paul with a cargo of supplies for the Fort Snelling garrison.[33] The 683
miles from St. Louis to St. Paul took no less
than twenty days, but the proof was that it
was possible to reach St. Paul by steamboat.
Navigation further upstream was impossible
because of the Falls of St. Anthony.

These early steamboats were small affairs,
flimsily built and with a primitive system of

propulsion, but progress was quick, and soon larger vessels (of 1000 tons and over) with batteries of boilers and high-pressure steam engines, driving enormous side-wheels, emerged. They easily caught the public fancy, with the hull low in the water, and the ornate, high superstructure of several decks, topped by two tall funnels, which spewed forth smoke and showered the boat with sparks. Most vessels burned wood, which was easily available along the rivers, but frequent stops were necessary to fuel up as the appetite for firewood was enormous. One thing all boats had in common was the light draft, with an almost flat hull, said to be riding *on* instead of *in* the water. Jokingly it was said of some of these boats that all they needed before they could float was a heavy dew.[34]

Steamboating on the Western rivers was a dangerous occupation and accidents were frequent. Snags were a constant danger. Heavy trees were often uprooted when the river was in flood, and their trunks, pointing upward, could easily tear open the flimsy wooden hull of a steamboat. Collisions with other boats were not infrequent, and fires, which could destroy the wooden boats in a matter of minutes, became all too common. Most dreaded were boiler explosions. High-pressure boilers, often without expert maintenance, and pressed just a little bit higher than was safe, to supply that extra pound of steam needed to reach a destination before the competition arrived, were a constant source of lethal danger. They exploded without warning with a most destructive force, which could reduce a large boat to splinters, covering crew and passengers with scalding water, steam, and red hot fragments of metal and generally causing great loss of life. When the *Moselle* blew up at Cincinnati in 1838, at least 150 persons lost their lives. In comparison, the explosion of the boiler of the steamboat *John Rumsey* lying at the St. Paul levee in 1864 took "only" seven lives, a relatively small af-

fair. It still caused a lot of damage to other boats and buildings on shore, though.[35]

One less dangerous, but annoying and annually returning, hindrance to navigation was ice. Between 1849 and 1866, on average, the navigation on the Upper Mississippi at St. Paul was closed for 143 days every year.[36]

Navigation on the rivers upstream from St. Louis was quieter and less spectacular than downstream. Boats were smaller, generally between 300 and 350 tons, and schedules less exacting. Regular once-weekly packet service to St. Paul began in 1847 after the organization of the Galena & Minnesota Packet Company, later reorganized as the Galena, Dubuque, Dunleith & Minnesota Packet Company. This outfit owned just one boat in 1847, but by 1857 it had thirteen boats running on the Upper Mississippi, chiefly in connection with the railheads at Dunleith, Prairie du Chien, and La Crosse, providing fast and regular thrice-weekly service to St. Paul. Twice-daily service was even offered between Galena and St. Paul from 1857 onward.

Successful as this company was, it is small wonder that competitors appeared on the scene in the shape of the Northern Line Packet Company for service between St. Louis and St. Paul. After a short time of fierce competition and rate cutting, a working agreement between the old and the new companies was reached in 1860, which resulted in a regular twice-daily service between St. Louis and St. Paul. Steamboats needed only eighty-eight hours for the trip upstream and sixty-seven hours downstream. This was a definite improvement over the *Virginia*'s accomplishment of twenty days in 1823.

In the same year, 1860, a third and more dangerous competitor showed up in the person of William F. Davidson and his La Crosse & Saint Paul Packet Company. He was supported by the La Crosse & Milwaukee Railroad and turned out to be a ruthless businessman, not for nothing nicknamed the "Jay Gould of Steamboating." But he did provide fast and superior service, and in three years he had acquired control of the old Galena Company. In opposition to Davidson's White Collar Line, other steamboat interests formed a Northwestern Line, but Davidson's influence was such that the two combined in 1866 into the Northwestern Union Line. Davidson extended his operations downriver to St. Louis, which brought him into fierce competition with the older Northern Line of St. Louis. Rate wars resulted again, and in 1873 the two rival lines merged into a new Keokuk & Northern Line Packet Company, under Davidson's management. By then, however, railroads had taken away the most valuable traffic from the rivers and the Keokuk & Northern line folded in 1881.[37]

The importance of the river traffic for St. Paul becomes clear from the average number of arrivals on the St. Paul levee at the foot of Jackson Street: in 1844–1845, there were 45; between 1851 and 1855, 280; between 1856 and 1860, 875; and between 1861 and 1865, 819. The top year was 1858 with a total of 1,068 arrivals. By 1866 the number had fallen to 777, and in 1874 a paltry 218 boats showed up at the St. Paul landing.[38]

Navigation on the other rivers in Minnesota was much less important. On the Upper Mississippi, Captain John Rollins started a steamboat line from St. Anthony to Sauk Rapids in 1851. All ironwork and machinery for his boat *Governor Ramsey* was manufactured in Bangor, Maine, and was shipped to St. Anthony by way of New Orleans. Carpenters from Bangor built the hull in St. Anthony, a very expensive procedure. More boats were added later.[39]

The Red River valley had been an important artery for traffic north to the Selkirk settlement and further on into the Hudson's Bay Company territory. With the Reciprocity Agreement of 1854 between the governments of Canada and the United States, the transportation of natural products across the border in both directions was freed from almost every duty and tax.[40] Ramsay Crooks, former owner of the northern outfit of the American Fur Company and then agent of the Hudson's Bay Company, in 1859 contracted with the St. Paul firm of Russell, Blakely & Company for the transportation of goods by way of the Red River valley.

This contract boosted traffic, and to speed things up, a certain Anson Northup, financially supported by the St. Paul chamber of commerce, hauled the machinery, boilers, and other ironwork of his boat *North Star* from St. Paul overland to the Red River, where a new hull was built. The new *Anson Northup,* a small stern-wheeler, was placed in service in 1859 and proved a huge success. In 1860 the boat was purchased by the firm of J. C. & H. C. Burbank of St. Paul, who renamed her *Pioneer* and operated her in combination with carts for the journey from St. Paul to the Red River. Despite low water, snags, ice, and other hindrances, traffic boomed and a second boat, the *International,* was placed in service in 1862.[41]

Success attracted competition, and in 1871 the St. Paul warehousing and transportation firm of Hill, Griggs & Company placed another boat, the *Selkirk,* in service on the Red River. Norman Kittson, already operating his transportation firm out of Pembina, bought the *International,* and in 1872 he and Hill, Griggs & Company joined forces and together incorporated the Red River Transportation Company. This monopolistic firm did very well and reputedly paid out 80 percent in dividends in 1876, money that the two could use very well in their entry into the railroad business (as we shall see later).

Winnipeg, at the confluence of the Red and Assiniboine Rivers near Fort Garry, was incorporated in 1873, and it quickly became the hub of a distribution system for the whole of Manitoba. The Canadian Pacific Railway was still in the future, and almost everything had to be brought up from St. Paul by way of the Red River. In 1876, five million pounds of freight worth over $800,000 were carried north, and furs valued at $794,868 were brought south. The first engine for the Canadian Pacific Railway, the *Countess of Dufferin,* was brought north on the *Selkirk* and landed at St. Boniface in 1877. Hundreds of tons of rails were also transported by this small boat, but when the railway from St. Paul at last reached Pembina and the Canadian border in December 1878, the steamboat era on the Red River was over.[42]

Other Means of Communication

Apart from steamboats, communication between St. Paul and the outside world was also facilitated by the opening of a telegraph line from Galena in 1860. Business made good use of this new, fast medium. Railroads from the South and East also crept slowly closer to Minnesota. The opening of the Chicago, Rock Island & Pacific line to Rock Island, in 1854, was occasion for a big celebration. A grand excursion from Chicago to St. Paul was staged and the party—including ex-president Millard Fillmore, the governors of Illinois and Missouri, historian George Bancroft, and a host of newspapermen from the East—traveled by train to Rock Island and there boarded a steamboat for St. Paul. In that city, just incorporated as such, a formidable reception awaited the party, sure to impress them with the amenities offered by the gateway to the North.[43]

Three years later, in 1857, the Milwaukee & Prairie du Chien Railway was finished, bringing the railhead a couple of hundred miles closer to St. Paul. In 1858 the railroad from Milwaukee to La Crosse was opened for traffic, again some fifty miles closer to the capital of Minnesota, but still over a hundred miles away. Only in 1867 was a direct connection by rail established, when the Minnesota Valley and the Saint Paul & Sioux City Railroads, under the aegis of the Chicago & North Western, opened for traffic. The Milwaukee & Saint Paul Railroad opened its river division from Winona to St. Paul in 1870 and finally the West Wisconsin Railroad provided a third outlet from St. Paul in 1872. By then, railroad building in Minnesota had started in earnest.

Jackson Street in St. Paul in 1869 as seen from Third Street looking down to the levee. Sidewalks were paved, but streets were still mostly mud. The ticket office in the left foreground was run by Alpheus B. Stickney, later president of the Chicago Great Western Railroad. (Minnesota Historical Society)

The First Railroads

"**A**mericans are born, not with silver spoons, but with iron rails in their mouths."[1] Thus was expressed the popular conception of the general clamor in the United States for railroads in the 1850s. Railroads were the cure for all evil, the sure way to riches for everybody, and the only means of elevating the population out of poverty and unemployment. Everywhere in the country the same sounds were heard, and Minnesota was no exception.

Before we turn to examine the development of railroads in Minnesota more closely, however, it is necessary to have a look at the general railroad situation in the United States around 1860. Just before the outbreak of the Civil War, the American railroad network was still not one single unified system, but more a collection of—sometimes loosely connected—regional or even local lines. Interconnection of railroads was often impossible because of difference in gauge. And even when the gauge used was in fact compatible with others, railroad managers often were not really willing to connect their line with any other, from the misguided idea that they were bound to lose their rolling stock. Passengers were said to have no objection to stretching their legs and boarding another train after many hours of travel, and freight had to be aired and checked too. Only

slowly did the idea of through trains become universally accepted.

In the South, most roads were laid in the Southern gauge of 5 feet, with some exceptions, and were badly interconnected or not at all. This was to cost the Confederacy dearly during the war. In New England and the Northern Atlantic states the English standard gauge of 4 feet 8.5 inches was generally in use, with the noteworthy exception of the 6-foot-gauge New York & Erie Railway and its extensions, the Atlantic & Great Western and the Ohio & Mississippi, which did stretch their broad gauge lines all the way to East St. Louis on the Mississippi River. And in the rest of the "Old" Northwest there were several different gauges in use, precluding a real transfer of cars and rolling stock. Ohio used a gauge of 4 feet 10 inches, which was not compatible with the standard gauge without some technical ingenuity. Here and there a so-called compromise gauge of 4 feet 9.25 inches was being introduced, which made possible the transfer of cars with wide wheel threads to accommodate gauges between the standard and the Ohio gauge. A makeshift solution, and not without its inherent dangers, it did work. Iowa, Wisconsin, and Illinois (apart from the Ohio & Mississippi line) knew only the standard gauge and so avoided the nuisance of transshipment from one gauge to another.[2]

By 1861 the railroads had reached north as far as Appleton, Wisconsin, west to

Prairie du Chien and La Crosse on the Mississippi River, and into Iowa as far as Waterloo. Only northern Illinois and southern Wisconsin could show a fairly integrated railroad network, with Chicago and Milwaukee as the main hubs. Into Iowa only short fingers, yet unconnected, ran out into the West. Only one railroad bridge crossed the Mississippi River, at Rock Island–Davenport. Everywhere else passengers and freight had to be ferried over.

Farther west there was almost nothing, just empty land. The only railroad really leading at least a little distance into the West was the isolated Hannibal & Saint Joseph, which stretched all the way across northern Missouri to St. Joseph on the Missouri River. St. Joseph and nearby Weston became favorite jumping off points for transcontinental wagon trains. Although the possibility of a transcontinental railroad had been discussed for decades, no actual work had been done, apart from several thorough surveys for the best route. Political stalemate between North and South in Congress and antagonism between the advocates of the different routes prohibited any decision. Only the defection of the Southern states from the Union made it possible to decide for the central route the Union Pacific was to follow.

In Minnesota

In Minnesota the development of railroads elsewhere in the country had been followed closely, of course. Land transportation was slow and laborious and therefore expensive, while river transportation was only possible during certain times of the year. Railroads were the obvious solution to the existing problems, and the new mode of transportation had proved its worth in other parts of the country. The iron roads were slowly creeping up through Iowa and Wisconsin toward Minnesota, and it would be only a matter of time before they reached

all the way to the Red River and beyond. Surveys had even been made for railroad routes to the Pacific and if such a transcontinental road was to become a real possibility, and few doubted its ultimate success, then railroads for Minnesota would be feasible as well.

The chief stumbling block for building railroads in the West was the chronic lack of capital. Although the early railroads in the East had been financed chiefly with local capital, the vast sums needed for building into largely uninhabited country needed other forms of financing. By 1860 Eastern capitalists had taken over from local or regional groups of businessmen. But what capitalist in his right mind would be willing to risk his money in a venture that could at best give him some small profit in a distant future?

To facilitate construction of railroads in undeveloped and sparsely inhabited regions, Congress had found a new tool—the land grant. First used for the building of the Illinois Central and the Mobile & Ohio Railroads in 1850, this later became a favorite means of making public aid available for railroad construction. Railroad companies with land to sell could then try and attract private capital by issuing loans—secured by a mortgage on the land grant, which was considered safe enough, indeed much safer than a mortgage on a jerry-built railroad line from nowhere to nowhere in particular.[3]

The Minnesota territorial legislature, impressed by the results of the donation of land elsewhere in the country, pressed Congress in Washington for a land grant for railroad building, and with success. On March 3, 1857, Congress passed a bill for a generous land grant in Minnesota. It made the land available—but not to the territory itself, to be distributed as the territorial government saw fit, which would have been usual. Instead, the bill outlined a basic network of railroads for Minnesota and designated the

The St. Paul levee, circa 1873, with the steamboat *Lake Superior* of the Keokuk Northern line at the landing. The railroad tracks are just visible on the right, and the Wabasha Street bridge is in the distance. Freight was apparently dumped in the open before being carted away. (Photo by W. H. Illingworth, Minnesota Historical Society)

territorial (and later state) government as agent for the distribution of this land to these railroads only. Odd-numbered sections, six sections in width and alternating on both sides of the road, were set apart and could be given over to the railroad company as building progressed. If not sold in ten years, the lands were to revert to the United States.[4]

The network, as proposed by Congress, followed fairly closely the available transportation routes. The first line was to cross the state from St. Paul in a westward direction; the second was to run northwest from the capital to the international boundary at St. Vincent or Pembina on the Red River. A later writer's statement that these two lines, forming the Saint Paul & Pacific and the nucleus of the later Great Northern Railway system, were "poorly conceived geographically" seems odd and ill-founded.[5] After all, these lines followed very closely the established transportation routes by land and water and were indeed a great success. The other lines as envisaged by Congress for Minnesota (which need not occupy us here) were designed to run south and southwest to connect with projected railways in Iowa and Wisconsin.

In 1857 the Minnesota legislature accepted the terms of the Federal land grant, and in the same session the Minnesota & Pacific Railroad Company was incorporated and empowered to build a line from Stillwater via St. Paul and St. Anthony to Breckenridge on the Bois de Sioux River, with a branch from St. Anthony to St. Vincent at the mouth of the Pembina River by way of Anoka, St. Cloud, and Crow Wing. Other new companies were set up, or existing ones empowered, to build the other lines as named in the act of Congress. All lands designated by Congress were to be passed on to the railroad companies under certain conditions. A first installment of land could be transferred to the company with each ten-mile stretch of line graded, while the rest was to be given out when the railroad actually opened the line for regular traffic.

Another stipulation was that the companies were to pay into the state treasury 3 percent of their gross earnings annually, in lieu of all taxes. All seemed set for a rapid building of the railroad lines people had been awaiting for so long. Expectations ran high, but then the commercial and financial crisis struck the country in August 1857. All credit dried up, commerce came to a virtual standstill, and the Minnesota & Pacific could not raise a single dollar to begin the survey of its lines.

State Bonds

Before continuing with the actual incorporation and construction of the first railroad in Minnesota, we need to look into the further actions of the Minnesota legislature to obtain a rail network. As lack of capital seemed to be the chief problem, the legislature in April 1858 passed a law by which the state was empowered to issue bonds in aid of the railroad companies. These bonds were to bear 7 percent interest and could be distributed to the tune of $100,000 per ten miles of road graded and ready for ties and rails. The total of this issue was to be $5 million, hence the nickname "five million dollar loan."

This law did not pass unopposed. A clause in the new Minnesota state constitution expressly forbade that the credit of the state should be given—or loaned—to any individual or corporation. This difficulty was obviated by adding an amendment to the constitution, to be laid before the voters, which would allow the state to loan its credit to the railroad companies in question. And despite warning voices, the people of Minnesota were so eager to have railroads that they passed the amendment with an overwhelming vote.

The railroad companies then set to work most earnestly, and by 1859, 239 miles had been graded and 2,275 state bonds had been delivered to the several companies. The contractors who had done the actual grading had been paid with these bonds, as was usual in these years when a young railroad had no cash available. But not a single rail had been laid and no locomotives or rolling stock had been delivered. By the end of 1859 all activity came to an end, with the coffers of the railroads still empty and no line of railroad in operation, but with the credit of the state greatly impaired. It is not necessary to follow the history of these state bonds closely, and it is enough to state that they never contributed much to the growth of the railroad network in Minnesota. Despite many influential advocates of repudiation of these bonds, the state never took this drastic step and in the end honored its obligations in full. It took some time, however, for only in 1881 were the state railroad bonds redeemed by a new issue of state bonds.

State Banks

Not only the state's but also the general financial situation was unsatisfactory in Minnesota in the 1850s. Before 1850 banks scarcely existed in St. Paul; the first was chartered only in 1851. Specie payments were much preferred, and when no coin was available, as was often the case, people resorted to barter. The only money readily available were notes issued by private banks of sometimes doubtful integrity and solidity. The notes circulating in Minnesota in those years were chiefly from out-of-state banks, many of them in the South, and were generally accepted at a discount, depending on the known (or supposed) solidity of the bank in question—all of which exacted great caution on the part of the bankers accepting them. There were advocates in St. Paul for the incorporation of a note-issuing bank of its own, but the legislature could not be persuaded to issue a charter for such a bank. The short boom period

after 1855 caused many new private banks to be set up, often without any real, solid foundation and backing, and during the panic of 1857 most of these closed their doors again.

The Minnesota Banking Act of 1858 meant some improvement, and the new state banks set up under this act started issuing notes secured by the state railroad bonds. But as these bonds soon depreciated, the banknotes were hardly circulated outside Minnesota and were only accepted and redeemed at great discounts, sometimes as low as 16.25 cents on the dollar.

By 1863 the situation looked better with seven state banks in operation, which had their notes mostly secured by safe U.S. Federal bonds. The National Banking Act of 1863 found little favor in Minnesota, but a First National Bank of St. Paul was organized in December 1863, the first in the state. Soon all state banks were converted into national banks. A new boom in Minnesota followed after the end of the Civil War, and remarkably enough, the national crisis of 1873 had only slight repercussions in the state. No bank had to close its doors, few businesses failed, real estate was depressed for some years only, and the only real result of the crisis was the almost complete stop to railroad building. When considering the slow growth of railroad mileage in Minnesota, it is good to keep this confused regional financial situation in mind.[6]

St. Paul as Commercial Center

The city of St. Paul, situated on the high bluffs above the muddy Mississippi landing, was a real frontier town. Many small ravines, cut into the banks by small creeks and streams, provided access from the landing to the town above, but with great inconvenience. Small hills and bluffs remained in the town itself and were only much later removed and the spoil used to fill the ravines. The actual levee, where the steamboats put ashore, was too low during flood stages of the river but was only much later raised. Jackson Street, unpaved as all other streets, was the main thoroughfare to the landing. Muddy in summer and slippery in winter, it was not a very satisfactory way of getting to and from the riverboats.[7]

Three hotels, of which the Metropolitan was the most fashionable and the Merchant's of 1853 the oldest, catered to the weary traveler. Over a hundred saloons and grog shops (no less than 140 in 1869) offered amusement of a different kind to a less elegant public—the carters, boat crews, and artisans who thronged the levee.[8] Native Americans were fatally attracted to these bars, which resulted in many fights and shootings in the streets of St. Paul. There was virtually no policing, so the citizens themselves had to keep order. For the more spiritual needs, twenty churches were available of every possible denomination, and to keep the young men out of the bars and saloons a YMCA and a library were soon established. More than thirty doctors had practices in town, and lawyers were present in even greater numbers.

The population of the city continued to grow, despite the setback of the 1857 crisis. From five thousand in 1855 it had already doubled by 1860; it reached almost thirteen thousand in 1862 and some twenty thousand in 1869. Flour mills had been established (five in number in 1869), with two

iron foundries and two sawmills as well, and a large number of other, smaller industries and workshops employed hundreds of workers. The mercantile business of the city reached as far as Winnipeg and was valued at $15 million annually.

Late in the 1860s St. Paul was beginning to find its commercial position being challenged by Minneapolis. Attracted by the cheap waterpower that was readily available, industrialists set up flour mills at the Falls of St. Anthony. Originally winter wheat was the number one wheat used for flour, but the invention of a new milling process by a Frenchman, N. LaCroix, in the 1860s made Minnesota spring wheat the favorite. Americans copied the LaCroix methods, and soon enormous mills were built alongside the falls, grinding the wheat grown on the newly broken prairies of western Minnesota and on the "bonanza farms" of the Dakotas. Waterpower was gradually supplemented by steam power, when cheap coal became available in large quantities. Only by means of the transportation facilities offered by the railroad network and the extensive system of grain elevators set up along these new lines of communication could this industry be fully developed. Consequently, by 1880 Minneapolis had passed St. Paul in population, but as the seat of government and the headquarters of big companies the capital remained an important center.[9]

The Minnesota & Pacific Railroad Company

A railroad between St. Paul and St. Anthony had been incorporated and its charter approved by the territorial legislature in 1853. Nothing had been done because of lack of capital, however, and the charter lapsed.[1] Then, on May 22, 1857, a new attempt was made when the state chartered the Minnesota & Pacific Railroad Company to build a line from Stillwater to St. Anthony by way of St. Paul. In St. Anthony the railroad line was to divide: one line (later known as the Main line) going to the west and northwest by way of Minneapolis to the Red River at or near Breckenridge (about 220 miles), and the other (later called the Branch line) going northwest via St. Cloud and Crow Wing to some place, yet undefined, on the Red River (428 miles). At first the northern terminus on the Red River was left undecided, as no real knowledge about the terrain was available, but soon St. Vincent was named, to be opposite Pembina and close to the international boundary.[2] Capital stock of the new company was set at $5 million, with power to increase this to $20 million. Another clause of the charter had the following provision:

> A bell of at least 30 pounds weight, or a steam whistle, shall be placed on each locomotive engine, and shall be rung or whistled where said roads shall cross any other road, and be kept ringing or whistling at intervals until it shall have crossed said road or street, under a penalty of fifty dollars for every neglect, to be paid by said corporation, one half to go to the informer, and the other half to the Territory or future State of Minnesota, and to be liable for all damages by reason of such neglect.

At such crossings warning boards were also to be put up, with lettering of at least nine inches high: RAILROAD CROSSING: LOOK OUT FOR THE CARS. Authority was also given to construct and operate a telegraph line along the tracks.[3] The standard gauge of 4 feet 8.5 inches was prescribed for all railroads in Minnesota.

Edmund Rice, first president of the company, was the leading force among the original incorporators and he remained the heart and soul of the undertaking. He was born in Waitsfield, Vermont, in 1819, came to Minnesota by way of Michigan, and settled in St. Paul in 1849. He was a lawyer and a member of the firm of Rice, Hollinshead & Becker until 1855. In 1857 he became president of the Minnesota & Pacific and remained in that position—and president of its successors—until 1872. He also served several terms in the Minnesota legislature and was considered one of the leading citizens of St. Paul. He was nicknamed the "Father of the Minnesota Railroad System." He died in White Bear Lake, Minnesota, in 1889.[4]

Another director of the young company

Edmund Rice, first president of the Minnesota & Pacific and Saint Paul & Pacific Railroads. (James J. Hill Papers)

was Alexander Ramsey. Born in Harrisburg, Pennsylvania, in 1815, he was active in the politics of his state, serving in Congress in Washington from 1843 to 1847. In 1849 he was appointed governor of the Territory of Minnesota by President Zachary Taylor and remained as such until 1853. In 1855 he was mayor of St. Paul, from 1860 to 1863 governor of the state of Minnesota, from 1863 to 1875 U.S. senator, and finally from 1879 to 1881 secretary of war under President Hayes. Always an active promoter of railroads, he died in St. Paul in 1903, having played an important role in Minnesota history.[5]

Francis Roach Delano was also among the first directors of the Minnesota & Pacific. Born in New Braintree, Massachusetts, in 1823, he came to Minnesota as a lumberman in 1853, and settled in St. Paul in 1860. Later he became general superintendent of the Saint Paul & Pacific and then right-of-way agent of the Saint Paul, Minneapolis & Manitoba. He also served in different capacities with the Great Northern Railway. He was a member of the Minnesota legislature in 1875 and died in St. Paul in 1887 (his name will be encountered again in this story).[6]

William Crooks, U.S. Army engineer from West Point, was engineer in chief until July 1857, when he was succeeded by David C. Shepard, who stayed on as such until June 1860.[7] Crooks meanwhile was in charge of one of the surveying parties of 1857 and returned to his post as engineer in chief in

1860. In this capacity he supervised the construction of the first miles of railroad in Minnesota; then he left for the battlefields of the Civil War as colonel of the Sixth Minnesota Infantry regiment in 1862. He returned to St. Paul in 1864.[8] Crooks must have been familiar with Minnesota before he came to St. Paul, as his father, Ramsay Crooks, had been agent of the American Fur Company in Minnesota and later director of that company in New York, which may well explain why the son went west to make his career.

First secretary of the Minnesota & Pacific was James W. Taylor, who was apparently already living in St. Paul. Taylor had a remarkable career after he gave up his post at the general office of the Minnesota & Pacific. In 1859 he was appointed representative of the U.S. Treasury Department at St. Paul with the express duty of watching the trade of the Hudson's Bay Company there, an official spy as it were. He did his work well, apparently, for ten years later he also got a special commission from the State Department to report on American-Canadian relations and trade in the area. In the same year 1869 he also was commissioned as public relations officer, press agent, and official lobbyist for the Northern Pacific and the Saint Paul & Pacific Railroads, something that could well be combined with his duties as government watchdog. In 1870 he was sent to Winnipeg as the first American consul there, but he still remained active for "his" railroads.[9]

Still in 1857 the line of the Minnesota & Pacific was roughly located in the terrain as far as Big Stone Lake in the west on the Main line, and from St. Anthony to St. Cloud and Crow Wing on the Branch line.[10] Hopes for a speedy completion ran high, and David C. Shepard, the engineer then in charge, reported in January 1858 to the directors in favorable terms. The terrain was nowhere really difficult, and land proved to be very fertile and fit for agriculture after clearing off the timber. For the development of the territory the construction of this railroad was imperative, and its financial prospects favorable. The land grant of 2,457,600 acres at an estimated $8 per acre gave, according to Shepard, a basis of $30,720 per mile, "a sum sufficient to cover every expense incident to construction and a full equipment, and leave a large margin to apply on interest and discount accounts independent of the earnings of the road."[11]

The addition of the word *Pacific* in corporate names of American railroads in those years was not uncommon but was generally only wishful (or at least too optimistic) thinking. The connection with the Pacific was something people were dreaming about, and it was seen as a way to lure potential investors. As a matter of fact several surveys had already been made for a real transcontinental railroad, connecting the Atlantic and the Pacific. In the case of the Minnesota & Pacific the word *Pacific* in the company's corporate title was probably not quite a hollow claim or a mere optimistic thought. From Shepard's remarks in his report about British interests, which were then considering building a line to the Pacific in connection with the Minnesota line, it becomes clear that the Pacific was seen as a possible terminus for the railroad in the future. And indeed, Lieutenant Matthew F. Maury— superintendent of the U.S. Navy Depot of Charts and Instruments at Washington, D.C., and a scientist of note who had already reported on Pacific railroad routes back in 1847—in 1858 advised a citizens' committee of St. Paul about possible routes from Minnesota to Puget Sound.[12] Moreover Isaac I. Stevens, governor of Washington Territory, who in 1853 had surveyed a railroad route from the Mississippi to Oregon, thought that a future Canadian railroad to the Pacific could never be built north of Lake Superior because of the geographical obstacles there. He thought it would have to follow the road through Minnesota instead.[13] Indeed, for optimistic souls, a possible connection between Minnesota and the Pacific at the time did not seem too remote.

Surveys of the railroad were finished in 1857, for both Main and Branch lines, and actual grading work on the ten miles between St. Paul and St. Anthony was started on October 1 of that year by the contractor Selah Chamberlain of Cleveland, Ohio. Selah Chamberlain, together with his brother Joseph, had already done much railroad work in the area, on a part of the Milwaukee & Mississippi among other lines.[14] He was to be paid $22,000 per mile after completion of the road, but after one month of grading he stopped work as no money was forthcoming. By then most of the grading of those first ten miles must have been finished, as the line, apart from the descent to the levee at St. Paul, was generally level and

The surveys for the Minnesota & Pacific Railroad lines as executed in 1857. (From Hidy, Hidy, Scott, and Hofsommer, *The Great Northern Railway*, 1988, courtesy of Harvard Business School Press)

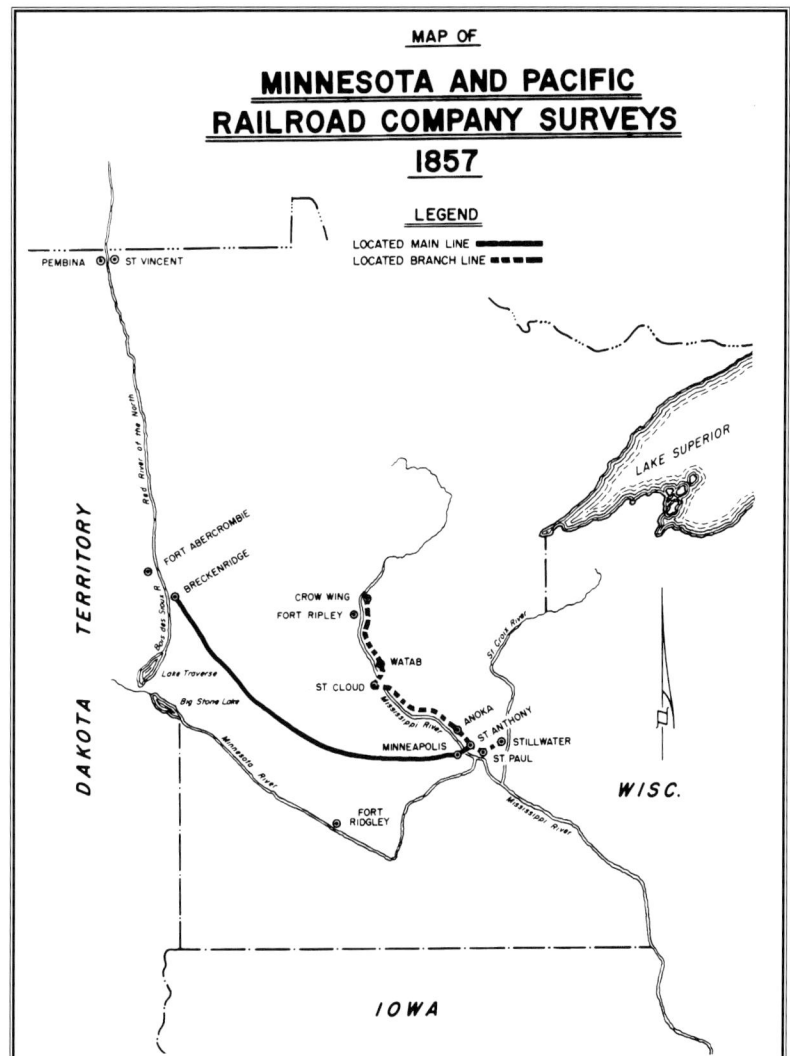

without any great obstacles. The St. Paul end was left open for the time, as no clear title to the right-of-way had yet been obtained. A new contract with Chamberlain was made in April 1858 for the extension of the Branch line from St. Anthony to Anoka and Big Lake. By that time the legislature had passed the act for state help, and the contractor was to be paid in the new 7 percent state bonds to the tune of $20,000 per mile, plus $3,000 in railroad bonds.[15]

A further contract, covering the extension of the line to Sauk Rapids, was signed in June 1858, and Chamberlain was to get $18,000 in state bonds plus some cash for this easy, level stretch. Altogether a total of $800,000 in state bonds was issued in support of the Minnesota & Pacific, after the grading had been finished. Some 62 miles of the Branch line were graded and bridged, and a large part of the necessary ties had been delivered.[16] But still not a single rail had been laid when the contractor had to stop work. His state bonds had depreciated so much that he was unable to sell them even at a large discount.

Altogether Chamberlain held 967 state bonds (of $1,000 each), for which he claimed to have done enough work to consider them as having been given out at about par value. When he later sued the state for redemption of these bonds at par plus interest, a neutral expert figured out that the 120 miles of grading done by him for all railroads in Minnesota had cost him $341,211 ($2,843 per mile), so that the bonds had actually cost him only about 30 percent of par. His bonds were redeemed accordingly to that amount only.[17]

Because of nonpayment of interest on the state bonds by the several railroads in Minnesota, including the Minnesota & Pacific, all their charters were revoked by the legislature in 1860 and all land grants were forfeited. Moreover, the deadlines for finishing the lines had not been met, as no railroad had yet laid any rails or run any train at all. The situation seemed desperate. Not every-

thing was lost, however, as in March 1861 the possessions, franchises, and privileges of the Minnesota & Pacific were returned to the company on the same terms as before. Only then, a sum of $10,000 as a guarantee of good faith had to be deposited with the governor, which was to be forfeited if the terms of the charter could not be met by the company. Of all the railroads concerned, only the Minnesota & Pacific managed to lay hands on this sum and deposit it with the governor. But if the company could open the line from St. Paul to St. Anthony before January 1, 1862, remained to be seen.[18]

It was clear that outside financial help was needed to get the railroad running. This was nothing unusual, as around this time it had become clear that most new railroads needed such vast sums of construction capital that local or regional capitalists were not able to supply enough. And in undeveloped regions such as Minnesota this lack of capital was even more marked than elsewhere in the nation. Eastern financiers had already taken over former local roads in the Northwest, such as the Chicago, Burlington & Quincy, the Chicago & North Western, and others, after local or regional capital had failed to materialize in the necessary amounts. The sums involved were becoming simply too large for the local businessmen, and the big fortunes in New England and New York were willing to risk their money in Western railroads in the hope of profits. And not only American capitalists were interested, but English and Dutch investors also had found a way to American railroads. The young Illinois Central had already attracted large amounts of foreign capital, and a large majority of its stock was held in London and Amsterdam. Other railroads were soon to follow this trend.

A well-informed man like Edmund Rice must have been aware of this change, and he contacted J. Edgar Thomson, president of the mighty Pennsylvania Railroad.[19] In the 1850s Thomson was extending his road into Ohio and possibly further west all the way to the Mississippi River, so Rice could well have been right in thinking that Thomson might be the man to help his ailing Minnesota & Pacific. And indeed, Thomson was so interested that he sent an engineer, Oliver W. Barnes, out to Minnesota to check the plans of the road and go over the proposed lines. Barnes's report was favorable enough for Rice and Crooks to be summoned in person to Philadelphia in May 1861 to talk things over with Thomson. Governor Alexander Ramsey of Minnesota, then in Washington, joined Rice and Crooks to put still more weight behind the Minnesota & Pacific, and talks with the Philadelphia parties went on well into June 1861. However, there were clouds on the political horizon that made Eastern financiers wary, and the outbreak of the Civil War soon put an end to all negotiations. Thomson was no longer able to help.[20]

All was still not lost, however. After leaving Philadelphia for New York, and without much hope remaining because of the impending war, Crooks met with a representative of Messrs. Winters & Harshman, bankers from Ohio, who were negotiating a deal for building the Winona & Saint Peter Railway with "Colonel" Andrew DeGraff. For this purpose the Ohio firm had associated itself with Elias F. Drake, a lawyer from Dayton, Ohio, and a director of the Dayton & Cincinnati Railroad.[21] Drake became the acting partner of the triumvirate and was to be from then on much involved in railroad construction in Minnesota. Later, as a director of the Minnesota Valley Railroad, he was instrumental in finishing that road all the way to Sioux City.[22]

After long talks with Rice and Crooks, the firm Winters, Harshman & Drake agreed to furnish the necessary means of building the line from St. Paul to St. Anthony. The Ohio firm deposited the required $10,000 with the governor and signed a formal contract: they were to complete the grade, lay the track, and furnish rolling stock in return for $12,000 per mile in 8 percent gold bonds of

the railroad (total $120,000) plus all lands to which the railroad could make title at that time, which amounted to some 76,800 acres, mostly in Hennepin County.[23] One problem remained, in that no clear title to the right-of-way in St. Paul had been obtained, which caused new delay. The line was to be opened to the public before January 1, 1862. Because of all delays, actual construction finally began only in the fall of 1861—probably too late to finish before the deadline stipulated in the contract.

Other conditions of the contract were indeed met, however: on September 9, 1861, the steamboat Alhambra delivered the first shipment of rails and other construction equipment at the Jackson Street landing in St. Paul. Half a mile downstream some thirteen hundred feet of track had been laid, using very light iron rails weighing not more than forty-five pounds to the yard. At this temporary end-of-tracks, the first locomotive was delivered. From Paterson, New Jersey, where it was built, the engine was transported on its own wheels to La Crosse, Wisconsin, the nearest railhead. There it was transferred to a barge towed by the Alhambra and brought upriver. With great difficulty the locomotive—Minnesota & Pacific number 1, named the Wm. Crooks—was unloaded, put on the short stretch of track provided, and run into a shed, where it was to be stored for the winter. Together with the engine, some freight cars were also delivered. A second engine—Minnesota & Pacific number 2, the Edmund Rice—was ordered by the contractors and delivered to St. Paul on September 28, 1861, by the same boat. As there was no work for it to do it was also stored for the winter.[24] Minnesota had its first railroad, but it was only thirteen hundred feet long, with two engines stored away in a shed and no traffic. The legislature considered this as not complying with the deadlines mentioned in the charter, and all possessions, franchises, and privileges of the Minnesota & Pacific were declared forfeited once again.

The first, primitive station at St. Anthony during the early years of operation. Minneapolis is in the distance and Nicollet Island is in the middle, with the road bridge connecting the two visible in the right background. The boxcar standing on the house track is still lettered for the Minnesota & Pacific. (Photo by Upton, Minnesota Historical Society)

The Saint Paul & Pacific Railroad Company

Although a serious attempt had been made to open the line of the Minnesota & Pacific, at the beginning of the year 1862 the state of Minnesota had not a single mile of railroad in operation. True, it did possess two steam locomotives, never used, and a couple of freight cars, but this was all. With the failure of the (second) Minnesota & Pacific Railroad Company to open its line from St. Paul to St. Anthony before January 1, 1862, all its possessions and privileges had been forfeited and returned to the state. But the state was not in a position to operate a railroad of its own, and the legislature was willing to listen to interested parties who wanted to take over the defunct Minnesota & Pacific lock, stock, and barrel.

So, on March 10, 1862, the legislature turned the possessions and franchises of the former Minnesota & Pacific over to a new company, the Saint Paul & Pacific Railroad Company, which was incorporated on the same day. In reality, this was the same old company, with the same directors and officers, only in a new external appearance. In all probability it was given a new name only to make potential investors forget the misfortunes of the earlier unfortunate Minnesota & Pacific. Edmund Rice was president again, with Delano among the directors as before and George Becker doubling as a director and land commissioner. Becker had come to St. Paul in 1849 and practiced law together with Rice. He had withdrawn from the law firm in 1857 and become active in the railroad business.[1]

The new act stipulated again that a sum of $10,000 was to be deposited with the governor and was to be forfeited if the line between St. Paul and Anoka (on the Branch line) was not in operation by January 1, 1864. The company complied and offered to deposit the $10,000 in state railroad bonds, but the governor refused them on the grounds of insufficient security—clear proof of the very small value of those bonds.[2] The earlier contract with Winters, Harshman & Drake was renewed, and under the close supervision of chief engineer William Crooks, tracklaying was pushed vigorously ahead. The two engines, *Wm. Crooks* and *Edmund Rice,* were hauled out of the shed in which they had wintered and were fired up again to be used on construction trains. Two engines were not enough to pull all trains, however, as was clearly demonstrated after the *Wm. Crooks* collided with a team on a level crossing and was thrown into the ditch on July 22, 1863. It needed a new set of driving wheels, which arrived only in August. The engine was back in service in September, but for two months the company had only one serviceable locomotive. The contractors had placed an order for two more engines back in May 1863, but the engines were

RAILROADS

SAINT PAUL AND PACIFIC RAILROAD.

On and after the 18th inst., the trains will run to
and from Suspension Bridge on the following table

TIME TABLE NO TWO.

Leave St. Paul.	Arrive at St. Anthony.	Leave St. Anthony.	Arrive at St. Paul.
5.30 A. M.	6 90 A. M.	7.10 A. M.	7 30 A. M.
9.00 "	9.30 "	10.00 "	10.30 "
2.00 P. M.	2 30 P. M.	3.00 P. M.	3.30 P. M.
5.00 "	5 30 "	6.00 "	6 30 "

No Sunday Trains.

On and after the 16th September, the first morn-
ing train (5 30) wil l start from the head of Mississip
pi street. The last evening train from St. Anthony
will stop at the same place.

Stages wil connect with these trains.

CHAS A F. MORRIS,
Chief Engineer and Superintendent.

St. Paul, Sept. 1.   nov3–tf

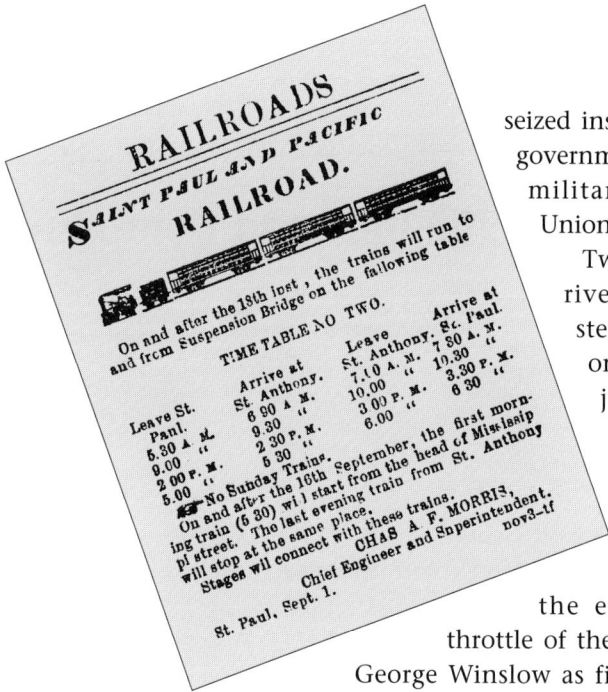

A newspaper clipping from September 16, 1862, displaying the second timetable of the Saint Paul & Pacific. (James J. Hill Papers)

seized instead by the U.S. government to serve the military needs of the Union army.[3]

Two carriages arrived on board the steamboat *Key City* on June 28, 1862, just in time for the formal opening of the line on July 2, 1862. W. C. Gardner was the engineer at the throttle of the first train, with George Winslow as fireman and J. B. Rice as conductor. John H. Randall was general ticket agent, accountant, chief clerk, and paymaster and, in case of sickness of the one conductor, also stand-in for this worthy. The rest of the staff consisted of a baggage master and two men in the engine house. More freight cars arrived later that year, so that by the end of 1862 the company was in possession of two engines, two passenger coaches, ten freight cars, and between fourteen and fifteen miles of track including side tracks. It was not much, but at least a small beginning, and Minnesota had its first railroad at long last.[4]

Winters, Harshman & Drake had fulfilled their part of the contract on time and were paid off accordingly on June 30, 1862. Altogether they got $325,000, chiefly in bonds and stocks.[5] At this time it was a common procedure to pay contractors in securities instead of cash. Newly opened railroads generally had no cash available until some traffic and revenues had been generated, and the only way to pay off the debts to the contractors was to give them securities of the railroad company. The contractors were then left with the problem of how to dispose of these bonds and stocks as best as they could. When the railroad in question was doing well, its securities could com-

mand a fair price on the market, but when it was slow in getting on its feet this paper could only be sold at a great discount. The risk was theirs, but usually some discount was already applied in the total to be paid.

The total sum received by Winters, Harshman & Drake works out at $32,500 per mile but, of course, includes the locomotives and rolling stock. The two steam locomotives would have cost about $11,000 apiece including shipping, the ten freight cars maybe another $5,000 all told, and the two coaches $1,500 each, leaving $295,000 for the construction of the line and building of depots, engine sheds, and such—still a generous sum per mile. It is most probable, however, that the bonds and stocks surrendered were not valued at par but at a great discount.

The first timetable, issued on July 1, 1862, showed three daily trains between St. Paul and St. Anthony, taking a leisurely twenty-five minutes for the ten miles of light iron rail. The fare was sixty cents one way—a lot of money for most people, when an unskilled laborer in St. Paul made only $1.75 a day and a skilled artisan about double that wage.[6] Trains left St. Paul at 6 and 9 A.M. and at 6 P.M. Trains in the opposite direction left St. Anthony daily at 7 A.M. and at 2 and 7 P.M. Because thirty-five minutes to service and turn the engine at St. Anthony after the first morning run turned out to be not enough, the departure of the first train out of St. Paul was fixed at 5:20 instead of 6 A.M. starting on July 3. On Sundays only two trains were run.

The first, temporary depot in St. Paul was built close to the levee at the foot of Rosabel Street and was a very modest affair, measuring only seven by nine feet in all. From there the line ran due east across swamps and creeks, mostly on trestles, before turning north, and after a stiff climb out of the river bottom it turned west toward St. Anthony. The first station there was situated on the prairie at the back of the first buildings of the University of Minnesota.[7] In later years, starting in 1863, the swamps along the Mississippi at St. Paul were filled in with dirt obtained when some of the bluffs in town were leveled and the streets graded. The original depot building was soon vacated and a new, somewhat larger one more to the west was opened early in 1863. In 1864, after some legal wrangling about the right-of-way, the line was again extended along the river to the west to bring it closer to the business center. A new depot was built near the foot of Wacouta Street on the old island number 11 in the river, after landfills had made this possible. This depot building served until 1873, when a new one was opened on the same spot, together with a new emigrant house, eighty feet long, also to replace an earlier one.

In the winter of 1863 a freight warehouse was opened near the foot of Wacouta Street. The existing warehouse near Sibley Street of Hill & Griggs, the local freight agents of the Saint Paul & Pacific, was enlarged to two hundred by sixty feet in the winter of 1865. A grain elevator was built by contractor William B. Litchfield early in 1866 near the passenger depot.[8] Slowly, sloughs were filled in, creeks covered or bridged, and tracks and yards extended to serve the growing business at St. Paul.

General offices were built nearby, but unfortunately the building was lost in a fire on November 25, 1878, together with most of the corporate records.[9] An engine house with workshops and stores was erected north of town on vacant land near the extension of Jackson Street. These buildings did not last long: on June 23, 1867, the machine and car shops burned to the ground with a reported loss of no less than $150,000.[10] They were insured for only $30,000. Besides all the buildings and stores, one engine (the *Wm. Crooks*), two new baggage cars, and one boxcar were also lost. The *Crooks* was later repaired and in 1869 put back into service after an almost com-

plete rebuilding.[11] This misfortune must have hindered the maintenance of engines and rolling stock to a great extent, although friendly neighboring railroads undertook some work. All structures were rebuilt straightaway and were much extended over the years. Part of the Jackson Street shops, as rebuilt in stone by the Great Northern Railway, have recently been converted into office buildings and are still standing.

Extension of the Lines

The Branch Line

Of course, running three trains a day over ten miles of track was meant to be just a beginning, and the work of extending the lines was taken in hand immediately. James D. Skinner had been appointed chief engineer to succeed Crooks, who had moved south with his regiment, and Skinner was responsible for the construction of the Branch line to Anoka and beyond, and also for the Main line, including the bridge across the Mississippi River at St. Anthony. He was to stay with the company until 1868. A new contract was signed between the company and a certain Electus B. Litchfield of New York City to build the Branch line to St. Cloud.[12] He was to be paid in stock to the tune of $350,000; the actual construction work was to be done by his son William B. Litchfield.

Edmund Rice stepped down temporarily as president (Geo. Becker replacing him) and was appointed agent and attorney of the company and empowered to travel to Europe in 1863 to find financial backing (about which more later) and place orders

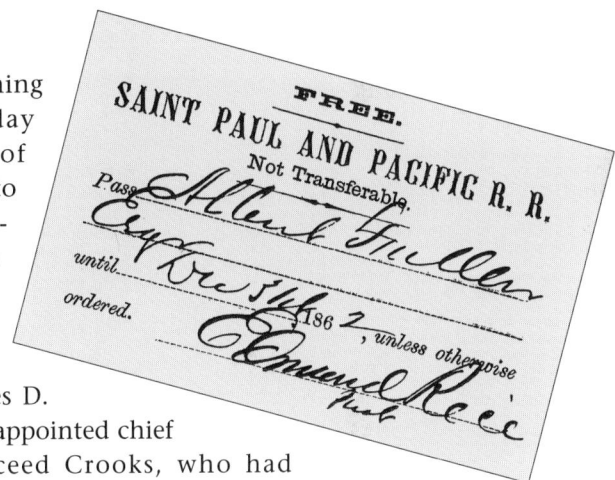

One of the first free passes from the Saint Paul & Pacific, issued to Mr. Albert Fuller and signed by President Edmund Rice. (Albert Fuller Collection, Minnesota Historical Society)

The St. Paul levee in 1866. Litchfield's grain elevator and James J. Hill's freight warehouse take up much of the available space. Boxcars of the Saint Paul & Pacific stand on the elevator spur. Note the steam boiler lying in the foreground. (Photo by Upton, Minnesota Historical Society)

for iron.[13] He went to London, the financial capital of the world, and came back with a contract for three thousand tons of iron rails. British ironmasters were used to accepting American railroad shares and bonds in lieu of cash payments for rails and other iron. Most young American railroad companies had little or no cash to spare, hence the payments in securities. When the stock market was good, these securities could then be unloaded on the public.

Despite the deliveries of iron, progress was agonizingly slow, even in the flat and easy terrain along the east bank of the Mississippi.[14] Anoka, seventeen miles beyond St. Anthony, was reached on January 1,

1864, and the deadline stipulated by the legislature was therefore only just met, although the first train for the public actually ran only on January 18 of that year. Elk River, twenty-nine miles from St. Anthony, was reached in October 1864; East St. Cloud, sixty-four miles from the junction in St. Anthony, only in September 1866. There the railroad builders, who must have been completely out of breath by this hair-raising speed of construction, had to stop for a moment, until the bridge over the Mississippi could be finished.[15]

Charles A. F. Morris, who had been city engineer of St. Paul in 1862–1863 and who was to be chief engineer of the railroad after mid-1871, had already assisted Skinner as engineer of the railroad, and he got the contract for building the bridge at St. Cloud, where the line was to divide. One extension was to go across the river and northwest toward Alexandria and St. Vincent, the other was to go due north to meet the Northern Pacific, then planning to build west from Duluth, at Brainerd. Sauk Rapids, on the Brainerd branch and sixty-six miles from St. Anthony, was reached in July 1867, but construction then stopped and the Saint Paul & Pacific would never extend as far as Brainerd. A few miles in the direction of Brainerd were laid as far as Watab, but that was all.

The towns along the new line were booming soon after the railroad came through. About fifteen hundred people were living in Anoka, and the town boasted of a furniture factory. St. Cloud, county seat of Stearns County, was much bigger, had thirteen hotels, a brewery, a distillery, and two weekly papers for its three thousand inhabitants, of which about two thousand were Germans, hence probably the brewery. St. Cloud was also important as a shipping point for the Hudson's Bay Company freight to the north, annually at least five hundred tons. It also boasted a wagon bridge over the Mississippi to connect with the railhead at East St. Cloud. Sauk Rapids was much smaller and could show a population of only five hundred in 1869.[16] At first only one daily train sufficed, but by 1872 traffic on the Branch line warranted two trains daily, which took a generous time of some four and a half hours to cover the seventy-six miles between St. Paul and Sauk Rapids.

The Main Line

Meanwhile, little or no work had been done by Litchfield on the Main line, and a new contract was signed between the railroad company and the firm of Andrew De-Graff & Company in 1866 for construction

The shops and round-house of the Saint Paul & Pacific at Jackson Street in St. Paul, circa 1875. The complex was later extensively enlarged and rebuilt by the Great Northern Railway. Everybody, including the man standing on the cab roof of the only locomotive in sight (middle left), seems to be following the movements of the photographer. (Minnesota Historical Society)

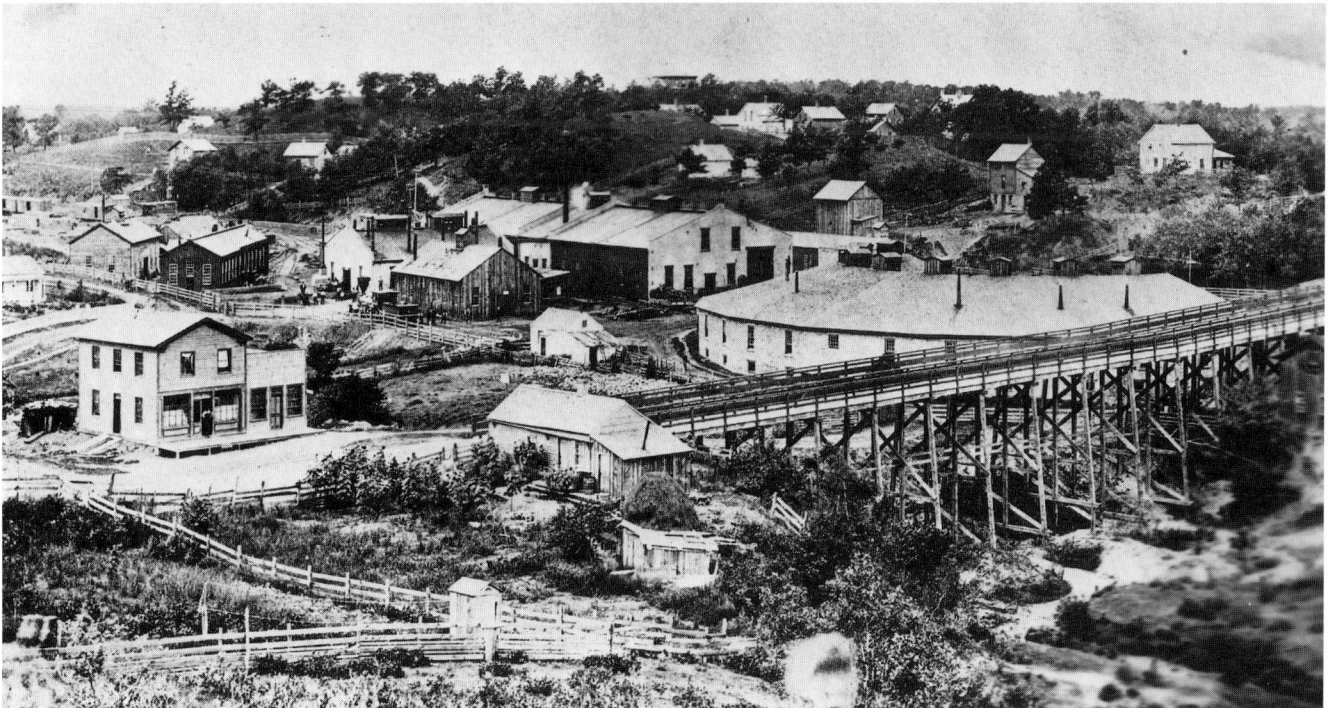

The depot of Sauk Centre as it looked in 1900, well into the days of the Great Northern Railway. (Minnesota Historical Society)

of that line.[17] William Crooks, after having returned from the war unharmed and been welcomed home as a hero, was partner in this DeGraff firm.

The first obstacle to be met was, of course, the bridge across the Mississippi. The original depot at St. Anthony behind the university had been replaced by one a little bit farther west, at the junction where the Branch line curved away to the northwest and the Main line turned south, following what was later Oak Street in St. Anthony down to the river. For bridging the river, a point had been chosen where Nicollet Island was situated, just above the falls. Skinner was engineer in charge, and he designed the bridge as a wooden Howe Truss, a type of bridge then much used. The shallow slough between the island and the north bank was bridged late in 1866 with two

spans of 150 feet each, on stone piers and abutments. Trestlework carried the line over the island, and the main channel was crossed with one span of 160 feet, three of 135 feet, and one of 80 feet close to the Minneapolis bank, again all on solid stone piers and abutments. The 160-foot span was the last to be finished, on June 10, 1867.[18] No movable spans were needed, as there was no navigation possible anyhow because of the proximity of the falls. Contractors for the bridge were Reynolds, Saulspaugh & Company and Boomer, Boynton & Company—probably one firm for the stone piers and the other for the wooden superstructure, but it is not clear who built what. Total cost of the bridge was low, only some $45,000.[19] Construction may have been too light, however, for already in 1874 and 1875 heavy repairs were necessary. At that time the 80-foot span was replaced by a trestle. The winter timetable for 1868–1869 showed three trains per day between St. Paul and Minneapolis, plus one from St. Paul to the end of the Branch line by way of St. Anthony.

The original depot in Minneapolis was again a simple wooden structure, without any luxuries or fancy decorations, as befitted a young frontier city. But soon extensions and improvements were necessary to cope with the growing traffic. A separate freight shed was erected, much bigger than the passenger depot, which itself was replaced by a larger, more elaborate one early in 1877. Several local firms worked on the new depot building: R. P. Russell & Company did all kinds of woodwork, to a total of no less than $1,062.06. James L. Spink supplied two hopper closets and two fancy marble tables, plus all the plumbing for $126.03, and Beck & Ranck did all the painting, glazing, and frescoing on the new building, which had a separate ladies' toilet among its amenities. His bill ran to over a thousand dollars. The existing scale for weighing freight trucks was repaired by Fair-

banks, Morse & Company, a firm famous for this kind of work.[20]

Building west of Minneapolis was easy, apart from the chronic lack of funds. Lake Minnetonka, already a popular holiday spot, was reached in August 1867, and the company at once advertised excursion trains to the lake. Delano, 40 miles from the junction at St. Anthony, was reached on October 14, 1868; Litchfield, 78 miles, in August 1869; Kerkhoven, 118 miles, in May 1870; Breckenridge, the end of the line 207 miles from St. Anthony, at last in October 1871.[21]

Toward the end of their contract, DeGraff & Company were really speeding up construction. In June 1871 more than twenty miles of track were laid, and eleven more the next month. In August eighteen more miles followed, plus some buildings: a dwelling ($1,250) and a handcar/section house ($550) at Douglass, the same at Moose Island and Herman, plus a second-class depot at Herman ($1,900). In September eighteen miles were laid, a two-stall engine house plus tank house erected at Herman ($2,840), a tank house with

The depot of Atwater, on the Main line west of Litchfield, in the 1890s. Fairbanks scales, used to weigh freight trucks, can be seen to the right of the telegraph pole. (Minnesota Historical Society)

The first railroad yard of the Saint Paul & Pacific at Washington Avenue and Third Avenue North in Minneapolis in 1873. The small building to the left is the passenger depot, and the bigger one in the middle is the freight depot. The engine standing with its train on the elevator spur could well be No. 12, the *Wayzata*, built by Danforth in 1869. (Don Hofsommer Collection, Great Northern Railway)

dwelling built at Gorton ($646), some more section houses at other places, and fourth-class depots at Gorton and Tintah ($1,250). Then in October the last fourteen miles were laid, plus many sidetracks at different places, which effectively completed De-Graff's contract.[22]

Litchfield was about the only township with a population amounting to anything. The houses of an earlier settlement on the Crow River, six miles to the north, were bodily moved to Litchfield when the railroad opened. But even an overoptimistic plunger

like McClung in 1869 could not say more about Meeker County and its "towns" of Litchfield and Darwin than that they were embryo towns, just laid out, on the railroad.[23]

After the line to Breckenridge was finished, one daily train covered the whole distance. The first time card of 1872 shows a train leaving St. Paul at 7:50 A.M. and supposed to arrive in Breckenridge at 7:30 P.M. The return train left Breckenridge at 6:15 A.M. and arrived at its destination at 6:15 P.M. One daily extra train from St. Paul to Litchfield and back was also scheduled, which took an ample four hours for the seventy-eight miles. Between St. Paul and Minneapolis two more daily trains were run, which took about forty minutes to cover the distance.[24]

The Saint Paul & Pacific in 1863 contracted with A. B. Smith and Z. G. Simmons of Kenosha, Wisconsin, for the construction of a telegraph line along the railroad for $90 per mile. With J. C. Burbank of the Northwestern Express Company of St. Paul a contract was signed in 1866 for the business of express goods: the railroad was to provide an express car, the other party in return was to pay $2,500 per annum for the exclusive right. Two years later the company contracted with W. J. Davidson, also of St. Paul, for the erection of grain elevators along the main line.[25]

That the word *Pacific* in the corporate title of the company was indeed not seen as wholly empty is proved by a survey made by Skinner in May–July 1871, before the track had reached Breckenridge. At the express order of President Becker, Skinner was to survey for a line from Breckenridge across the Dakotas to Fort Sully on the Missouri River, circa 250 miles long.[26] This reconnaissance, ending on July 17, 1871, was carried out by a party of twenty-six men under Skinner and included, apart from the usual surveyors, axmen, draftsmen, and cooks, also a certain J. Demarre, interpreter, along with Wambediwiaper, a Native American guide, the latter at $2 per day.[27] No actual results of this survey are known.

The short stretch from Stillwater to St. Paul, already included in the original charter of the Minnesota & Pacific and therefore also in that of the Saint Paul & Pacific, was never built by the company. All forces and available funds were concentrated on the construction of the Branch line to St. Cloud and beyond and of the Main line toward Breckenridge. The Stillwater line was quietly forgotten. It was certainly less interesting to

A view in 1882 of Benson looking northwest from Twelfth Street, displaying the vastness of the Minnesota plains. Benson was one of many towns that sprang up along the Main line of the Saint Paul & Pacific. (Photo by James Studio, Benson, Minnesota Historical Society)

A later photograph of the St. Paul levee. The grain elevator and freight warehouse are still evident, but the line has been extended to bring the passenger terminus, visible in the foreground, closer to the business district. The large stone freight house of the La Crosse & Milwaukee Railroad is apparently brand new. The trestle taking the Saint Paul & Pacific out of the river bottom is visible in the left background, and that of the La Crosse & Milwaukee is to the right of the elevator. (James J. Hill Papers)

THE SAINT PAUL & PACIFIC RAILROAD

the original railroad incorporators, as the land grant applied mostly to the lines west of St. Paul. In 1867 the powers for building that line were officially transferred to the Saint Paul & Chicago Railway, which in turn became part of the Milwaukee & Saint Paul Railway in 1872, then finally renamed the Chicago, Milwaukee & Saint Paul Railway in 1874.[28]

The Sioux Uprising

Field excursions into what was then former Sioux country, just opened up to whites, were only possible as a result of the Sioux Uprising or Dakota War of 1862. The Sioux had become restless on their reservations along the Minnesota River and in the western part of the state because of their justified complaints about the fraudulent execution of the treaties on the part of the American government.[29] The slow filling up of the land with settlers—legal and illegal—angered them even more. Since so many white men were away because of the Civil War in the South, some younger hotheaded Sioux leaders saw this as an excellent opportunity to get rid of the intruders once and for all and take back their native lands. In August 1862 they started a murderous campaign in the area of the Minnesota River, killing hundreds of settlers, burning houses and farms, and looting the whole area. Settlers fled in terror to the larger settlements and hastily assembled armed forces to stop the marauders.

A Sioux attack on Fort Ridgely, the American supply base on the Minnesota River, was repulsed without much loss of life, and a subsequent attack on the town of New Ulm, also on the Minnesota River, was also repulsed, but with greater loss of life. Governor Ramsey was instrumental in bringing together a substantial armed force, including the Minnesota Sixth Regiment under William Crooks, which had just been mustered but not yet sent south to fight the Confederacy. This force moved slowly forward into Sioux country and threatened the villages in the west. The Native Americans saw the futility of their attempt to stem the tide of white settlers, gave up their prisoners (mostly women and children), and scattered widely to avoid capture. Thousands later surrendered and were sent to reservations in the West. Thirty-eight of the ringleaders were hanged at Mankato late in 1862, and others were hunted down later. Small bands remained and continued to give trouble for some years, but generally Minnesota was open to white settlement since the Sioux had been removed from Minnesota soil. The former treaties with the Sioux were abrogated by Congress in February 1863, and the great majority of Sioux were removed to a reservation on the Missouri River.

This Dakota War, of course, was not the only cause of the slowness of railroad construction in Minnesota, but it did slow the westward movement of settlers and thereby diminished the demand for transportation. The chronic lack of funds was another, maybe more important cause of the snail's pace of construction of the railroad. A third problem was the lack of suitable labor. Labor had always been hard to get on the frontier and the Civil War meant a severe drain on the available manpower. No less than eleven infantry regiments were raised for the cause of the Union in Minnesota, plus two of cavalry and one of artillery. On the other hand, the war also meant that some industries were booming and new land was broken by the plow and converted into wheat fields to produce much needed foodstuffs. Laborers in these industries could make more money than by working on the railroad. The Saint Paul & Pacific tried hard to attract newly immigrated Irishmen in 1862 by offering them a wage of "nine shillings a day," apparently not bad for those days, but with little success.[30]

Officials of the Saint Paul & Pacific Railroad at Breckenridge in October 1871. The engine, *Wm. Crooks,* was the first locomotive of the company. Contractor Andrew DeGraff is at the very left in the top hat; director William B. Litchfield sits on the pilot of the locomotive; William Crooks is the bearded man leaning on the pilot; Leon Willmar, representative of the Dutch bondholders, is in the light suit in the middle; chief engineer Charles Morris stands on the right with his hands behind his back. The others in the group have not been identified. (Don Hofsommer Collection, Great Northern Railway)

Finances

To finance construction, the Saint Paul & Pacific resorted, as was commonly done in those days, to the issuing of loans. Capital stock was issued to those who were—and who wanted to remain—in control of the company, but it was hardly ever fully paid up, and in this case probably not at all. Some of it was even given to the Litchfields in payment for construction work done (which would cause a lot of trouble later on). Bonded loans were the usual way of raising construction and working capital until revenues from traffic were sufficient to cover expenses and leave something, if possible, for interest payments. A first loan was issued in June 1862, at 8 percent interest, running thirty years and being secured by a first mortgage on the Branch line. Total of the loan was $700,000. It is probable that Drake *cum suis* were paid off—at least in part—with these bonds. The bonds were not sold on the European market, and at the default of the company in 1873, $366,000 of this loan was still outstanding and taken over by the successor company.[1]

Trustees of this loan were Russell Sage and Samuel J. Tilden, both well known in financial circles. Russell Sage was at this time early in his career and still relatively unknown outside Wall Street, but he had al-ready made an unsavory name for himself by the many shady deals he had pulled off.[2] He had been very much involved in the La Crosse & Milwaukee and had enriched himself unscrupulously at the expense of the Wisconsin taxpayers. Bribery of the Wisconsin legislature had been practiced on an until-then-unprecedented scale. Together with Selah Chamberlain, later the contractor for the first line of the Saint Paul & Pacific and then receiver of the bankrupt La Crosse & Milwaukee Railroad, Sage also was a power to be reckoned with in the Milwaukee & Saint Paul Railroad, the successor to the La Crosse & Milwaukee.[3]

He was said by one of the later "muckracking" writers, Gustavus Myers, to have come away with millions from the Minnesota & Pacific venture, but it is difficult to get proof for this accusation.[4] True, he was trustee of the first Saint Paul & Pacific loan, and he will have made some money out of the deal, but that millions really disappeared into his pockets (as suggested by Myers) is hard to prove and probably not true. The New York office of the Saint Paul & Pacific was for a time housed in Sage's office at 25 William Street, but his name is not mentioned anymore in connection with later loans. Samuel Tilden, unsuccessful presidential candidate in 1876 and close friend of Sage, was trustee of some of the later loans.[5] Sage was certainly deceitful and corrupt to the core, but this was a time when corruption and bribery were more or less an accepted means of doing

Hennepin Avenue in Minneapolis in 1869, the view facing the river from atop the Nicollet House. The Mississippi River railroad bridge of the Saint Paul & Pacific is visible in the upper left. (Minnesota Historical Society)

business. The whole history of the Saint Paul & Pacific smacks strongly of corruption and shady deals, perpetrated by almost all parties involved, and Sage's share is hard to establish. His name is not mentioned even once in the later correspondence between the Dutch bondholders and James Hill and associates, nor in the voluminous correspondence between Hill and those associates. Thus Myers's accusations seem to be not too well founded in this case.

With the paying off of Winters, Harshman & Drake, little was left of this first issue for the extension of the lines. So on the same day, June 2, 1862, a second loan was issued, again running for thirty years and bearing 7 percent interest. The new loan was for $1,200,000 and was secured by a second lien on the Branch line and a first lien on part of the land grant. Sales of these bonds must have been sluggish and Edmund Rice, while in London, must have tried hard to sell them. A second lien on a property that was hardly existing (after all, the Branch line was nothing more than a

grade without rails at this time) could not have been very attractive to investors. Rice must have been very persuasive to get any of them sold at all. Now, he certainly could be most persuasive. He had already made a name for himself in 1864—when in Washington, D.C., on railroad business—when he tried to reach his goal by "distributing magnificent bouquets to the wives of members of Congress with a princely hand."[6] On that occasion he did succeed in persuading Congress to enlarge the company's land grant from six to ten sections of land.

In the end, the London firm of Robert Benson & Company—helped by E. Darwin Litchfield, who took care of the London side of the Litchfield family interest—took up the sale of the bonds. Benson had been involved in American railroad finance since he successfully undertook to market Illinois Central securities in Great Britain, and he had handled other American paper as well. In this case, he had little success at home but managed to unload a substantial portion of the bonds on a Dutch house.[7] Political reasons may have played a role here. The Confederate cause was fairly popular in England in the early years of the Civil War, and interest in "Yankee" railroads may have been flagging. American railroads were distinctly unpopular on the London stock market in those years.

The Dutch firm involved was the old, established stockbrokers' house of Kerkhoven & Company of Amsterdam and they managed to sell more than $625,000 of these bonds—first sections, as they were later known. But their introductory price of only 66 percent of par reflected the brokers' low opinion of the security offered by a second lien on a property of doubtful value. Kerkhoven, later assisted by other Dutch houses, was to remain faithful to the Saint Paul & Pacific Railroad to the end.

In 1864 the original incorporators of the Saint Paul & Pacific Railroad Company set up a new company, the First Division of the Saint Paul & Pacific Railroad Company. This was done ostensibly to facilitate the floating of new loans on foreign markets, as investors in England and Holland were supposed to be afraid of putting their money into a company with such an undefined and faraway goal as the Pacific. This rationale scarcely holds water, as foreign investors were generally well aware of what they were doing.[8]

Others have suspected that the intention was to set up a construction company, owned by the same stockholders as of the railroad and intended to finance and construct the railroad—to the personal advantage of the owners.[9] Indeed, the construction company was a favorite vehicle among swindlers, as it could easily be used for purposes of personal enrichment at the expense of the bondholders of the railroad company. But in this case, the First Division not only took over all possessions, franchises, privileges, and rolling stock of the original Saint Paul & Pacific but was to be the operating company as well. The original Saint Paul & Pacific Company became a sleeping partner,

owning no tracks and no rolling stock but still retaining its corporate identity and its rights to construct the remaining lines, such as the St. Vincent extension, as laid down in its original charter.

A new contract was entered into with William B. Litchfield & Company, which gave him about $850,000 worth of stock of the new First Division Company. All rights, franchises, and so on of the railroad, plus its complete administration, were transferred to him as well. For all intents and purposes the railroad was Litchfield's own private company, and he undertook to finish the remaining lines as soon as possible. The original stockholders of the Saint Paul & Pacific Railroad exchanged their old shares for shares in the new First Division Company, but they had only minority holdings. Largest among these were Edmund Rice himself with some $26,100 in shares, and Governor Alexander Ramsey with $10,000. Valentine Winters, Jonathan Harshman, and Elias Drake each also held some shares. George Becker became president of the new company, and William Litchfield vice president. The Minnesota legislature approved these changes on February 6, 1866.[10]

It is most probable that the incorporation of the First Division was done to give Litchfield the authority and the opportunity to build and operate the railroad. After all, the Litchfield brothers were a power in the land; together they could muster enough financial muscle to accomplish what local businessmen apparently could not. But the Litchfields were not willing to risk any of their own money, or rather, they were intent on making money out of the deal, so they continued to seek outside capital for construction.

George L. Becker, president of the First Division of the Saint Paul & Pacific, a new company formed in 1864 by the original incorporators of the Saint Paul & Pacific. (From Williams, *History of the City of Saint Paul*)

The two earlier loans issued by the Saint Paul & Pacific were clearly not enough to build the railroad, so more loans were required. In October 1865 the First Division Company issued another loan, this time of $2,800,000 at 7 percent, intended to retire the two earlier ones, hence it was called a consolidated loan.[11] That all earlier bonds were indeed retired is doubtful, as at least $625,000 of the first-section loan was still outstanding at the time of the default in 1873. This consolidated loan was secured by a mortgage on the Branch line (third lien) plus a first (partly) and second lien on the total land grant. Next came a loan—dated March 1, 1864, of $1,500,000 at 7 percent—secured by a first lien on 150 miles of the Main line. These bonds were not sold at all but were delivered to the trustees of a later loan of 1868. In 1866 a new loan was floated, $3,000,000 at 7 percent, and secured by a second lien on 150 miles of the Main line, plus a first lien on the corresponding part of the land grant. This loan was generally known as the second-section loan.

In 1868 the coffers were empty again and with the Main line not yet finished, another loan was issued, $6,000,000 at 7 percent, secured by a mortgage (first lien) on sixty miles of the Main line, plus a second lien on all other mileage and lands. As this loan was considered risky at best, the bonds of the earlier $1,500,000 loan of 1864 were delivered to the trustees of the 1868 loan as extra security. It will be seen that most of the mortgages, being second or even third liens on the property, were of doubtful value, yet the bonds were sold on the Dutch market with apparent ease.

The bonds of the consolidated loan of 1865 not needed for retiring the earlier loans—some 780 (of $1,000 each) in all—were again marketed through Benson in London, but there is no indication that he actually sold any. Kerkhoven, assisted by the firm of H. C. Voorhoeve of Rotterdam, marketed at least 760 of them at a price of 70 percent of par. To guarantee that at least for some years the 7 percent interest was to be paid, the Dutch brokers withheld 10 percent of their sales to be invested in "safe" U.S. bonds that could be sold to supply the cash needed for interest payments on the railroad bonds—a sure sign of the lack of solidity attributed by the brokers to the Saint Paul & Pacific.

The 1866 second-section loan was also marketed through Benson, but most of the bonds were immediately passed on to Kerkhoven and Voorhoeve and sold in Holland. A small number may have been kept in Britain, but at least one million (par value) turned out later to be held in Holland. The introductory price is not known but cannot have been much over 70 percent of par.

The 1868 loan of $6,000,000 was again placed chiefly on the Dutch market at 70 percent of par. Kerkhoven and Voorhoeve held back no less than 20 percent of the bonds and exchanged them for U.S. bonds to guarantee the interest payments for some years to come. But sales remained sluggish, and as an extra incentive early buyers were given an even lower price of 65.5 percent of par. In this way less than half of the nominal issue ended up in the coffers of the railroad company. Herman Trott, land commissioner of the railroad company, traveled to Amsterdam that year, no doubt to explain the slow progress of the tracks and the pressing need for more money.[12]

At the end of 1869 a total of $13 million (par value) had been invested in the Saint Paul & Pacific, but even with this large sum, the Main line was not yet in operation beyond Willmar, still more than one hundred miles from the intended terminus at Breckenridge, while the Branch line remained stuck in Sauk Rapids, with some more miles of rapidly deteriorating grade toward St. Vincent and Brainerd. The Dutch market seemed saturated with Saint Paul bonds. Yet more money was desperately needed to meet the deadlines stipulated in the contracts with the Minnesota legislature and as laid

The freight depot of the Lake Superior & Mississippi Railroad at Duluth, the eastern terminus of the Northern Pacific, in 1874. The Lake Superior & Mississippi formed the Northern Pacific's connection with St. Paul. (Minnesota Historical Society)

down in the original act of Congress. Originally the St. Vincent line was to have been finished not later than February 6, 1869!

This deadline was extended several times, but still, time was pressing. People in Minnesota were hopeful in 1869 that the lines would soon be finished. The *Winona Republican* boasted on August 22, 1869:

> The order given, the other day, over the Ocean Cable, by the European capitalists who own the main line of the St. Paul and Pacific Railroad, to complete that road to the Red River of the North, a distance of 225 miles from St. Paul, before the close of the present year, is an

event the full force and importance of which can scarcely be grasped at a single effort. It is a stroke of financial daring which, but a half dozen years ago, would have startled the people of the whole country.[13]

The paper was a bit too optimistic, as it turned out. It was still to take two more years before Breckenridge was finally reached.

Yet it took some daring to decide to put still more money into the road. After the company's consultations with Robert Benson and with one of the largest Amsterdam brokers, Lippmann & Rosenthal, as underwriters, they resolved in 1871 to issue one more loan, a very large one this time of no less than $15 million at 7 percent. Security was to be provided by a mortgage on the 293 miles from St. Cloud to St. Vincent and the 55 miles of line from Watab (just north of Sauk Rapids) to Brainerd. None of these lines could show more than some grades and a few dilapidated bridges, so the security thus given was of most doubtful value. Watab–Brainerd was actually never to be built by the Saint Paul & Pacific. Lippmann & Rosenthal was one of the foremost Amsterdam stockbroking and banking houses, much involved in American railroad finance. In these years they also advanced a lot of money to the company operating the state railways in the Netherlands.

Of course, the underwriters of this St. Vincent extension loan knew the real state of affairs quite well and therefore again withheld 20 percent of the total sales to guarantee interest payments until July 1874. Almost all the bonds were sold in Holland, at least $11.5 million. At a first price of 70 percent of par, minus the 20 percent security, minus the commission of the underwriting syndicate and brokers, less than half the nominal issue went to the construction account of the railroad. Brokers' commissions usually ran from 0.5 to 1.5 percent, but in the case of underwriting syndicates their commission could run much higher, sometimes as high as 10 percent, especially with securities that were considered hard to market. How much Lippmann & Rosenthal actually charged is not known, but they were later accused of exacting an exorbitant commission for their services.

It is hard to say what portion of all these loans actually flowed into the coffers of the railroad. Rumors of large-scale fraud flew about. One writer claimed later that no less than $8 million disappeared somehow, but this seems hardly possible.[14] It is worth trying to figure out how much of all these loans could in reality have reached the treasurer of the company to be spent on construction.

1. **1862** $700,000 at 70 percent = $490,000
2. **1862** $1,200,000 (1st sect.) at 66 percent = $792,000
3. **1865** $2,800,000 (cons.) at 70 percent = $456,000 (only the 760 bonds not used for redeeming the earlier loans)
4. **1864** $1,500,000 (given to trustees of number 6, whereabouts unknown)
5. **1866** $3,000,000 (2d sect.) at 70 percent = $2,100,000
6. **1868** $6,000,000 at 45 percent = $2,700,000 (sold at 65 percent but 20 percent kept back as extra security)
7. **1871** $15,000,000 (Ext.) at 40 percent = $6,000,000 (sold at 70 percent minus 20 percent security minus 10 percent brokers' commission)[15]

Of the first two loans (together $1,900,000), only $909,000 at the most was redeemed, for the rest was still outstanding in 1873. Of the consolidated loan (number 3), $909,000 may have been used to redeem numbers 1 and 2 in part, and $760,000 was sold in Amsterdam, making a total of $1,669,000, which leaves $1,131,000 of the consolidated loan unaccounted for. What happened to number 4 is not clear; it was never mentioned at the default, and it may have remained unissued and has therefore been omitted in the grand totals given here.

Of a grand total (par value) of $27,791,000 of loans issued (grand total of all loans minus the $909,000 of numbers 1 and 2 redeemed by number 3), at best only $12,548,000 may have flowed into the coffers of the railroad company. This figure assumes that all bonds have actually been sold, which may not be the case, and it leaves out the brokers' commission except in the case of the last loan, where the commission was known (and very high).[16] A figure of $12,000,000 may be on the safe side, and for just over six hundred miles of railroad planned, this should have worked out at $20,000 per mile, a most reasonable

Table 1   Actual Cost of the Lines of the Saint Paul & Pacific Railroad

Branch Line

Grading	76 miles at $3,000	$228,000
Bridges	638 feet at $25	16,000
Track	rail, 82 $^5/_8$ m., 80 tons per mile, at $90	594,900
	chairs, fishplates, bolts	44,000
	ties, 2,200 per mile at 36 cts.	65,439
	laying and ballast at $800 per mile	66,100
	switches	13,000
Right-of-way and fences		88,000
Engineering		38,000
Total roadbed and track, $15,200 per mile		**$1,154,000**
Buildings		50,000
Rolling stock	6 engines	54,000
	4 1st-class cars	20,000
	2 2d-class cars	6,400
	3 baggage cars	7,500
	40 freight cars	28,000
Grand total, at $17,400 per mile		**$1,320,000**[a]

Main Line

Grading and masonry	207 miles at $4,000	$ 828,000
Bridges	1,565 ft. at $25	39,125
	trestle, 7,263 ft. at $6	43,578
Track	rail, 217.5 m., 78.5 tons per mile, at $90	1,536,637
	chairs and spikes at $500 per mile	108,750
	ties, 2,200 per mile at 40 cts.	191,400
	laying and ballast at $500 per mile	108,750
	switches	16,600
Right-of-way		60,000
Snow fences		25,000
Engineering		103,000
Total roadbed, $14,800 per mile		**$1,962,000**
Buildings		60,000
Rolling stock	17 locomotives	153,000
	5 1st-class cars	25,000
	5 2d-class cars	16,000
	3 baggage cars	7,500
	196 freight cars at $700	137,200
Grand total, at $16,700 per mile		**$3,460,000**

Source: *Report of the Railroad Commissioners* for the year ending August 31, 1873, lxx–lxxi.

Note: [a] The depot grounds in St. Paul, which would be worth $500,000 as lots are valued, are not included above.

figure for a railroad in relatively easy terrain.

But, of course, the company never laid more than some 282 miles of Main and Branch lines before its default in 1873, and this makes a figure of $42,550 per mile, which is excessively high even when rolling stock is included. Somewhere, a lot of money must have disappeared—but much less than has been rumored. A Dutch visitor to St. Paul in 1873, who was allowed to consult the books and ledgers of the company and who spoke with President Becker and other officials, could find no proof of outright fraud, only of much free and careless spending and bad bookkeeping.[17] He was fully aware of the despair felt in Holland

and imagined poetically that the sighs of the desperate Dutch bondholders could be heard in the panting and hissing of the Saint Paul's locomotives.

It is possible to reconstruct the almost exact cost of the railroad by way of the reports of the Minnesota railroad commissioner, although the figures he gives were supplied by the railroad company and have therefore to be taken with a grain of salt (see table 1).[18] "Although the cost is low, this is a remarkably good piece of road, although the iron and bridges much depreciated."

Servicing a debt of the magnitude outlined in table 1 proved no easy task for the

Table 2 Lowest and Highest Prices of Saint Paul & Pacific Securities on the Amsterdam Stock Exchange (in percent of par)

	A	B	C	D	E	F
1864	63–65					
1865	29–63	50–54				
1866	48–62	45–55				
1867	55–59	44–51				
1868	58–73	49–67	59–71			
1869	68–70	63–70	65–67	66–69		
1870	56–69	50–68	52–68	52–70		
1871	65–71	63–72	63–71	64–73	70	
1872	72–77	64–77	63–74	64–76	64–76	
1873	26–65	15–65	13–65	16–66	12–66	
1874	27–32	12–16	10–16	11–20	5–10	
1875	25–45	14–21	10–20	7–17	3–10	59–65
1876	35–48	18–33	14–21	11–21	3–9	63–85
1877	39–61	18–27	15–20	16–31	3–9	85–94
1878	51–60	20–28	14–27	23–34	5–9	91–92
1879	59–78	24–32	23–25	25–37	5–14	98

Source: Archives of the Amsterdam Stock Exchange.

Notes: A = 7 percent first-section loan of 1862, $1,200,000.

B = 7 percent second-section loan of 1866, $3,000,000.

C = 7 percent consolidated mortgage loan of 1865, $2,800,000.

D = 7 percent loan of 1868, $6,000,000.

E = 7 percent St. Vincent extension loan of 1871, $15,000,000.

F = 10 percent receiver's certificates.

First Division Company. After all, the interest on the last loan, which netted only some $6,000,000, amounted to more than a million dollars annually, which was hardly feasible for an impecunious company with very limited earnings. In May 1873, even before the general crisis of that year really struck, the First Division Company had to announce that it was unable to pay the coupons due in May and July of that year of all loans except the 1871 St. Vincent extension, for which the guarantee was still good until July 1874. A receivership was applied for, and Jesse P. Farley, who had been managing several Iowa railroads and at the time was superintendent of the Iowa Division of the Illinois Central Railroad and an experienced railroad man, was appointed receiver by the courts per August 1, 1873. Upon the news of this default, prices of all Saint Paul & Pacific securities on the Amsterdam Stock Exchange fell disastrously to levels unheard of. And even the St. Vincent extension—for which interest was guaranteed until July 1874—fell from a high of 66 percent to an abysmal 12 percent of par in 1873 (see table 2).

After the crash of so many American railroads in 1873 the *American Railroad Journal* commented in its editorial of May 16, 1874:

> It is notorious that during the past ten years a vast quantity of railroad bonds has been sold in Europe, and especially on the Continent, which could not have been sold at home at all. . . . There was a time when the Frankfurt and Amsterdam bank offices were thronged with Americans, whose black bags were filled with railroad bonds promising to pay any rate of interest, anywhere, in any sort of money, and generally accompanied with liberal offers of shares and large commissions to the agents and first handlers of the loans.[19]

The editor made no specific mention of the Saint Paul & Pacific but may well have had this road in mind.

The Northern Pacific as Competitor

One other railroad company, which was to influence the fate of the Saint Paul & Pacific to a certain extent, must be mentioned here. We have already seen the surveys for a Pacific railroad along the northern route (see Chapter 3). As the central route was originally preferred by Congress, it was not until 1864 that the Northern Pacific Railroad Company was incorporated. Congress did give a land grant, which was bigger than that given the earlier central route—the Union Pacific–Central Pacific combination—but no straight subsidies. Because a land grant could only begin to bring in money after a portion of the railroad was actually in operation, construction capital had to be found elsewhere, just as with the Minnesota & Pacific. Little was done in this respect and the Northern Pacific project lay dormant until 1869, when the Philadelphia banking house of Jay Cooke & Company assumed control.[20]

Starting point for construction of the Northern Pacific was to be a place on the western shore of Lake Superior. From there two routes through Minnesota had been surveyed: one running from Superior City, Wisconsin, to Crow Wing River and from there to the Red River, and the other from Bayfield, Wisconsin, east of Superior City, by way of Sauk Rapids to Breckenridge on the Red River.[21] In the end a completely different and more northerly route was chosen instead, running from Duluth, Minnesota, on Lake Superior, westward via Brainerd to the Red River.

Actual construction started at Thomson Junction, twenty miles from Duluth, on the Lake Superior & Mississippi Railroad, which was then being built south from Duluth to St. Paul. And as this railroad was also in the hands of Jay Cooke, it was logical to avoid duplication and use part of the Lake Superior & Mississippi instead. To be sure of a permanent connection, the Northern Pacific

The Red River bridge of the Northern Pacific at Moorhead in 1879. Moorhead was a busy exchange point for the steamboats that plied the Red River. (Photo by Ole E. Flaten, Courtesy of the Clay County Historical Society, Minnesota Historical Society)

acquired a controlling interest in this road in 1872. The line from Thomson Junction to Brainerd was finished in 1871, and from there to the Red River (at what is now Moorhead-Fargo) was opened for traffic in February 1872.

It soon became clear to the leaders of the Northern Pacific that Duluth was not the ideal terminus for a transcontinental railroad as it lacked connections with other railroads to the south. True, Duluth had a fine natural harbor, but this was of little use for passenger traffic and general freight transportation by water. During the long Minnesota winters the harbor was frozen over and could not be used at all. The gigantic ore deposits close by were then still hardly known. St. Paul had already developed into the transportation center of the whole Northwest, but the only railroad connection between Duluth and St. Paul over the Lake Superior & Mississippi Railroad was fairly roundabout.

The Saint Paul & Pacific Branch line to Brainerd seemed to be of vital importance to

the Northern Pacific for this purpose, and so the directors contacted E. Darwin Litchfield in London, who had taken over his brother William's Saint Paul & Pacific shares. Early in 1870 a deal was closed: the Northern Pacific bought all First Division stock from the Litchfields for $500,000 in cash and $1,500,000 in old Saint Paul & Pacific bonds, which the Northern Pacific had already acquired. In April 1870 the directors also purchased the capital stock of the St. Vincent extension for $75,000 in Northern Pacific first-mortgage bonds. William Litchfield remained in charge of operations of the Saint Paul road but as a front for the Northern Pacific. The actual connection by way of Brainerd was not yet finished, however, and it would take many more years before it could be used.[22]

In 1873 Jay Cooke & Company had overextended and had to close its doors, which precipitated a general crisis of unknown severity in the United States. Without Cooke's support the Northern Pacific was unable to survive and it defaulted as well. And as the Northern Pacific had never completely fulfilled the contract with the Litchfields, the capital stock of the Saint Paul & Pacific and of the First Division had to be returned to the Litchfields. After the Northern Pacific was reorganized in 1875, it did not buy the stock again, but later built the Brainerd branch itself—through a subsidiary—and contracted with the Saint Paul & Pacific and its successor for running rights over the Sauk Rapids–St. Paul line and the use of terminal facilities in St. Paul.

Dutch Interests in Minnesota

The reader may have wondered by now why the Dutch, of all people, invested so heavily in the Saint Paul & Pacific. Did they have any special relationship with Minnesota? Or were there special reasons for them to concentrate their attention on that state?

Dutch investment in the United States was nothing new at the time. The Netherlands—before 1795 officially the Republic of the Seven United Netherlands and after 1815 the Kingdom of the Netherlands, with a short interlude of French domination—were a small nation, but a rich one, and Dutchmen had always looked for profitable investment outside their own borders. Although the political links with the original Dutch West India Company settlements of New Amsterdam and the Hudson Valley may have been severed in 1666, economic, religious, and cultural connections had remained strong under British rule and these became even stronger after American independence. After all, the Dutch Republic was the only example in the world of a reasonably successful republican state—there were some serious flaws and errors in its constitution that the American leaders tried hard to avoid. Progressive Dutch leaders of the late eighteenth century also recognized these flaws and did their best to reform their own country, but in vain, and they saw in America the ideal state taking shape. The Dutch Republic was the first state to recognize the United States as an independent, sovereign state, and the special relationship between the two republics continued for many years.

After American independence, Amsterdam bankers with loans to the Federal government helped their sister republic across the Atlantic Ocean to get on her feet, and as the financial record of the new state proved most positive, they remained interested in investments there. Thomas Jefferson's Louisiana Purchase of 1803 was largely financed from Amsterdam, although the London house of Baring's had taken the lead in that particular deal. Other Dutch capital had flowed into American land, through the Holland Land Company of Amsterdam, for example, in upstate New York.

This company had its American headquarters in Batavia, New York, with a second New Amsterdam, later known as Buffalo, as its most important town, and it owned some five million acres in New York and Pennsylvania.[1] Although from the standpoint of the original investors it was never a source of riches, the influence of this Holland Land Company on the development of upstate New York was great and its activities were not wound up until the late 1850s.[2] Other land companies with a Dutch financial background had flourished (and sometimes withered) elsewhere in the United States. Both the First and the Second Banks

A 600-guilders ($240) bond issued in 1878 by the Minnesota Land Company, a limited company headquartered in The Hague, Netherlands. It was one of several Dutch companies active in boosting Minnesota at the time. (Author's Collection)

of the United States had Dutch capital behind them. Internal improvement schemes in several states had attracted Dutch investors, with sometimes disastrous results when the states in question defaulted on their interest payments after they had overextended themselves. Canal or river improvement companies had also attracted Dutch monies, and from there it was but a small step to railroads.

During the latter part of the eighteenth century and despite French occupation also in the early years of the nineteenth, Amsterdam trading houses had conducted a lively trade with the young United States and a lot of personal relations had been built up over the years. American colonial traders—mostly from New England—who had done business in the Dutch East Indies (Indonesia) had established contacts in Amsterdam, which could also be used to attract Dutch capital for purposes other than trade. David E. Neal, a Boston trader in China and Indonesia, was the first to solicit Dutch capital for railroad building. Neal was a director of the Illinois Central and the Michigan Central Railroads,

and soon after his visit to Amsterdam in 1851 Dutch bankers became interested in both railroads. After this example had been set, a flood of American railroads sought Dutch capital for construction purposes. A large number of bankers and brokers in Amsterdam and Rotterdam started to handle American railroad shares and bonds, and the public, attracted by the high yields possible, poured their money in. It has been estimated that by 1873 more than $130 million in Dutch capital had been invested in American railroads alone.[3] Yet even with these enormous sums the Dutch trailed far behind the English, who invested much more. Despite this second place, during the nineteenth century Amsterdam was always a very important market for American railroad securities, more so than Paris or Frankfurt am Main.

High yields, sometimes more than 12 percent, could be attained and this was the most attractive point about American "rails" (*spoortjes* in Dutch), as these railroad securities were popularly called. A certain speculative or gambling element played a significant role too. New issues could suddenly rise or drop, and for many, gambling on this aspect was a kind of sport. Fortunes could be made or lost in a very short time. That the risks were high, too, was generally forgotten in the excitement of the moment. There were lots of unsound schemes among the many stocks offered, railroads that could show nothing more than a prospectus describing in glowing words the endless possibilities of the road and the great future of the country it traversed. That there was nothing solid behind such a scheme was only discovered when the inevitable crash came. Bankers and brokers (and certainly not only Dutch ones) failed to check the soundness of the securities offered by unscrupulous American railroad promoters, and only after the crash of 1873 and the following general worldwide crisis, when American and foreign investors suffered great losses, were bankers becoming more cautious when offering these American railroad securities to the public. They then regularly sent out observers of their own to check over the property in question before deciding to take the plunge.

English and Dutch investors tended to concentrate their capital in a limited number of roads. The Illinois Central for many years was almost completely owned by English and Dutch shareholders; likewise the Chicago & North Western and the Chicago, Milwaukee & Saint Paul had attracted large amounts of foreign capital and had English- and Dutch-appointed directors on their boards. The first lines of the Denver & Rio Grande, the fabled narrow-gauge road of general William Jackson Palmer in the Colorado Rockies, was exclusively financed from Amsterdam. The Missouri, Kansas & Texas was likewise strongly dependent on Dutch capital, as were many other Midwestern and Western roads. The railroad company with the most issues of bonds and shares listed on the Amsterdam Stock Exchange before 1914 was the Southern Pacific system with twenty-nine different securities, including those of its predecessor and constituent companies such as the Central Pacific, the California & Oregon, and others. Runner-up was the Union Pacific with twenty-six, again including constituents. Third place with twenty-three different issues of shares and bonds was held by the Great Northern Railway, with its predecessors the Saint Paul & Pacific and the Saint Paul, Minneapolis & Manitoba, and others in the Hill empire.

Ownership of American stocks and bonds in the Netherlands was widely spread among the population. Because of their generally small denominations of sometimes a hundred dollars (250 guilders) or even less, they were deemed suitable for the small saver. And when bonds of $1,000 were issued, the Dutch brokers and bankers often split these into smaller certificates of $100, a sum small enough to be attractive to people of modest means. To cater for these small capitalists Amsterdam bankers and brokers had already set up early investment funds,

probably the first of their kind in the world, back in the 1770s. In 1869 the first investment fund, explicitly doing business in American railroad securities, was started by Amsterdam firms—Kerkhoven & Company and the Boissevain Brothers—and when this proved successful, others soon followed. Certificates of participation could be bought for as little as 50 guilders ($20) and they carried 5 percent interest. Bonds of the early Saint Paul & Pacific issues were included in this first investment fund.[4]

Dutchmen were—and still are—great savers, and a lot of money was available for investment. Savings banks hardly existed at the time, and the Dutch national debt was small and did not yield more than 3 percent. Industrialization of the country came late in the nineteenth century, and opportunities for investment in the East Indian colonies were few until the 1880s, when tobacco (the Deli Company) and oil (Royal Dutch) lands

---

THE FIRST DIVISION OF THE

St. Paul & Pacific Railroad Company.

LAND DEPARTMENT.

THE COMPANY NOW OFFERS FOR SALE

1,000,000 ACRES OF LAND,

Located along their two Railroad Lines, viz: From St. Paul, via St. Anthony, Anoka, St. Cloud, and Sauk Rapids, to Watab; and from St. Anthony, via Minneapolis, Wayzata, Crow River, Waverly, and Forest City, to the Western Boundary of the State.

THESE LANDS COMPRISE

TIMBER, MEADOW, AND PRAIRIE LANDS,

And are all within easy distance of the Railroad, in the midst of considerable Settlements, convenient to Churches and Schools.

INDUCEMENT TO SETTLERS.

The attention of persons whose limited means forbid the purchase of a homestead in the older States, is particularly invited to these lands. The farms are sold in tracts of 40 or 80 acres and upwards, at prices ranging from $5.00 to $10.00 per acre. Cash sales are always One Dollar per acre less than Credit sales. In the latter case, 10 years are granted if required.

EXAMPLE:—80 acres at $8.00 per acre, on long credit—$640.00. A part payment on the principal is always desired, but in case the means of the settler are very limited, the Company allows him to pay only One Year's Interest down, dividing the principal in ten equal annual payments, with seven per cent. interest each year on the unpaid balance:

		Int.	Prin.				Int.	Prin.
1st payment,		$44.80		7th payment,			$17.92	$64
2d "		40.32	$64	8th "			13.44	64
3d "		35.84	64	9th "			8.96	64
4th "		31.36	64	10th "			4.48	64
5th "		26.88	64	11th "				64
6th "		22.40	64					

The purchaser has the privilege to pay up any time within the 10 years, thereby saving the payment of interest.

The same land may be purchased for $560.00 cash. Any other information will be furnished on application in person, or by letter, in English, French or German, addressed to

LAND COMMISSIONER,

First Division St. Paul & Pacific R. R. Co.,

Saint Paul, Minn.

36

A price list of available railroad land. Land could be bought for cash, credit, or in exchange for railroad bonds. (From McClung, *Minnesota as it is*)

A panoramic view, taken in 1892, of Kerkhoven on the Main line of the Saint Paul & Pacific. The town was named for the Amsterdam banking firm but was mostly settled by Scandinavians. (Photo by C. L. Merryman, Minnesota Historical Society)

were developed. Before this development foreign investment was the only way out to make the surplus capital realize some profit. British consols were secure but carried a low yield. Other foreign countries were less safe, but the United States had a very good financial record. Shares in well-run railroad companies such as the Illinois Central, the Chicago & North Western, and the Rock Island were considered blue chip investments and deemed eminently suitable for spinsters and orphans. Other railroads may have been less safe, but their promised yields were attractive to the more adventurous souls among the Dutch investing public. But whatever their character, all American railroad securities were widely spread among the Dutch investing public in many individual small holdings.[5] The Saint Paul & Pacific was no exception to this general rule.

Why Minnesota started to attract so much Dutch capital is not really clear, but once begun, more investment tended to follow the first, and with the influx of capital came schemes for emigration companies on a large scale, which focused even more attention on Minnesota. The first idea of investing in the Saint Paul & Pacific probably came from Robert Benson and E. Darwin Litchfield in London. Benson had been active in marketing Illinois Central shares and bonds in London, and he must have been aware of the great Dutch interest in that road. So, when Benson could not find

enough customers for the Saint Paul & Pacific bonds on his hands, it was only natural for him to turn to Amsterdam. And once success had been obtained there, it was nothing out of the ordinary to try again with the next issue of Saint Paul & Pacific bonds. Dutch brokers knew very well that they were taking risks with the Saint Paul & Pacific bonds. Willem van Oosterwijk Bruyn, one of the partners of Kerkhoven & Company, put it this way: "as long as both lines are not yet finished, it [the Saint Paul & Pacific loan] will remain a speculation, but a speculation with a better chance of profit and less risk than most others."[6]

The Dutch had by then been thoroughly alerted to the possibilities of a developing state like Minnesota and the opportunities offered there to enterprising young Dutchmen. A steady flow of travelers and writers paid attention to Minnesota and promoted its land and industries. Already in 1866 two young Dutchmen visited St. Paul and were well received. They were Claude A. Crommelin, of an old trading and banking family of Amsterdam, and Hendrik J. de Marez Oyens, scion of an old banking family. Together they went over the railroad, discussed the value of the land grant, and later reported back to their Amsterdam relatives.[7]

With the enormous land grant of the Saint Paul & Pacific available for settlement, it is small wonder that Dutch farmers were attracted. One of the advantages claimed for buying Saint Paul & Pacific bonds was that they could be exchanged at par for land. One bond of $1,000 was good for two hundred acres, and with the average purchase price of bonds at 70 percent, this worked out at circa $3.50 per acre, not bad for land of this excellent quality. However, there is no indication that Dutch farmers settled in large numbers on railroad land, although individual cases are known.

Minnesota was actively boomed by Dutch officers of the Saint Paul & Pacific Railroad Company. Johan H. Kloos (whom we shall meet again later) was most active in this respect and wrote a couple of books and articles on the subject.[8] Another Dutchman, Johan Knuppe (brother-in-law of Johan Carp, the secretary of the Dutch bondholders committee, whom we shall meet in later chapters), eventually settled on a farm near Crookston, no doubt on railroad land, and wrote in glowing terms of his experiences there.[9] The one real colony of Dutchmen, however, settled in Benton County in the middle 1860s, was not on railroad land, and apparently had little to do with the railroad investment.[10]

In 1866 a "Maatschappij van Grondbezit in Minnesota" was founded in Amsterdam. Commonly known as the Minnesota Land Company, it tried hard to make the lands of the Saint Paul & Pacific popular in the Netherlands, but with slight success, even though H. Kloos (brother of Johan Kloos) was director of the land company. A couple of years later, an emigration society was set up in Rotterdam with the express purpose of settling poor Dutchmen in Minnesota.[11] Initiator of this scheme was G. P. Ittman, Jr., who also for some years edited a journal named *Landverhuizer*.[12] Ittman was Jay Cooke's agent for peddling securities of the Northern Pacific in Holland, so his aim was to settle Dutchmen on Northern Pacific land, not Saint Paul & Pacific land. Another Dutchman, M. E. d'Engelbronner, a civil engineer and member of the prestigious Royal Institute of Engineers in the Netherlands, was for a time land agent in Minneapolis, but it is not clear if he acted on his own or in some connection with the Saint Paul & Pacific railroad.

Another booster of Minnesota was a certain Dr. S. R. J. van Schevichaven, who wrote a very practical guide, full of tips on what to do and what to avoid, for prospective emigrants to Minnesota.[13] He had been to Minnesota in person in 1870–1871 and had been informed by Johan Kloos about the land available. He waxes lyrical about the rapid growth of St. Paul and sees endless opportunities for enterprising Dutchmen there. His success must have been slight, however. According to the 1875 census, of the 14,364 foreign-born persons living in Ramsey County, of which St. Paul is the county seat, only thirty were Dutch.[14]

A visitor and writer of a somewhat different kind was the Reverend Martinus Cohen Stuart, protestant minister at Rotterdam, who traveled to the United States in 1873 as a Dutch representative at the meeting of the Evangelical Alliance, held in New York City in that year. After the meeting was over, Cohen Stuart traveled around, and as every Dutch clergyman, he first visited the Dutch protestant colonies in Michigan and Iowa, then boarded a train of the Saint Paul & Sioux City Railroad at East Orange, Iowa. He was pleasantly impressed by the wooded valley of the Minnesota River, although it was the end of November, and he found St. Paul, where he arrived late at night, a most interesting place.[15] Although the entry into the city was hindered by dark and unpaved streets, open ravines, and strangely situated hills, he saw St. Paul as the city of the future, where Dutchmen could well make their careers. In his interview with President George Becker of the Saint Paul & Pacific, he noticed a great deal of carelessness on the part of the directors and officers of the railroad. But, on the other hand, he blamed the unfortunate Dutch investors for foolishly having expected a good rate of return on their investment right from the start. They should have known that a railroad in a developing country like Minnesota could only make money in the long run. For a clergyman, this was certainly an enlightened standpoint.

After the default of the railroad in 1873, more Dutchmen descended on St. Paul, but for very different reasons. These were no more curious amateur visitors or optimistic boosters, but hardheaded businessmen, come to save something from the wreck of the railroad. Their activities will be covered in a later chapter.

The spartan interior of one of the early emigrant coaches of the Saint Paul & Pacific, circa 1875. Note the woodburning stove in the corner, a definite necessity in the harsh Minnesota winters. (Minnesota Historical Society)

Traffic and Operations

The first traffic figures of the Saint Paul & Pacific are not known, but operations over the first ten miles of road must have been simple in the extreme. At first there were only two locomotives available, and when one engine needed a boiler washout or repairs, as was the case with the *Wm. Crooks* after its accident, the other had to be pressed into full service to prevent traffic from coming to a standstill. With the primitive facilities for maintenance on hand, it must have been a hard job to keep at least one engine in operating condition all the time.

Freight traffic was probably soon more important than the passenger side of the business. The small and inadequate passenger depot at St. Paul was considered sufficient for many years, but for freight transfer more room was needed. For this purpose the First Division Company entered into a contract with Canadian-born James J. Hill, then an active shipping and forwarding agent living in St. Paul. First, in February 1866, they leased his transportation company some land to erect a freight transfer shed between the river and the railroad tracks, and next they contracted with Hill and his partners for the handling of freight at the St. Paul depot.[1] With the gradual extension of the lines, business became better almost every year and Hill must have done extremely well out of these contracts.

What kind of freight was actually carried in the early years? This is hard to establish because no detailed figures have been found, but grain, lumber, and flour must have made up the bulk of outgoing shipments of most stations. Incoming freight was probably mostly miscellaneous merchandise, finished products, hardware, and household goods.

Detailed figures have been found for one station only: Elk River, about halfway between St. Paul and St. Cloud on the Branch line.[2] In the first month of operations, August 1863, the princely sum of $10 was generated in incoming freight—agricultural products, tools, nails, and other hardware. One year later a healthy growth is visible. The area served by the station was much larger and stretched as far as Fort Abercrombie on the west bank of the Red River in what is now North Dakota. Local grocers and hardware and dry goods stores had everything shipped in by rail. D. McCauley at Fort Abercrombie ordered a complete store inventory in November 1864: tobacco, soap, salt, painkiller, strawberries, sugar, whiskey, powder, oysters, brooms, crackers, and hundreds of other items. His total charges came to $441.20. In later years agricultural implements, hardware, boats, furniture, liquor, door and window frames, and miscellaneous merchandise made up the bulk of freight shipped in. James Campbell of Elk River received his piano (boxed, weighing one thousand pounds) in August 1865, for a charge of $3 from St. Paul. Income from freight varied wildly, from a low of $84.50 in April 1865, to a high of over $1,000 in September of that year.

Outgoing freight from Elk River was very different: lots of lumber and lumber products, such as shingles and staves, chairs and other furniture from the factory established there, and wooden shoes. Cattle, hay, feed, deer, hides, eggs, and cranberries were shipped to St. Paul in 1869, and also one McCormick reaper, possibly for repairs. The Albee Mills were a regular customer for shipping flour by the carload (one hundred barrels) all the way to New York by way of Chicago. Their rate to St. Paul for one carload in 1869 was $30. Another customer was E. P. Mills, who also shipped one carload of flour (weighing twenty-two thousand pounds) to Langdon & Burleigh of Boston, but their rate to St. Paul came to only $22 in 1873. Was this a case of preferred customer rates? An unusual transport were three batteaux, the light boats used on the Minnesota lakes and rivers, complete with paddles and oars, weighing three thousand pounds in all, to Sauk Rapids in 1873 for $9.90.

From 1872–1873 onward the annual reports of the railroad commissioners give details of freight handled at all stations. On the Main line, of all thirty-five stations, Willmar was easily the most important for wheat shipments, closely followed by Atwater, Litchfield, and Benson. As is to be expected, Minneapolis was the greatest shipper of flour in barrels, followed at a distance by St. Anthony, with Litchfield and Swede Grove far behind. For lumber Wayzata was the most important, followed by Minneapolis, which also generated the most miscellaneous freight. In the fiscal year ending August 31, 1873, in tons forwarded and received Minneapolis led the way, with 29,461 and 56,497 tons respec-

tively, but Delano shipped no less than 20,300 tons in that same year, mostly in grains other than wheat and in forest products other than lumber. All other stations trailed far behind, with Willmar the biggest of the smaller stations.

For passenger traffic Minneapolis was again easily the leader, with 82,682 passengers leaving and 87,264 arriving. St. Anthony came second, with 15,365 and 14,647 respectively, and Wayzata and Litchfield came third and fourth but with only about a third of the number of St. Anthony. At the bottom of the list, Randall—a flag stop only—saw three people arriving and two leaving.[3] Altogether passenger trains ran 154,138 miles, and freight trains 113,979 miles. The line was blocked by snow no less than seventy-three days!

On the Branch line there were eleven stations, including St. Paul but without St. Anthony, which was considered to be on the Main line. Of these eleven, St. Paul was easily the most important in almost every respect. St. Cloud shipped most wheat and flour, Anoka was strong in lumber and other forest products. In tons received (97,761 tons), St. Paul easily outdid them all, though Anoka (with 40,975 tons) topped the list of freight forwarded. No less than 94,583 passengers left the capital by train, with 89,495 arriving.[4] Even the unimportant flag stop of Coon Creek saw 242 passengers arrive and 147 leave. Passenger trains ran 71,490 miles, freight trains 52,162. The conclusion is that on the Branch, passenger traffic was relatively heavier than on the Main line, with 238,568 passengers carried on a line of 76 miles, compared to the 269,685 on 207 miles of Main line. Occasionally traffic between St. Paul and St. Anthony must have been extremely heavy because of festivities such as state fairs. One traveler, in 1872, complained about his long passenger train being overcrowded between the two stations for that reason.[5]

Table 3 Passengers and Freight Carried

	Branch	Main	Branch and Main
Passengers			
1869			148,723
1870			195,000
1871	90,599	106,647	
1872	104,484	129,052	
1873	238,868	269,685	
1874	124,143	149,547	
1875	102,486	127,579	
1876	191,993	230,540	
1877	201,282	230,408	
1878	185,668	196,421	
1879	not given		
1880	not given		
Freight (in tons)			
1869			76,793
1870			78,250
1871	53,170	99,302	
1872	66,650	146,947	
1873	77,764	113,879	
1874	115,864	115,750	
1875	65,831	137,713	
1876	84,527	186,194	
1877	92,178	138,342	
1878	107,491	129,719	
1879	not given		
1880	St.P.M.& M.		550,450

Source: *Poor's Manual,* consecutive years.

Table 3 shows that after 1873 the number of passengers carried declined dramatically. The figures for freight are less dependable, and those for 1874 even suspect, as a change was made in the definition of the fiscal year. The general crisis brought an end to almost all commercial traffic for a time, and the invasion of grasshoppers in several consecutive years stopped agriculture in large parts of Minnesota. These insects were not really grasshoppers but Rocky Mountain locusts, living mostly in the foothills of the Rocky Mountains and adjoining plains. For some reason still not sufficiently known, they suddenly swarmed out to the east in uncounted millions and arrived in Minnesota around June 1873. Over the next years they pressed even farther east, almost as far as the Mississippi River, and they devoured everything green in their way, leaving whole counties ravaged. Farmers under these conditions gave up every attempt to grow some crop, as countermeasures proved largely ineffective. The year 1877 was the last of the plague, and then the insects disappeared as mysteriously as they had come.[6] This invasion, combined with the effects of the general crisis, did much to diminish the amount of traffic on the railroads, although the country traversed by the Saint Paul & Pacific was less hit by the locusts than other parts of Minnesota.

Traffic picked up again soon after the effects of the 1873 crisis wore off. In 1876 the number of passengers was again above the level of 1872, and the freight tonnage the same. The year 1877 saw a slight dip for the Main line only, but for some unexplained reason the year 1878 was bad over the whole line. Passenger traffic declined substantially on both Branch and Main lines, and freight tonnage on the Main line showed a further decline, with only the Branch showing some gains.

A terrible accident happened in Minneapolis in that year and may have caused part of the decline of freight traffic. On May 2, 1878, the Washburn "A" flour mill in Minneapolis, one of the largest mills then in existence and opened only in 1874, exploded without warning. The mill itself was completely obliterated, and many others in the neighborhood were destroyed or severely damaged and put out of use for many months. Eighteen workers were killed instantly and many others were injured. The explosion was caused by flour dust accumulating in the building, which was not equipped with enough ventilators. It took months before the volume of flour milled was back to the pre-explosion level.[7]

Rails—Iron versus Steel

The Saint Paul & Pacific was distinctly backward when compared to other railroads in the use of steel rails, then coming into vogue. From the very beginning many different brands of iron rails had been bought, apparently when and where available. War exigencies had made undamaged rails a strategic, sought-after material and had driven prices up. Rails were imported from England and Belgium, but the Belgian rails did not wear well: the company complained in 1867 that a batch of newly laid Belgian rails shattered in cold weather.[8] Moreover, the many different sizes of rails caused problems with the joints.

Table 4 Earnings and Operating Expenses, Branch and Main (in dollars)

	Earnings (gross)	Expenses	Earnings (net)
1866	169,539	100,129	69,410
1867	254,965	158,899	96,066
1868	305,027	162,183	142,844
1869	373,448	235,037	138,411
1870	477,464	308,689	168,775
1871	649,870	382,985	266,885
1872	682,560	not given	
1873	796,050	629,687	166,363
1874	848,471	632,395	216,076
1875	750,083	593,745	156,338
1876	1,006,045	641,755	364,290
1877	861,439	544,659	316,780[a]
1878	1,124,766	650,844	473,922[a]
1879	2,009,946	1,003,466	1,006,480[b]

Source: Poor's Manual for several consecutive years.
Notes: [a] Includes St. Vincent extension figures.
          [b] St. Paul, Minneapolis & Manitoba figures.

Only in 1877 did the company begin laying steel rails, with a modest 10 miles on the Branch, plus a short distance of 1.75 miles on the Main line the next year. The weight of this new rail was only fifty-six pounds per yard, but its superior quality and strength meant that it was not necessary for steel rail to be much heavier than the earlier, soft, iron rails. Most of the new rail then came from the Cambria Iron Works at Johnstown, Pennsylvania. A first payment of $27,569.68 to the Cambria Works for 501 tons of steel rail at $55 per ton has been found for March 28, 1877.[9] But as late as June 10, 1878, receiver Farley contracted with the same firm for 8,600 tons of iron rail, 50 pounds to the yard and 30 feet long, known as Cambria section number 79.[10]

After Hill and his associates took over the line, they set to work immediately to improve the quality of the track. This was really necessary, too, as the Branch was pronounced definitely unsafe to run. George Stephen ordered five thousand tons of steel rail plus fastenings from the North Chicago Rolling Mill Company in December 1878, which was raised to six thousand tons in March 1879.[11] But even then, the discussion about the use of iron or steel rails had not ended (see Chapter 13).

Rolling Stock
Freight

Although money was always tight (even more so than usual after 1873), the rolling stock had to keep pace with the extension of lines and the growth of traffic. The fleet, only 2 engines in 1862, had already grown to 7 by 1867, together with 6 passenger cars, 3 mail, baggage, and express cars, 1 four-wheel caboose, 25 boxcars, and 25 flatcars.[12] In 1870 the number of engines had reached 16, with 12 passenger, 4 mail and baggage cars, 50 boxcars, 145 flatcars, and 5 cabooses. At the time of the default of 1873,

DELAWARE CAR WORKS,
JACKSON & SHARP COMPANY.
WILMINGTON DELAWARE.

Manufacturers of Sleeping, Saloon, Drawing Room, and Passenger Cars.
EMPLOY 1,000 MEN. SPECIAL ATTENTION GIVEN TO NARROW-GAUGE CARS, AND SECTIONAL WORK
FOR EXPORTATION.
New York Office: 115 BROADWAY.

The Delaware Car Works of Wilmington, formerly known as Jackson & Sharp, one of the largest manufacturers of rolling stock in the United States. (From Poor, *Directory of Railway Officials*)

there were 23 locomotives on hand, with 20 passenger cars, 6 mail and baggage cars, 218 box- or stock cars, 156 flatcars, 134 service cars, and 5 snowplows.[13] As traffic continued to grow, receiver Farley was authorized by the court to buy new engines when needed, and by 1878 the number of engines had reached 34, with 21 passenger cars, 14 mail and baggage cars, 289 boxcars, 202 flatcars, and 10 stock cars. In April 1878 business was for a time so heavy that the company could not muster enough motive power and had to borrow two engines from the Saint Paul & Duluth Railroad. The last time that *Poor's Manual* lists the Saint Paul & Pacific's rolling stock separately, in 1880, it counts 46 engines, 34 passenger cars, 16 mail and baggage cars, 404 boxcars, 302 flatcars, plus some service cars.

These figures tally well with a handwritten list in the Great Northern archives, compiled at the time of the transfer of all property to the Saint Paul, Minneapolis & Manitoba Railroad.[14] On hand on June 30, 1880, there were 407 boxcars—of which

157 were built in the railroad shops at St. Paul, numbered 2–338 (even numbers only), with numbers 250–72 being stock cars; 36 were built by Barney & Smith in 1872 for $750 each, numbered 340–410; 120 were built by Haskell & Barker in 1878 at $405 each, delivered in Chicago, and numbered 412–710; 64 were built by Barney & Smith in 1878, numbered 712–874 plus some random higher numbers. Of the total 407 boxcars, 14 were destroyed in accidents and collisions, 2 were converted into tool cars, and 2 were converted into cabooses.

Also listed were 306 flatcars—of which no less than 206 had been built in the railroad shops, the last 50 in 1878; 50 more were built by Haskell & Barker in July 1878. Of the total, 65 were damaged or destroyed in collisions and not rebuilt. Also on hand on June 30, 1880, were 37 stock cars—of which 12 had been built in the railroad shops, and numbered 250–72; 25 more were built by Haskell & Barker in 1878 and numbered 812–60. In 1880, of the original 37, 11 were still in service, 2 had been destroyed and

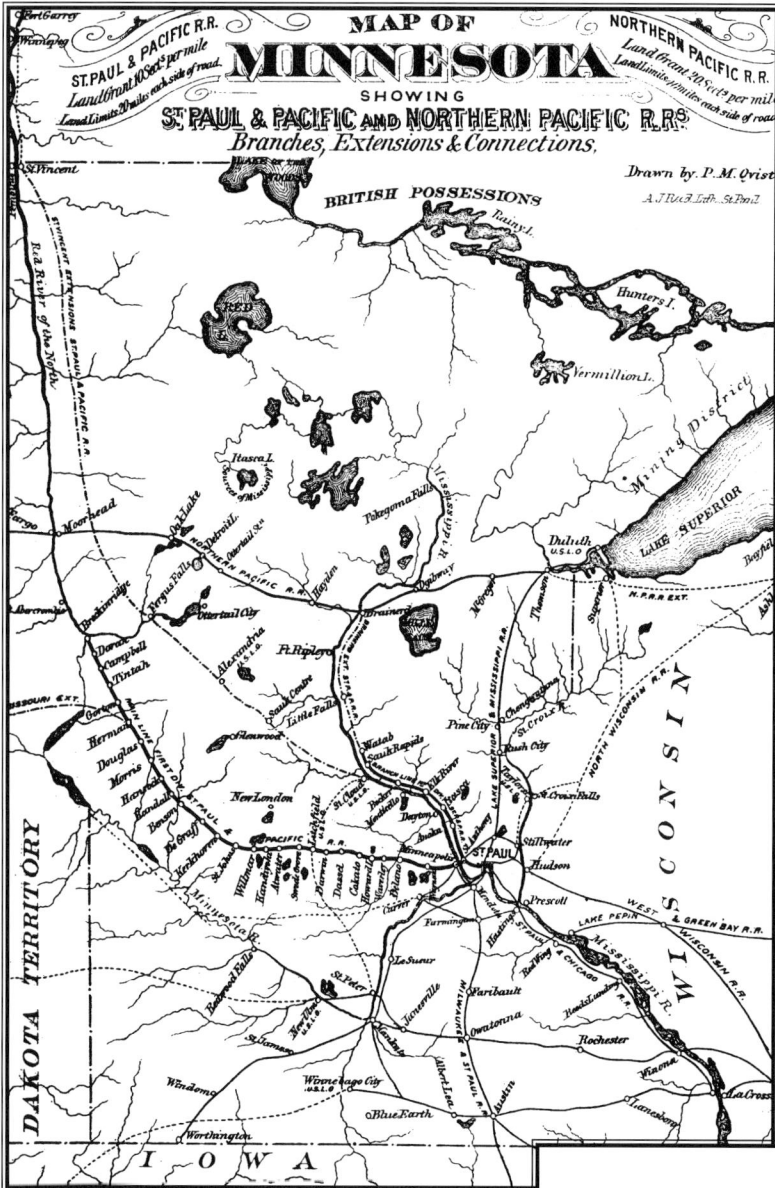

(left) Map from the *Guide to the Lands of the First Division of the Saint Paul and Pacific Railroad Company* of 1872. (Author's Collection)

(below) The construction of the Saint Paul & Pacific completed by 1870. The Main line stretched as far west as Benson, while the Branch line was in operation to Watab. (From Hidy, Hidy, Scott, and Hofsommer, *The Great Northern Railway,* courtesy of Harvard Business School Press)

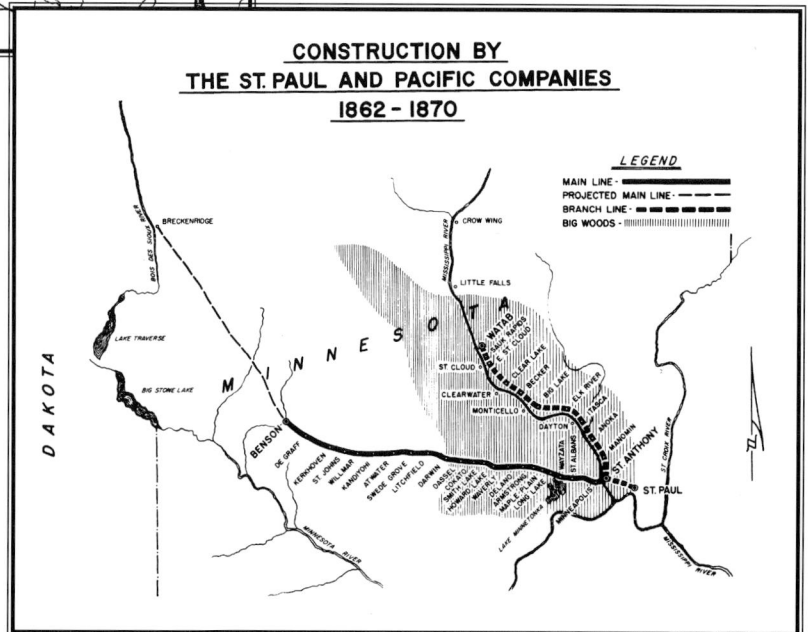

scrapped, and 24 were rebuilt into cabooses, mostly in 1880 and 1881. There were 10 cabooses, 6 built new by Haskell & Barker in 1879 for $1,000 each, and the rest converted in the railroad shops from box- and stock cars. No service cars are listed, apart from one shop-built derrick, but from records of accidents it is clear that several snowplows were on the premises, and no wonder, in the harsh winters of Minnesota.

That so many cars were home-built at St. Paul would indicate that the shops were fairly well equipped. But car construction at that time was still fairly simple and straightforward and did not ask for extensive equipment. Most cars were constructed completely from timber, including frames and truck bolsters. The most common size was thirty feet long, with a capacity of between twelve and fifteen tons for both box- and flatcars. Stock cars, then coming into universal use, did not differ greatly in their dimensions and were also of all-wood construction. Frame trusses, couplers, wheels, and the greatest part of the trucks were made of iron.[15] Brakes were hand-operated only and simple in the extreme; couplings were the infamous link-and-pin devices. In the case of cars built in the St. Paul shops, all wheels, axles, and other iron parts were bought from outside suppliers such as the Cleveland City Forge & Iron Company and the firm of May, Swallow & Company, who were paid $1,216.40 (charged to the Branch line account) for one hundred car wheels of different sizes in 1876.[16] Axle brasses came from A. F. Hodge & Company, who in 1876 were paid $442.30 for 225 brasses for cars of two different sizes.

The two main suppliers of rolling stock, apart from the shop-built cars, were Barney & Smith and Haskell & Barker. The first was founded in Dayton, Ohio, by Eliam E. Barney and Preserved Smith in 1864 and was also called the Dayton Car Works. It was very successful, for many years the largest car-building firm in the country. The firm of Haskell & Barker was established in Michi-

gan City, Indiana. Under the leadership of John H. Barker, the son of one of the founders, it became one of the leading railroad-car manufacturers of America. Later it was taken over by George M. Pullman and continued as part of his empire.[17]

Roads were not necessarily too independent-minded but shared their resources according to circumstances. During car shortages many cars were borrowed from other railroads, at a fee of one cent per mile, but payments for these rentals ran into the thousands of dollars. Most cars came from neighboring roads such as the Milwaukee & Saint Paul, the Central of Iowa, or the West Wisconsin. Another regular supplier of extra cars was the Pittsburgh, Fort Wayne & Chicago, not really a close neighbor. After the West Wisconsin Railway reached St. Paul from the east, the Saint Paul & Pacific took care of the station business for them, and also took the West Wisconsin trains on to Minneapolis over its own metals. After the West Wisconsin had become part of the Chicago, Saint Paul & Minneapolis, which in turn was controlled by the Chicago & North Western, this arrangement continued for some years, until the Union Depot was opened in St. Paul.

Passenger Cars

The same handwritten list of June 30, 1880, gives the number of passenger coaches in 1880 as thirty-three. From six in 1867, twelve in 1870, and twenty at the time of the default, the fleet had grown to thirty in 1878, and thirty-three at the time of the transfer to the Saint Paul, Minneapolis & Manitoba. Apparently the Saint Paul & Pacific at first used the same numbers for both Branch and Main lines, which must have caused a lot of confusion. Of these thirty-three, two (numbers 2 and 6) had been built at an unspecified time in the St. Paul shops. Two new first-class cars were delivered in November 1866 and were highly praised in the local press for their luxurious appointments, especially for the plush seats with patent flexible backs, separate for each individual passenger. They cost no less than $7,000 apiece.[18] They must have been among the eight cars (for example, numbers 3–5 and 7–9, plus number 3 of the Branch) supplied by Barney & Smith. Four more cars (numbers 12–14 plus number 5 of the Branch) were delivered from Bowers, Dures & Company of Wilmington in January 1873 at a price of $5,000 each. In May 1878 Jackson & Sharp delivered numbers 17–20, which were followed by numbers 21–27 from Barney & Smith in July and August of that same year. Six emigrant cars (numbers 28–33) came from Jackson & Sharp in February 1879 at $2,850 apiece. Freight charges to bring cars to St. Paul from the East were high: delivery of two cars at La Crosse cost $814, plus $100 for the river transportation to St. Paul.

Jackson & Sharp was one of the larger American firms in the field of car builders and was established in Wilmington, Delaware, in 1863 by Job H. Jackson and Jacob H. Sharp. Sharp retired in 1870 and the company became a joint stock corporation under the name of Delaware Car Works, although the old name stuck, apparently, as it was still being used in the Saint Paul & Pacific records as late as 1879. In Wilmington they were located next door to another big car-maker, Harlan & Hollingsworth. About the other firm that delivered passenger cars to the Saint Paul & Pacific, Bowers, Dures & Company, less is known. T. Wesley Bowers was another early Wilmington car builder, who, together with Jackson & Sharp and Harlan & Hollingsworth, helped to make that town the leading place for that industry for many years.[19]

Toward the end of the independent existence of the Saint Paul & Pacific, the need for night trains arose, which necessitated the use of sleeping cars. In September–October 1878, Jackson & Sharp delivered four sleeping cars, numbers 28–31, soon renumbered

200–203 and named the *St. Paul, Minneapolis, Winnipeg,* and *Selkirk*. From these names it is clear what kind of traffic they were intended to accommodate. They cost a hefty $7,000 apiece. The company seems to have operated its sleepers for its own account, without having any contract with the Pullman Company or others, and a certain Mr. E. H. Brown was superintendent of the sleeping-car operations of the Saint Paul, Minneapolis & Manitoba.[20] Since 1866 Pullman had been operating the sleeping cars on the lines of the Chicago & North Western and the Chicago, Burlington & Quincy, among others, but a large number of railroads either contracted with other sleeping-car operators, such as Wagner or Woodruff, or had their own cars.[21] Much later the Great Northern went over to Pullman, but in 1885 the Saint Paul, Minneapolis & Manitoba was still running its own sleepers, under superintendent Brown.[22] Dining cars came only in 1888, and before that year the Saint Paul & Pacific operated its own eating houses, at Willmar and Breckenridge on the Main line, and at Glyndon and Crookston on the Branch line.[23] All trains stopped there for half an hour or more to give passengers and crews the opportunity to eat lunch or dinner.

A directors car, also costing $7,000, was ordered from Jackson & Sharp and delivered in 1878. It was numbered 32 but was soon rebuilt into the sleeper car *Itasca*. It lasted until 1884 when it was destroyed in an accident.

Few records survive of the nineteen mail, baggage, and express cars. Three were apparently built by the company at an unknown date, but *Poor's Manual* for 1869–1870 mentions three such cars in that year. Six more were built in 1878, numbers 33–34 by Jackson & Sharp at $2,000 each, and numbers 35–38 by Barney & Smith. A pay car, number 16, had been supplied by Barney & Smith in 1871; it was rebuilt in 1881. Nothing is known about numbers 21–24 and 31–32, only that they were on the premises in 1880. Most cars were soon rebuilt by the Saint Paul, Minneapolis & Manitoba company, but between 1880 and 1883 no less than fifty-nine old Saint Paul & Pacific cars were destroyed or scrapped. The list does not mention if these fifty-nine were only passenger cars; cabooses and freight cars may have been included as well.

Most passenger cars will have followed the familiar pattern of the times. The monitor or clerestory roof was just coming into vogue in the early 1860s, and surviving photographs show that the Saint Paul & Pacific did indeed have clerestories on its passenger cars. Better lighting and ventilation and more headroom were the chief reasons for using the more expensive clerestory, although the roof was structurally weaker than a flat or simple arch roof. The first baggage cars on the Saint Paul & Pacific still had flat roofs.

Heating was by means of wood-fired stoves, one at each end of the car, with all the adherent dangers and disadvantages of this time-honored system. Passengers nearby roasted while those farther away froze, but stoves were considered better than nothing and in the Minnesota winters they were obviously needed. The terrible consequences of having a red-hot stove on board in case of accidents, which were all too common on other roads, were fortunately never experienced on the Saint Paul & Pacific. For all these reasons the vastly superior hot-water heating system developed by William C. Baker around 1865 soon became popular, but its initial expense prevented installation on a really large scale. It is probable that the sleeping cars of the Saint Paul & Pacific were equipped with Baker heaters, as the higher fares charged for night travel could outweigh the extra cost of installation.[24]

At night coal oil (kerosene) lamps provided some light. At that time candles were also still being used on many lines, sometimes in quite elaborate fixtures, and they were certainly not yet considered outdated.

In the Saint Paul & Pacific purchase books, however, no mention is ever made of candles for coach lighting, so presumably this company used kerosene lamps, also for lighting the offices and city depots. In Germany a system of compressed-coal-gas lighting was already being developed by Julius Pintsch, and after 1870 it was in use all over Europe. In America the Erie was one of the first to use the Pintsch system, from 1882 onward. Widespread use came only after an American subsidiary was set up in 1887. From then on the Pintsch gaslight became the most common system on American railroads.[25]

Couplers in use, for both passenger and freight cars, were of the simple, almost universal, but crude and dangerous link-and-pin system. Conductors and brakemen on coupling up had to guide the link of one car

A typical link-and-pin coupler from the 1860s. (From Bendel, *Aufsätze Eisenbahnwesens in Nord Amerika*)

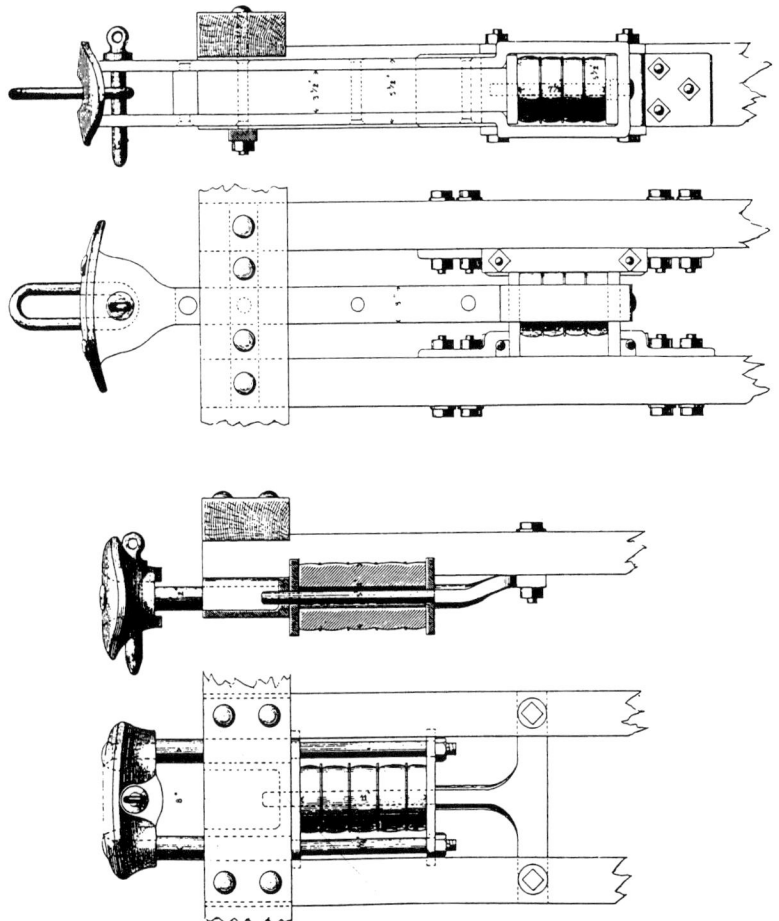

into the hollow end of the coupler of the other and then drop a pin at the right moment to fix it there. This system was cheap and simple to install, but expensive in human cost because of the accidents common with this system. For freight trains the link-and-pin remained in use for decades after 1860. For passenger trains something better had been evolved, because there was one more drawback of the link-and-pin coupler then in use on passenger trains. Apart from the rough jolts on starting and stopping, there was the frequency of telescoping in accidents. When meeting a sudden obstruction, passenger cars often telescoped one into another, with disastrous results and often great loss of life.

Colonel Ezra Miller, a New York politician, militia officer, and engineer, devised a new system eliminating all these drawbacks. He used a strong, heavily reinforced platform, at the same height as the car floor, with a single sprung buffer in the middle and a hook-style automatic coupler. Cars were drawn closely together with their buffers compressed to do away with the then common swaying of individual cars, and the platforms all at the same height prevented telescoping in case of accidents. The whole train moved as one and stopped as one, making rail travel a lot more pleasant for the general traveler. Miller's system was so simple and so efficient and its advantages so obvious to everyone that there was no reason not to use it. Even so, some conservative railroad managers found it hard to accept that this invention was really much better than earlier equipment and fully worth the extra financial outlay.[26] Despite this opposition from some railroads, the Miller system found widespread use after its first introduction on the Erie in 1866, and by 1874 85 percent of all American passenger cars had been so equipped. On the Saint Paul & Pacific its first use is recorded in 1873, when eleven Branch line and fourteen Main line coaches are reported as being equipped with the Miller platform and coupler, at $100 per car.

Brakes on passenger and freight cars were worked by hand only. On a signal from the engineer, brakemen turned the handles on platforms and roofs of the cars, and the train came to a slow halt. In emergencies the engineer could also reverse his engine, but this could have disastrous results with the train piling up against the locomotive, when the brakemen did not screw down their brakes in time. Over the years many hopeful inventors experimented with mechanical gadgets—especially for fast-running passenger trains, where the lack of brake power had first made itself felt. Steam, water, vacuum, and air had all been tried as a means of braking a complete train at once, but only the latter two had been reasonably successful in actual practice.

George Westinghouse started working on his version of the air brake in 1868. Two years later it was declared beyond the experimental stage and was introduced on a fairly large scale. Improvements were made to eliminate the initial defects and to make it automatic in operation in case of a train parting. For this purpose the triple valve was developed, an amazing small piece of machinery, later much improved by one of Westinghouse's collaborators, a young Dutch engineer and mechanical genius named Albert Kapteijn, who was later (from 1882) director of the European branch of the Westinghouse Air Brake Company in London. By 1880 the Westinghouse air brake was almost universally in use on American railroads.[27]

On the Saint Paul & Pacific the use of air brakes is first mentioned in the report to the railroad commissioner for 1878. In 1879 it is stated that all passenger equipment is equipped with this brake. It is not known how many of the locomotives were outfitted with the necessary steam pumps and other equipment; probably only those that were in regular use for passenger trains. Freight trains for decades to come continued to use hand brakes only.

The Wood Train

All engines were wood-burners, and regular supplies of firewood were needed along the line. Most wood was supplied by farmers living nearby, who must have considered this a most profitable sideline, especially in slack times in winter when farmwork was impossible. Hundreds of payments, mostly in small sums and to many different persons, were recorded in the company's books. A lot of wood was needed to fire the locomotives. In 1875 some twenty thousand cords were used for Branch and Main lines together, which must have cost around $55,000. Out on the line it may have been possible to secure a regular supply from local farmers, but at the main stations of St. Paul and Minneapolis supply could not be achieved this way, and in 1876 a special wood train was organized to supply stations that had no regular deliveries of their own. Apparently this still did not suffice, for next year a special fuel agent was appointed with some men, sixteen in all, stationed at several places along the lines.[28]

The company never used coal as fuel, although many of the railroads in the area started to do so. The Iowa coalfields were being opened up at the time, so coal, suitable as locomotive fuel, could be had at good prices. The Milwaukee, the Winona & Saint Peter, and the Northern Pacific all used coal for locomotive fuel (at least in part) from 1874, but the Saint Paul & Pacific never did. One of the first changes James Hill made, after taking over the company, was to switch to coal for fuel. But then, he had personal interests in the coal mines of Iowa.

Fares, Rates, and Tickets

The first passenger fare must have been around 6 cents per mile, as a one-way ticket between St. Paul and St. Anthony cost 60 cents. Later the fares fluctuated considerably. The report of the railroad commissioner for 1872–1873 gave 5 cents per mile, with a minimum of 25 cents per ticket. Later figures vary: for 1875 the fare was 3.28 cents per mile, for 1876 it was 4.09 cents, for 1877 it was 4.27 cents, and for 1878 it was down to 3.60 cents.

Freight rates differed according to distances and quality of goods carried. Stone and coal had the lowest rate and miscellaneous goods the highest, with grain and lumber in between. As usual elsewhere on the American railroads, the shorter the distance, the higher the rate. A ton of grain carried five miles was charged 24 cents per mile, but for the entire line only 4.5 cents a mile, and it was the same with all other classes of freight. Shipping a bushel of grain from Willmar to St. Paul in 1875 cost 13.2 cents, and from Breckenridge to St. Paul 17.1 cents. All rates had a tendency to fall after that year, and by 1885 most freight rates had almost halved.[29]

There was a lot of opposition to the supposedly high rates for freight traffic, aimed not only at the actual rates but also at the alleged discrimination against small shippers. Big operators, such as Oliver Dalrymple of the "bonanza" farm in the Red River valley, could claim substantially lower rates than a small farmer elsewhere along the line.[30] Also, Dalrymple did not have to wait for cars when he wanted to ship, whereas others often had to wait days or even weeks during the frequent periods of car shortages.

Another source of complaint was the monopoly of the elevator companies along the railroad lines. Most railroad companies did not themselves operate elevators but contracted with other parties for this purpose. The Saint Paul & Pacific signed a contract with William Litchfield in 1866 to provide storage facilities at stations, which gave him the exclusive right to receive, store, and ship grain. Two years later Litchfield sold his rights and elevators to "Commodore" Davidson, the steamboat operator. Davidson set up a new firm, the Delano, Davidson & Kyle Company, and by 1874 he owned thirty-six out of thirty-seven elevators along the Saint Paul & Pacific.[31] The Delano of this firm was none other than Francis R. Delano, the general superintendent of the railroad. No one seems to have bothered about a possible clash of interests here.

These circumstances gave rise to many complaints from farmers, first in individual cases, which soon led to a more or less organized resistance. This movement—the National Grange of the Patrons of Husbandry, founded in 1867—was particularly strong among Minnesota farmers. The Grangers, as they were generally known, felt oppressed by monopolistic corporations such as the railroads, who charged too high rates for the transportation of grain and so prevented the farmers from getting a fair price for their products and making a decent living. The Grangers called for legislation to establish fair and uniform rates, and to keep the railroads from giving rebates to preferred customers.[32] The state of Minnesota was pressed to act, and in 1871 a railroad commissioner was appointed, with commission to collect statistics and to enforce the laws. At the same time maximum rates for freight and passengers were established by law. The railroads contested the validity of this law as they held that in their charters as issued by the state the power to establish rates was given to the railroad companies themselves, not to the state.

In 1874 a new law was enacted, establishing a board of three commissioners with powers to fix a maximum rate based on mileage only, without any discrimination. The railroads complied under protest—and raised their rates everywhere to the allowed maximum. The Saint Paul & Pacific, which was charging three cents per mile between St. Paul and Minneapolis, raised that fare to five cents, the maximum allowed. Loud protests were heard, of course, not only from farmers and other shippers but also from railroad executives. Among the latter was Elias Drake, president of the Saint Paul & Sioux City Railroad, who said: "It may as well be laid down at once as a maxim, that no money will be furnished by capitalists from abroad or at home, to build roads, until by judicial decisions or otherwise the absolute control of roads when built will belong to those who built them."[33] His and other protests resulted in a change of the law in 1875. The board of commissioners was abolished and one person was consid-

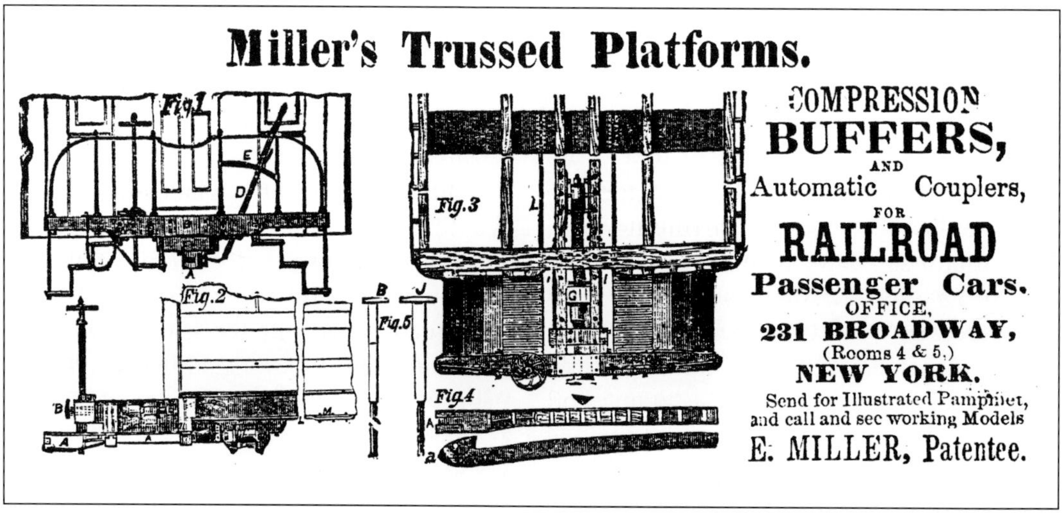

An advertisement illustrating Miller's new system, consisting of a strong, reinforced platform and a hook-style automatic coupler. Miller widely promoted his system in the railroad press of the day. (From *American Railroad Journal,* 1875)

Miller's Trussed Platforms.

Fig.1 Fig.2 Fig.3 Fig.4 Fig.5

COMPRESSION
BUFFERS,
AND
Automatic Couplers,
FOR
RAILROAD
Passenger Cars.
OFFICE,
231 BROADWAY,
(Rooms 4 & 5.)
NEW YORK.
Send for Illustrated Pamphlet, and call and see working Models
E. MILLER, Patentee.

ered enough to do the work. He was supposed to report on and to investigate into all railroad matters, including the setting of rates, but without power to change them. To all purposes the railroads were free again to make their own rates.

The first commissioner in Minnesota was Alonzo J. Edgerton, in 1874–1875, to be assisted by William R. Marshall, ex-governor, and John H. Randall.[34] Randall had been general ticket agent of the Saint Paul & Pacific from the very beginning and could be considered friendly to the railroad interest. He continued to serve as only commissioner after 1875.

Tickets were probably the already common kind of preprinted cardboard pieces, as invented by Edmondson in England. Thousands of tickets for the Branch line came from the New York firm of Sanford, Harroun & Company in 1864, at a total cost of $86.69. Two conductor's punches were bought from Jesup, Kennedy & Company, Railway Equipment & Supplies, of Chicago at $3 each. Jesup also provided three dozen white conductor's lanterns for $48 and one dozen red ones for $36. In 1876 more tickets were bought in bulk from Rand McNally & Company, also of Chicago: for most destinations they supplied one thousand consecutively numbered tickets, plus twenty-five hundred for the trip Minneapolis–St. Paul and two thousand for the opposite direction. The total bill came to $10.62.[35]

The Land Department

For all land grant railroads the income generated by the land department was a most useful source of income. In the early days of a railroad, traffic was generally light and revenues from that source negligible. On the other hand, title to lands granted could be obtained only after the completion of a certain mileage. It was the duty of the land department to bring these lands on the market as soon as title had been obtained.

Wild schemes were evolved occasionally, such as the one to settle no less than twenty thousand French *communards* on Northern Pacific land in 1871. These men—and women—had taken part in the Commune, the violent socialist-communist revolt of 1870 in Paris; after the revolt had been suppressed, with much bloodshed, it was deemed necessary to get rid of these people.[36] Settling them in America far from civilization seemed, to some reactionaries then in power, to be as good a solution as any, but fortunately nothing came of the scheme. Parisian artisans and laborers would never have made good farmers.

Land commissioner of the Saint Paul & Pacific was Hermann Trott, a German engineer living in St. Paul, and he became active in advocating the company's lands. A problem was the presence of early settlers or squatters on lands assigned to the railroad. Settlers who already occupied such lands were called upon to make arrangements with the company for formal possession.[37] If they were unwilling to settle somehow with the company, they were threatened with eviction, but it is not clear if Trott really ever went as far as that.

Land could be bought on credit, with very easy terms. Most new settlers had little cash available, and the company was willing to wait until after the third crop before exacting payments. Railroad bonds were also accepted at par in lieu of cash, and since most of these bonds quickly depreciated on the market to far below par, land could be bought cheaply in this way.

Whatever form the payment would take eventually, it was necessary to advertise the lands available to attract settlers. Numerous brochures were printed that explained in detail which lands were for sale and at what prices, and what had already been done in the way of building towns and constructing grain elevators, schools, and churches. These brochures were printed in many languages and distributed widely in America and Europe. Most commonly found is the *Guide to the Lands of the First Division of the Saint Paul and Pacific Railroad Company,* which went to at least three editions between 1870 and 1872, and probably more, with separate booklets for the Main and Branch lines. A German edition of 1871 has also been found: *Beschreibung der Laendereien der Ersten Division der Saint Paul und Pacific Eisenbahn-Compagnie;* both *Haupt-linie* and *Zweig-linie* booklets have been found.[38] In all these pamphlets Trott announced that requests for more information could be addressed to him in English, French, German, Dutch, or Scandinavian.

Brochures alone were not enough to reach a really large audience, however, and personal attention proved necessary. This was nothing new in itself, as the Northern Pacific had done the same thing on an even larger scale, with agents in several European countries. The Saint Paul & Pacific did not go that far, but it did appoint a certain Eduard Pelz as its representative in Germany. Pelz was a friend of Hermann Trott, hence probably his appointment.[39] Little is known about his activities.

More important in this respect was the contract with a Swede, Hans Mattson, to act as the company's land agent.[40] Mattson was a well-to-do farmer-lawyer in Red Wing, Minnesota, and had been the state's chief immigration officer for several years. In 1868 the Saint Paul & Pacific appointed him as its land agent, especially with the aim of attracting Scandinavian settlers. For this purpose Mattson advertised in the appropriate newspapers such as the Chicago-based *Svenska Amerikanaren* and *Hemlandet* or the St. Paul *Svenska Monitören,* but also in local papers in Sweden. And when this journalistic activity turned out to be not enough, he traveled in person to his homeland late in 1868 to enlist recruits for the lands of "his" Saint Paul & Stillahafsbanan, as the railroad was called in Swedish. He was quite successful in this respect and managed to attract

hundreds of settlers, who bought land mostly along the Main line in Meeker, Kandiyohi, and Wright Counties. And not only farmers came from Scandinavia. Single young men also emigrated and took jobs with the railroad company. Between 1868 and 1871 Mattson did indeed succeed in settling hundreds of Swedes along the Saint Paul & Pacific. Cokato, Dassel, Litchfield, and Swede Grove (later known as Grove City) had a strong Scandinavian element among the early settlers, thanks to his activities.[41] Mattson ended his contract with the Saint Paul & Pacific late in 1870 and then acted in the same capacity for the Northern Pacific and the Lake Superior & Mississippi Railroads.

Another important figure in the settlement along the Saint Paul & Pacific lines was John Ireland, Roman Catholic coadjutor-bishop of St. Paul. Ireland was born in Ireland in 1838, came to America as a young man, and was appointed pastor of the Cathedral parish of St. Paul in 1852. In 1888 he became the first archbishop of St. Paul. When still in the East, he was appalled by the awful quality of life of the poor Irish immigrants in the American cities, and after coming to Minnesota, he decided to do something about this situation. In 1864 he founded, with others, the Minnesota Irish Emigration Society in St. Paul, but initially this organization had little success.

After becoming coadjutor-bishop of St. Paul in 1875, he had more authority to do something about the lot of the poor Irish, and he then evolved a scheme to settle them in Minnesota. He reached an agreement with the Saint Paul & Pacific in 1875, whereby seventy-five thousand acres of railroad land along the Main line were reserved for Irish settlers selected by him. No others were allowed to buy this acreage, but Ireland had to pay the railroad only after a settler had actually selected a place to farm. In this way he avoided a large initial outlay of capital to buy land, which he never had,

TRAFFIC AND OPERATIONS 77

and he could keep out land speculators at the same time. He was allowed to set up an office in the St. Paul railroad depot and was appointed the railroad's exclusive agent for Swift County, west of Willmar (with Benson as county seat). Ireland's new organization, the Catholic Colonization Bureau, was indeed most successful in attracting Irishmen—not the kind of poor city dwellers he had in mind but the more affluent immigrants, who had some previous experience in farming. Communities such as DeGraff and Clontarf in Swift County were settled by Ireland's Irishmen, and he provided them with priests and schools right from the start to ensure continued success.[42]

The Saint Paul & Pacific Railroad helped Mattson's and Ireland's (and others') attempts at colonization in several ways. It built immigrant houses in a couple of places, where settlers could stay free of charge while selecting a farm. These houses were equipped with cooking stoves and other amenities and each offered shelter to several hundreds of people, while functioning at the same time as a kind of information center. When no longer needed in one place, they were taken down and reassembled farther along the line. Litchfield had one in 1872, as did Willmar, Benson, and Morris in the same year, while one was under construction at Breckenridge. On the Branch line Pleasant Valley and Clear Lake, both northwest of Big Lake, boasted an immigrant house.[43]

Other small gestures complemented this general benevolent attitude of the railroad toward the settlers. The early farmers at De-Graff were helped in 1876 with a supply of firewood, at cost, when nothing was available in their neighborhood. When citizens of Benson complained about the muddy streets, the railroad offered to haul sand and gravel free of charge in empty cars going west. Leading citizens of all colonies were invited to the annual grand ball at the Ryan Hotel in St. Paul as guests of the railroad. Special low-fare excursion tickets were issued to players and spectators of the regular ball games. When the grain elevator (not railroad-owned) at Benson was filled in 1877, and with still more grain coming in, the railroad boarded up its depot to serve as a temporary storage. Perhaps most important of all, when the grasshoppers devastated the crops in some areas in 1876 and 1877, payments for land were deferred until better times, at the request of Bishop Ireland.[44]

By mid-1872 total land sales of the railroad company amounted to $337,674, mostly in cash, with expenditures amounting to $131,739.[45] By 1873, at the time of the default, the proceeds of land sales amounted to over $1 million, at an average price of $6.66 per acre. During the fiscal year 1876–1877 revenue from land sales on the Main line alone amounted to $1,560,677. Gross earnings from traffic on that line came to only $475,579 in the same year, so the importance of the land department for the financial well-being of the company is clear.[46] The Branch line added some $285,000 in land sales to the total. At the time of the transfer of the Saint Paul & Pacific to the new Saint Paul, Minneapolis & Manitoba in the summer of 1879, total revenue from all land sales up to that date (July 1, 1879) was $4,334,358.97 for the Main line and $450,600.59 for the Branch. And only about half of the lands of those two lines had been sold by then, while the more than 1.5 million acres of land grant of the St. Vincent extension had not even been touched.[47] Small wonder that the remaining lands of the several grants were seen as a valuable asset.

Management and Staff

Even a small rural railroad company just starting up needed some form of organization to run it properly. And although the staff at first was very small indeed, the setup followed a fairly commonly used form. The great authority on railroad management in those years was Daniel C. McCallum, former general superintendent of the New York & Lake Erie Railroad. In 1856 he had outlined and defined a clear system of duties and responsibilities of all officers of his road and spelled out the lines of authority and communication.[1] And although the Saint Paul & Pacific was then still a minute system compared to the sprawling New York & Lake Erie, its organization closely followed the guidelines laid down by McCallum.

The most important officer was the general superintendent. William Crooks, the chief engineer, seems to have doubled as such originally, but after he left for the battlefields of the Civil War he was succeeded by William B. Litchfield, who operated the road more or less as his own. Litchfield was, in turn, succeeded by Francis R. Delano, who held office until 1872. His successor as superintendent was Edmund Q. Sewall, with "Jud" Rice as his assistant.[2] Rice had been the first conductor of the company back in 1862, and his career on the Saint Paul & Pa-

cific and its successor was to be long and honorable.[3] Sewall stayed on until 1876 when, with the appointment as general manager and receiver of Jesse P. Farley, former merchant and steamboat owner, no superintendent was deemed necessary anymore.[4] Sewall moved on to the position of secretary treasurer of the Saint Paul & Duluth, while Rice stayed on as Farley's assistant. When the St. Vincent extension was partly opened in 1877, Farley was appointed receiver and manager of that line also, still separate from the rest of the network, with William H. Fisher as his assistant there.[5] By 1879 Fisher was superintendent of all lines of the Saint Paul & Pacific, but in that same year he was discharged by Hill and was succeeded by E. B. Wakeman.[6]

Under the McCallum system the chief engineer was the first officer under the general superintendent, and in chronological sequence these were D. C. Shepard, William Crooks, James S. Skinner, and Charles A. F. Morris (from 1871 onward). Morris is last named as such in *Poor's Manual* for 1878, with no immediate successor then being mentioned. In 1881 the chief engineer of the Saint Paul, Minneapolis & Manitoba was Charles C. Smith, an old hand at this game who back in 1857 had already located part of the line of the Minnesota & Pacific.[7]

The ticket agent was the man responsible for all matters pertaining to the passenger traffic, and John H. Randall was the first serving as such until 1875, when he became railroad commissioner of the state of Minnesota.[8] In the very beginning he also doubled as cashier, conductor, and general handyman when anybody was sick or on leave. He was succeeded by W. S. Alexander, who is first mentioned as freight and ticket agent in *Poor's Manual* for 1879.[9] First freight agent, responsible for all matters concerning freight operations, was James W. Doran, who for some years after Randall's departure also doubled as passenger agent. He is last mentioned as such in 1878, and his successor was A. L. Mohler.[10] Both ticket and freight agents were responsible for setting rates and fares, and for organizing the cooperation with other carriers, both railroads and others. They were also supposed to solicit new traffic and potential customers, and for this aspect of their duties they had to be men of good standing, well known in the community, in order to perform their work adequately.

For a railroad with an extensive land grant such as the Saint Paul & Pacific, the land commissioner was a man of great importance. If he did his job well, he could generate a large amount of income, and at the same time attract new traffic from the settlers on railroad land. Herman Trott, an engineer of German extraction, served as land commissioner almost from the beginning, and he did more than just sell land.[11] He served as treasurer of the First Division Company for some time, was even on the board of directors, but returned to the land department in the 1870s. He also traveled to the Netherlands at least once, in the fall of 1872, to reassure the Dutch bondholders that everything was to come out right and to defend the company's policy of halting all construction during the severe Minnesota winters.[12]

Johan Knuppe, a Dutch army officer and brother-in-law to Johan Carp (whom we'll meet again in the next chapter) was land commissioner for the St. Vincent extension in 1878 and 1879. He also did odd jobs in the offices of the company at St. Paul and seems to have made himself generally useful. Among other jobs he translated Dutch texts and letters into English. He later settled on a farm near Crookston in the Red River Valley and wrote a brochure full of hard facts and useful tips for his countrymen who might be thinking of emigrating to Minnesota.[13] Still later, in 1912, he was partner in the Netherlands–American Land Company in St. Paul.

There are few details available about the salaries earned by the top-ranking men in the company. Payrolls of some years have been found, but they do not always give the amounts paid every man.[14] In 1876 Farley as general manager made $583.35 a month, and his assistant manager Fisher earned $208.35. Assistant superintendent J. B. Rice made $170 a month, while dispatcher F. E. Merrill earned $100, and the few clerks in the general office made around $45. In 1871 Charles Morris, the chief engineer, earned $200 a month and his chief draughtsman, J. S. LaCare, made half that sum. In all, nineteen persons worked at the general office.

Serving under the chief engineer were the master mechanic, in charge of the rolling stock and locomotives, and the road master, in charge of the track and bridges. *Poor's Manual* for 1869–1870 gives some names. Charles N. Parker was master mechanic; Robert Walker was road master of the Branch line and O. L. Dudley of the Main line, both at $100 a month; C. B. Boynton was in charge of the car shops. Parker is mentioned as master mechanic for the last time in the 1872–1873 edition of *Poor's*, but other sources indicate that he was already replaced in 1867 by John C. Munro, only twenty-four years old, who made $150 per month. Munro was fired in September 1876; he was succeeded by Geo. W. Turner, who in turn was succeeded in 1882 by Harvey Middleton.[15]

The Rank and File

The men serving under these division heads are sometimes hard to identify and their duties are not always clearly defined. Most sources have been destroyed or lost over the years. Some personnel records do remain, however, and it is possible to reconstruct the mechanical engineering department between the years 1873 and 1877.[16]

The master mechanic (Parker, Munro, and Turner, in succession) had under him a chief clerk, at $125 a month, and several clerks, at between $40 and $81 per month depending on length of service and responsibilities. From 1871 onward shop foreman in St. Paul was Thomas W. Heathcote, at $150 per month. From 1867 onward his colleague in Willmar was William H. Slichter, at $110 per month, but he was discharged in 1875 and was succeeded, apparently temporarily and at only $95 a month, by A. B. Smith, a locomotive engineer who quit voluntarily in 1879. From 1867 onward, there was one "stationary engineer" at St. Paul, Geo. H. Prescott, at $75 per month. He was supposed to fire up "cold" locomotives in time for the first train they were scheduled to haul, and to clean out the ash pans and fires of incoming engines. The regular boiler washouts were probably also part of his duties. Prescott died "in insane asylum Fergus Falls."[17] Patrick Gillen was another veteran; from 1863 onward he served as watchman in St. Paul at $50 per month.

As was common on other railroads, lower personnel were paid by the day instead of by the month. A veteran locomotive engineer such as Charles W. Dearing, who had entered service in 1864 when he was twenty-nine years old, made $3.50 a day. He was still in service in 1879. George Chrysler came to the Saint Paul & Pacific in 1866, also at age twenty-nine, and remained in service with the company (finally the Great Northern) until his death in 1899. William E. Noyes was engineer from 1868, when he was only twenty-one years old, until he quit in 1878. Engineers appointed after 1871 generally made only $2.50 or $2.75 a day, and many quit or were discharged in 1873 after the default. Some were discharged for carelessness, some for "incompetency," some others have the remark "dead" behind their names—one was burned to death in a hotel fire in Willmar. Addiction to alcohol has not been found as cause for discharge, although on many other railroads this was the most common reason for being fired. Liquor often was the only escape from the harsh operating and living conditions, and in Minnesota things cannot have been very different from those found elsewhere. Extremely cold, dark winters could be seen as a valid reason to take to drink, and even railroads in more temperate climes such as the Santa Fe were plagued with drunkenness among their workers.[18] Yet drunkenness is not mentioned even once in the surviving Saint Paul & Pacific records.

The workforce must have been cut back severely after 1873: only twenty-three locomotive engineers remained listed in 1875, with twenty-six firemen. Firemen made between $1.50 and $1.75 a day. In 1876 the number of engineers was down to eighteen, with the whole locomotive department including firemen and engine wipers at fifty-four men, and not all of them fully employed. The shops employed another seventy-eight men in that year. No less than thirty car repairers at between $2.75 and $3.50 a day were needed to keep the rolling stock in running order. Laborers, helpers, and pattern-makers made up the rest of the shop force.

Wages paid by the Saint Paul & Pacific were certainly not low, and the $3.50 per day for the first engineers compares favorably with the national average of between $3.08 and $3.38 for these years. The $2.50 made by engine men after 1873 was definitely low when compared to the national wages, however, but it did follow a downward trend in railroad wages in general during the years 1870–1874. Firemen nationwide generally made around $1.80 per day, and the Saint Paul & Pacific was not far below this level.[19]

Unskilled laborers made much less than the engineers, generally between $1.50 and $1.75, which tallies well with other wages paid locally in St. Paul in those years: laborers from $1.50 to $2.00, carpenters from $2 to $3, and masons between $3.50 and $4.50.[20] Machinists in the St. Paul shops were hired at between $2.50 and $4.00 per day, painters at between $1.75 and $3.75 (one painter, Charles Slausen, in service since 1874 "killed himself on the steps of First Baptist Church").[21] The wages of the machinists were very high—elsewhere these men did not make more than between $2.60 and $2.90 per day. They must have been in short supply in St. Paul. In 1876 the workforce was cut back again: of the thirty-five machinists then serving, fourteen were discharged for want of work, five left of their own volition, two were discharged with no reason given, and one was transferred to another job, leaving only thirteen in place. Again, nothing unusual here, as railroads generally cut back on staff in slack times.[22]

Altogether these records, scanty as they are, give an impression of a high turnover—especially in the lower ranks, but also among locomotive engineers. Men came and left continuously, often of their own free will, and moved on to other jobs and other companies. This was not unusual on the frontiers, where a man could easily find better work or higher pay when he found his present situation unsatisfactory. Most were young, unmarried men, who could easily pack up their few belongings and move on to new horizons. On other pioneer railroads, especially on those in the West such as the Atchison, Topeka & Santa Fe, matters were very much the same. Some workers on this road were hired for the sea-

son only; the seasonal workforce often consisted of nonskilled laborers such as students, real estate agents, farmers, and such, and they were never supposed to stay on the job for long.[23] Things will not have been very different on the Saint Paul & Pacific.

But even skilled railroaders were often migratory for a variety of reasons. Boomer railroaders, as they were commonly called, were a familiar sight all over the western parts of the United States, and railroad superintendents did not hesitate to hire these men as long as they had some experience, were not blacklisted for earlier strike action elsewhere, and had no known criminal record. The high turnover was nothing unusual when even on Eastern railroads a period of two years of service in one company was considered long. In general the higher the rank, the longer the service. Unskilled station and track laborers were always the most transient.[24]

A good example of such a boomer railroader is Horace P. Breed, born in Norwich, New York, in 1843. He entered service with the Saint Paul & Pacific in 1863 as a brakeman and was promoted to freight conductor one year later, then to passenger conductor in 1866. In 1872 he left St. Paul to become superintendent of the New York, Kingston & Syracuse (later part of the Ulster & Delaware), where he lasted until 1874, whereupon he became a passenger conductor again, this time on the Long Island Railroad, which would seem to have been a demotion. He stayed on the Long Island for two years, then his whereabouts are unknown until 1882 when he returned to St. Paul as general superintendent of the Saint Paul & Duluth.[25]

Not everybody was as restless as Breed and other boomers were. Some even made a lifetime career on the Saint Paul & Pacific and its successors. A. Guthrie for instance, a Canadian born in 1843, started his railroad career as a tracklayer in 1866, moved on to clerk, brakeman, conductor, purchasing agent, and assistant superintendent; he finally ended up in 1881 as superintendent of the Northern Division of the Saint Paul, Minneapolis & Manitoba at Crookston. Charles H. Jenks, one year Guthrie's junior, joined the ranks of the Saint Paul & Pacific in 1870, at age twenty-six, and served as brakeman on freight trains, construction trains, and finally passenger trains until 1882, when he became train master of the Northern Division of the Saint Paul, Minneapolis & Manitoba. One year later he was promoted to assistant superintendent on the same Northern Division, where he served at Crookston under Guthrie.[26]

Uniforms were unknown at first, just as on other pioneer lines. People knew each other, and insignia of rank or function were not needed. Conductors sometimes wore a distinctive hat, but ordinary clothes. Only in 1882 were uniforms introduced for train staff on the Saint Paul, Minneapolis & Manitoba, a sure sign of having reached a certain level of civilization! Blue was worn by conductors, gray by brakemen and baggage men.[27]

Out on the Road

The Branch Line

The Branch line was divided into nineteen sections under road master Robert Walker; of the nineteen foremen at between $45 and $60 a month, three could not write their names. Every section had between three and six laborers (there were seventy in all) and twenty of them were illiterate. Judging by the names most were American or Irish, but there are many Scandinavian names and a few German, Dutch, or other. Irishmen made up a large part of the railroad workforce in Minnesota, but were never as numerous as the Scandinavians.[28] Section 11 of the Branch was a Scandinavian preserve: P. A. Ostergren was foreman and J. P. Jonson, L. Peterson, and N. P. Nelson laborers. Section 12 seemed more Italian: J. Costello was foreman, and out of five

laborers two more were also named Costello. It is most probable that many of these men were related to each other. It was not unusual that fathers, sons, and brothers served on the same company, and the Saint Paul & Pacific will have been no exception. Family connections apparently played an important role in securing employment on any railroad.[29]

Train staff on the Branch in 1876 consisted of four conductors at between $75 and $85 per month; six brakemen at between $45 and $50; four baggage men at $50; the St. Paul yardmaster, H. Snyder, at $100; and several flagmen, watchmen, and yardmen—thirty men altogether. Station agents on the Branch made between $60 and $80 a month. St. Cloud had the largest staff apart from St. Paul: agent, assistant agent, operator, bridge tender, and pumper. Total station staff on the Branch, again excepting St. Paul, was only thirty men. St. Paul was easily the most important station of the whole network. Agent H. W. Burk, at $135 a month, had thirty-six men under him: a cashier, several clerks, yardmasters, foremen, flagmen, and switchmen.

It was fairly usual that railroad depot buildings also contained living quarters for the agent and his family. When a railroad was built ahead of civilization, there were no towns to speak of where suitable quarters could be found for an agent, and many companies constructed depots with a second story for living quarters.[30] Many Midwestern railroads such as the Chicago & North Western and the Chicago, Milwaukee & Saint Paul habitually did so, but it is not likely that the Saint Paul & Pacific followed this trend. The few surviving photographs of early depots show single-story wooden buildings, with no provision for the agent and his family. Apparently he was expected to find accommodation for himself and his family elsewhere in the village or town. On the other hand the Saint Paul & Pacific may have followed the example of the Chicago, Burlington &

Quincy, which hired only single men for its rural agencies in the West, to avoid the necessity of providing living quarters for families.[31] Available data are not sufficient to draw any conclusions on this point.

The depot generally was the center of the town or village. More often than not, in newly opened country, it was the first permanent building in town and the rest of the business structures were clustered around it. The station agent was an important person. He was in connection, by way of the telegraph, with the outside world, and he was the source, often the only source, of news from the rest of the world. With few trains running daily, the agent's job was hardly a full-time occupation, but he had to be on hand twenty-four hours a day in case of emergencies, hence the popularity on many lines of in-house living quarters for him.

The Main Line

The Main line in 1876 had two road masters: O. L. Dudley, at $100 per month, for sections 1–19 and John Clint, at $75 per month, supervising sections 20–38. Dudley's nineteen sections each had a foreman and between four and seven laborers, making the total for his part of the line 112 men, plus an extra crosstie gang of six men. Of this total, twenty could not write their names but signed with a cross. Clint had eighty-three men for his sections, six of them illiterate. Here also, some sections seem to have been wholly operated by Scandinavians, as shown by section 16: foreman was B. Olson, with laborers C. Olson, N. Knutson, and O. W. Sundblad. Section 18 had C. Nelson as foreman, with J. Mattson, J. Carlson, and J. Thorson as laborers.

The Main line boasted eight conductors, four baggage men, and thirteen brakemen, not all fully employed. At Minneapolis agent J. W. Henion, who made $125 a month, had nineteen men serving under him. At the other end of the scale, most sta-

tions had only one agent, at $40 per month, as did Cokato, Dassel, Swede Grove, and Hancock, or one agent and a pumper/woodpiler, at $20–25 per month, as in Kerkhoven. In between was Willmar, with one agent and four other men. Total station staff for the whole line was sixty-eight, all able to write their names.

The Main line also had an extra gang of thirteen bridge carpenters under foreman W. F. Hills, probably chiefly for the Mississippi bridge. The wood train was in the charge of conductor John L. Kellogg, at $100 per month, who had one brakeman and nineteen laborers for supplying all stations with locomotive fuel. Apparently this was not enough, for in 1877 a fuel agent, H. W. Armstrong, is listed in the payrolls, at $90 per month, plus some fifteen fuel agents spread out along both Main and Branch lines, at between $40 and $50 per month. Only the fuel agent in Delano made $100 a month; he may have been in charge of the gravel pit there as well, which would explain his high wages.

The payrolls surviving from 1879 clearly show the growing traffic on all lines of the Saint Paul & Pacific. Wages paid are generally the same or somewhat lower than before, apart from a sharp rise in the monthly salaries paid to the conductors. The general offices had expanded to thirty men, and station agent Burk at St. Paul had sixty-nine men working under him. His colleague J. H. Henion at Minneapolis had seen his staff grow to thirty-two, and only the smaller stations still had only one agent with sometimes a pumper and/or woodpiler. Master mechanic George Turner and his shop foreman, Henry Hinkins, had nineteen machinists and six blacksmiths at the St. Paul shops, plus one wheel presser, seven boilermakers, clerks, apprentices, car repairers, cleaners, and such (altogether 131 men), mostly in St. Paul, but a few also elsewhere on the system. Foreman of the car shops was Charles B. Moritz, at $90

A view in 1880 of the Melrose depot, opened in 1872, with the section gang standing on their handcar. (Minnesota Historical Society)

per month, and foreman boilermaker William McTeague, at $80.

The number of locomotive engineers had grown to thirty-six, with thirty-seven firemen and thirteen engine wipers in St. Paul alone, plus twenty-two at other stations on the system (a grand total of 115 men). Charles W. Dearing is still the first on the roll, and still at $3.50 a day. The number of pumpers, at $30 per month, to supply the engines with boiler water had grown to twenty-five at nineteen different stations. T. S. Nickerson was pump repairer and made $60 a month. The new fuel agent Wm. M. Russell had twenty-three woodpilers working at eighteen stations.

The total station staff of the Branch then numbered twenty-four, excepting St. Paul. Most stations were still one-man affairs, with only St. Cloud, Alexandria, and Anoka having more than one person. The number of conductors on the Branch had grown to six, and their monthly wages had been raised to between $70 and $100. Brakemen numbered

twelve, with two baggage men, generally at the same rate of pay as before. The two road masters—William Ray for sections 1–14 and J. A. Mayer for sections 15–26 (the road had been extended to St. Vincent by then)—had small gangs of three or four section men, making only a dollar a day.

The Main line station staff including Minneapolis totaled seventy-five men. Conductors numbered twenty-two, each with his regular crew of between two and nine brakemen (altogether 104 men). J. Costello was road master of sections 1–19 at $75, with 102 men under him. Flint had seventy men for the rest of the line to Breckenridge. Section 18 was completely Scandinavian: P. Nelson was foreman and N. Carlson, O. Nelson, J. Carlson, and S. Anderson were laborers (the latter all illiterate). Other names were mostly American or Irish, again with a sprinkling of German and other. A few Dutch names are found: N. A. van Meter was agent at Kandiyohi, P. L. van Cleve at St. Johns, and H. S. van Cleve at Kerkhoven.

The wood train was still operating under conductor Kellogg, who was making only $90 a month, with a brakeman and forty laborers, some of whom were part-time. This must have been a labor-intensive and fairly expensive business. It is difficult to understand why the company did not switch over to burning coal in its locomotives instead of wood.

There is no indication that railroaders of the Saint Paul & Pacific took part in the early stages of organization of labor. The Brotherhood of Locomotive Engineers had been in existence since 1863 and had seen a rapid development, but apparently St. Paul was at that time still too far out for the Brotherhood's propaganda to reach. The Brotherhood of Locomotive Firemen came some ten years later, but again, there is no indication that the firemen of the Saint Paul & Pacific took part in its early growth. The great railroad strike of 1877, which started in the East on the Baltimore & Ohio Railroad in July of that year and spread as far as Iowa, never did reach Minnesota. A general 10 percent cutback in wages was the direct cause of the strike, but some roads, such as the Northern Pacific, did not follow the nationwide trend and so escaped from harm. The Chicago, Burlington & Quincy was struck toward the end of July and suffered damages to its shops in Chicago and in Burlington, Iowa, and to its rolling stock. There is no indication that any of the railroads operating in Minnesota was seriously affected by the strike.[32]

Working for the railroad was a respectable and generally much sought-after job. The pay was not bad compared to other industries, and life on the railroad, especially for the train personnel, could be varied and full of adventure. But working hours were long, conditions in the harsh Minnesota winters very exacting, living accommodations primitive, and job security uncertain. Accidents were frequent and insurance nonexistent. Pension plans for old employees came only much later in the American railroad industry and in this respect the United States lagged far behind Europe, where insurance and pension plans for railroaders were already common in the 1860s.[33]

Adding up the numbers of employees as given above, and allowing for some omissions and duplications, the total staff of the Saint Paul & Pacific must have counted between 900 and 950 at the end of its corporate existence, which places it very close to the category of largest railroads with over 1000 employees in 1880.[34] Of all American railroad companies 12 percent belonged to this exclusive class. So even before James Hill took charge in 1879 and greatly expanded the road, the Saint Paul & Pacific was no longer a small, unimportant regional railroad but was ranking among the larger companies, though only just so. In 1876 the number of employees had stood at around 670, and growth had been steady, not only in the length of the network, but also in the intensity of its traffic and the number of personnel needed to operate this growing traffic.

The cramped railroad yards at St. Paul in the early 1880s, where accidents were bound to happen. Hill's transfer shed and Litchfield's early elevator are visible in the distance. (Minnesota Historical Society)

Accidents

O
n every railroad, and certainly on pioneer railroads in undeveloped country, accidents were common, and the Saint Paul & Pacific was no exception to the rule.[1] Accidents, sometimes involving loss of life, did occur frequently, but the company seems to have avoided the worst crashes and the most glaring disasters. No bridges ever fell under the weight of a train, as did the Mississippi bridge of the Northern Pacific at Brainerd on July 17, 1875, when two spans collapsed under a freight train. Northern Pacific engine number 45, ten flatcars with rails, twelve boxcars, and the caboose fell into the river, killing the engineer and fireman and three passengers in the caboose.[2] Shortly before, an experienced traveler had crossed this bridge and pronounced it one of the best of its kind he had ever seen.[3] In contrast, the Mississippi bridge at Minneapolis stood the test of time.

Of course, traffic was light and speeds were slow: thirty miles per hour was the permitted maximum for passenger trains, which gave an average speed of nineteen miles per hour, including stops, and the trains hardly ever ran even that fast. Freights were allowed fifteen miles an hour maximum, resulting in an average of only ten miles per hour. On the other hand, maintenance of rolling stock left much to be desired, the roadbed was rough and uneven, and with the high turnover in labor inexperienced trainmen and depot personnel made many mistakes or simply did not care, so it is only to be wondered at that nothing really serious ever happened.

The track was in bad shape in places through hasty construction and lack of maintenance. The 1871–1872 report of the Minnesota railroad commissioner stated that the track of the Main line between St. Anthony and Wayzata was made up of old, light iron rails, badly worn, and with the roadbed soft and subsiding. Between Wayzata and Darwin, the iron rails were bent and again very much worn, and only from Benson to Breckenridge (the stretch finished shortly before) was the roadbed found smooth and in good shape, with heavier iron rails in good condition. The old iron rails weighed only fifty pounds to the yard, connected with wrought-iron shoes, whereas the newer rails, although still iron, weighed fifty-six pounds to the yard and were connected by the much better fishplates.[4]

Steel rails were already common by that time and, although much stronger and longer lasting, were also more expensive. The Saint Paul & Pacific only started laying steel rails toward the very end of its corporate existence. The superior qualities of steel were already fully known by that time,

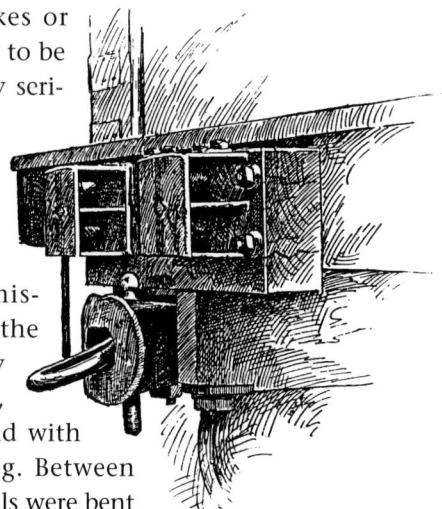

The infamous link-and-pin coupler, the cause of many mangled hands and bruised limbs. (From Clarke, *The American Railway*)

The dangerous practice of coupling cars while standing between them. The link of one car had to be guided into the slot of the other, and the pin was dropped at that precise moment. (From Clarke, *The American Railway*)

and American and foreign foundries and blast furnaces were doing a roaring trade in steel. Trade journals of the time were full of advertisements of American agents for British iron and steel. Steel tires and wheels, made by Friedrich Krupp of Essen, were being imported as well.[5] There is no indication that a poor company such as the Saint Paul & Pacific could afford these new high-quality products. Complaints were heard that the company instead bought stocks of iron rails of no less than thirteen different kinds, which made a smooth track scarcely possible.[6] Many minor derailments must have resulted from this policy of buying only the cheapest available, a fault that continued to plague the railroad for many years to come.

The most common accidents by far were collisions with animals on the track. Although the railroad companies were by law obliged to fence their tracks, they hardly ever did so in the sparsely settled areas. Paying compensation was apparently cheaper than fencing the whole line. Generally such collisions resulted only in the death of the cow or steer, but now and then a train was derailed as a result, which disrupted service and damaged track and rolling stock. Locomotives and cars were light and sometimes unstable and could easily be thrown off the tracks in an unlucky encounter with a large animal.

The first recorded accident involving an animal was the collision between the *Wm.*

Crooks and an ox at the Lake Como crossing on July 22, 1863. It must have been a hefty beast, for the locomotive was derailed and fell into a ditch, which damaged its driving wheels beyond repair. A new set of wheels had to be ordered, and the engine was out of service for several months.[7] Next, the snowplow ran over a cow belonging to Mrs. Eliza Phillips of St. Anthony, in January 1866. How rustic must that place still have been in 1866 that cows could wander onto the tracks. The company paid Mrs. Phillips $15 "for damage to cow."[8] Later, a regular tariff was established for such mishaps; they were so frequent that in some years the expenses could run into thousands of dollars in compensation paid. Derailments following running over animals were fortunately rare, but one happened to the Litchfield accommodation train in June 1872. After hitting a cow near Howard Lake, the train derailed, injuring two passengers.[9]

Another all too common accident was the crushing of fingers, hands, or feet of brakemen and conductors while they were trying to couple railroad cars. The link-and-pin coupler then in use was a dangerous device and caused thousands of injuries to railroad personnel nationwide. Operating the coupler required the brakeman to step between the cars, guide the link of one car into the draft box of the other, and drop the pin in place at the right moment. But brakes were not very precise or dependable, locomotive engineers often could not see very well what was happening at the far end of a long line of cars, and brakemen all too often were run over or had their fingers smashed between the cars. Many inventors tried their best to introduce some kind of automatic coupler, but only in 1893 did Congress make the automatic Janney coupler mandatory for all cars and locomotives in interstate traffic.[10]

The Saint Paul & Pacific did not escape this particular danger. Early figures are not available, but of the four accidents causing injuries mentioned in the railroad commissioner's report for 1873, three were coupling accidents. On December 18, 1872, John Roberts was caught between a shifting engine and caboose at Minneapolis when trying to couple up and had two ribs broken. On April 30, 1873, P. Gallagher, employed in shifting at East Minneapolis, had his hand crushed while trying to couple two cars. On May 14, 1873, Thos. Conners, freight brakeman, had his foot hurt at Kandiyohi.[11]

In later years the list continues. On October 31, 1874, Geo. Maguire, freight brakeman, lost two fingers while coupling cars at Rice Street, St. Paul. The last months of 1875 were particularly bad in this respect. On November 5, 1875, Samuel Brown, brakeman, was killed. He fell from a moving train while attempting to turn a "summersault" from one car to another. On December 7, 1875, conductor O. P. Huntington lost two fingers while coupling cars. On December 23 of the same year, Chas. Lawson, brakeman, was killed while coupling cars. Early in the next year, Frank Love, brakeman, fell from a boxcar of a moving train and was injured.[12]

On April 12, 1877, $20 was paid to Doctor O. J. Evans for operating on the hand of F. Mulholland, "breakman," injured at Minneapolis. On June 26, 1877, $26 was paid out to D. L. Dunham, M.D., at Anoka, for professional services to A. J. Manley, brakeman, injured while coupling cars at Anoka on May 11. Ten visits of $2 each, plus six visits of $1 each, were needed for Manley's treatment. Charles Ball was killed while working in the gravel pit near Delano, on August 4, 1877. His coffin cost $17, and Charles Eppel, the undertaker at Delano, was paid $9.75 for "sundries" for Ball's burial. On November 7, 1877, brakeman Charles Quinn lost one finger while trying to couple cars. On August 5, 1878, brakeman Charles Otto was fatally injured while coupling up the engine of the wood train at Delano. Apparently he lived for some days, as $11.70 were paid to a certain M. A. Chance—probably the local druggist—for

medicines supplied to Otto, and later Charles Eppel of Delano was paid $6.52 for material furnished for Otto's funeral. Undertaker Eppel must have done a good business with the railroad.[13]

One of the worst crashes involving loss of life was on March 21, 1872. The snowplow train, returning to Benson after having cleared the track near Hancock, became separated. When the engine reversed to catch up with its lost work cars, it could not stop in time and crushed the caboose. Three men, among them the road master E. M. Sullivan, were killed instantly and two others were seriously injured.[14]

A potentially dangerous accident happened on June 28, 1878, at St. Anthony Junction, at the only crossing with any other railroad. A train of the Minneapolis & Saint Louis Railway running on the rails of the Saint Paul & Duluth (the former Lake Superior & Mississippi River) rammed into a Saint Paul & Pacific Branch line train at the crossing. One passenger car and one baggage car were thrown off the track and their trucks broken, but there were no injuries reported.[15] Accidents of this kind could have been infinitely worse, and the Saint Paul & Pacific was certainly in luck here.

In a country without roads the railroad right-of-way was often used by people to walk from one place to another. With the few trains running this was no real problem, but when a train came along, people were often careless or too late in getting off the track, resulting in death or severe injuries to the unlucky trespasser. John Walker was walking across the tracks in St. Paul yard when he was struck by an arriving train on August 20, 1874. J. J. Terwell, an aged—and probably deaf—resident of Delano, was struck by the snowplow while walking the track. On December 4, 1876, Austin Hanson was killed near Swede Grove while walking on the track. An unknown tramp, asleep under a car in St. Paul yard, was injured by a train. A certain Scott, while lying in a fit on the tracks near Cedar Lake, had his foot crushed by a passing train on March 23, 1878.[16]

Generally these accidents were attributed to a lack of caution on the part of the persons injured or killed, without any consequences for the company. But now and then the company was considered to blame for not having used the locomotive's bell or whistle when crossing public streets, as prescribed in its charter. On November 27, 1875, young Oliver Beaudoin was struck and killed by a switching engine at the lower levee of St. Paul. One year later the company paid his father, Vital Beaudoin, $1,000 in compensation for "damages."[17] In this case the railroad was apparently found guilty of neglect.

Another common source of accidents leading to injuries or deaths were attempts to jump onto moving trains for a free ride. When they could not afford the regular fare, people were often found trying to catch a free ride, sometimes with dire consequences. These hoboes traveled free all over the country, mostly on freight trains in empty boxcars or under the cars, "riding the rods." On the Saint Paul & Pacific things were much the same, apparently. A certain Fleming was injured while trying to board a passing freight train at Howard Lake on July 5, 1875. Two years later on March 1, 1877, Comstock, no employee, had his foot crushed while trying to jump on a moving freight train at St. Anthony. In the same year John LeClair had the same misfortune while jumping a train at Delano. One year later a boy named Treat was killed when he missed his foothold while jumping a train near St. Anthony Junction.[18]

And then there were those passengers who by their own carelessness or foolishness lost their lives or were seriously injured. It took some time before travelers and bystanders adjusted to the new phenomenon of moving trains and fully realized that the iron horse was very different from a horse

and buggy and could be very dangerous. Speeds may have been low, but even then, jumping off the train before it stopped could be fatal. Crossing from one car to another was prohibited because of the danger involved, but it was done despite these warnings. Particularly unfortunate was passenger A. S. Pruitt who, while drunk, tried to cross from one car to another while the train was on the Mississippi bridge at Minneapolis. On February 7, 1874, he fell between the cars, through the timbers of the bridge, landed on the ice of the river, and was killed instantly. Another passenger under the influence, Duncan McMillan, fell from a moving train west of Willmar and was killed. No compensation to dependents was mentioned in the reports. The company was certainly not to blame on December 2, 1876, when E. Hazard threw himself in front of a train at Minneapolis in an apparent suicide.[19]

Big smashes occasionally happened without loss of life, but with a lot of material damage. A broken rail caused the derailment of the westbound passenger train at milepost 20, west of Minneapolis, on August 31, 1874. Damage to the cars was extensive; a Mr. Cahill and three women, Mrs. Anna Thingstead and the Misses Godfrey and Dassel, were much cut and bruised. On December 12, 1877, in a dense fog, the wood train ran into the rear of a freight train near Atwater. The engine of the wood train had its smokestack and headlight knocked off and the caboose of the freight was much damaged, but no injuries were reported. On March 12, 1878, ten cars of a freight jumped the track, cause unknown; on September 22 of that year four cars with wheat were derailed by a broken brake beam and destroyed, two miles west of Cokato. Less than one month later, on October 17, two extra freights collided head-on between Litchfield and Grove City (Swede Grove as was). Both engines were seriously damaged, but again no personal injuries were reported. Both crews must have bailed out in time.

In respect of safety the Saint Paul & Pacific was no better and no worse than other railroads of the time. It had its share of accidents, but most were minor affairs without loss of life. And in many years the company could proudly state that no passengers lost their lives other than through faults of their own. But there must have been a lot of irregularities and minor accidents that never reached the ears of the railroad commissioners and so have escaped detection. Especially during the years after the bankruptcy, when money was scarce and the staff limited in numbers, maintenance of both track and rolling stock was cut back to a minimum, and small mishaps must have been an almost daily occurrence. Even after things improved significantly during 1878, after James Hill and his associates concluded the deal with the Dutch bondholders, Hill was exasperated about conditions on the road. He wrote to his associate George Stephen on December 26, 1878:

> Since you left here we have had four trains off the track—one passenger and three freights—one of the freights damaged 14 cars more or less with their contents and the other damaged 4 cars—we think only the engine. The passenger train was caused by a broken rail and the air brakes saved the train—only the mail, express and baggage cars getting off.[20]

And even two years after Hill took over as general manager and started improving the situation, his diaries are still full of such minor mishaps and irregularities.[21]

January 1881.
Thursday 6: train off track at trestle bridge east of Dassell
Friday 7: Broken wheel in engine 23 about 5 miles west of Alexandria

The Northern Pacific's Mississippi River bridge at Brainerd, which collapsed in 1875. (From Beadle, *The Undeveloped West*)

Monday 10: Car 988 & 1290 ends stow up, bad switching
Tuesday 11: Combination car 43 just out of shops with flat wheels. Reported today that worktrain on Fergus Falls line with broken flange broke 30 rails and ditched train
Wednesday 12: Report that no bell was ringing when eng. struck Faben's team on Main Street, St. Anthony
Thursday 13: Engines are being run without oil box covers & engineers say they have reported it but no covers are at either Crookston or Fergus Falls. Gravel cars have more or less box covers lost. Eng. 37 badly leaking was not able to handle her train on B.V. [Barnesville?] line and for that reason had to lie near Big Muddy all night. This run must have an engine in prime order.

Engineer ran eng. off turntable at Benson. Costello says that table was not fastened. Coaches in all trains mismatched. Trainmen should report every wheel that is off track whether from open switch or otherwise.

This small selection of mishaps in one week only was apparently nothing out of the ordinary; it should have been enough to drive any sane man crazy. Not so Hill, as he methodically set out to rectify all abuses and errors.

The *Wm. Crooks* as refurbished in 1908, with James J. Hill on the tender steps. (James J. Hill Papers)

Locomotives

Before we look at the locomotives of the Saint Paul & Pacific Railroad, there is a general remark that should be made. A lot of the available records are incomplete or conflicting, and some of the following notes are thus, of necessity, somewhat conjectural. As early as 1880 the people in charge of the locomotive department were already confused. The list of rolling stock on hand on June 30, 1880, one year after the takeover by the Hill interests, has this penciled remark: "Note, engine record very incomplete as to Saint Paul & Pacific engines. The earlier locos were designated by a name as the *Wm. Crooks* and cannot find record of changes from names to numbers."[1] And indeed the list mentions only numbers 9–11 and 20–46, twenty-seven engines altogether, which had cost $233,404.77, giving an average cost per engine of $8,644, which seems on the low side. Or was the word *cost* here meant as valuation at the moment of transfer to the Manitoba? The list then simply continues with the statement that twenty-two engines, numbers 1–8 and 12–19, which had cost another $190,181.44 (same average price), are not accounted for.

The first locomotive of the Saint Paul & Pacific was already on the premises at the time that the Saint Paul Company took over from the Minnesota & Pacific in March 1862. It was the then famous Minnesota & Pacific (later Saint Paul & Pacific) number 1, *Wm. Crooks,* named for the chief engineer of the Minnesota & Pacific. The engine arrived by rail from the East in Prairie du Chien, Wisconsin, and as there was still no rail connection with St. Paul at the time, it was loaded with some cars and rail on a barge towed upriver by the steamboat *Alhambra*. It landed at St. Paul on September 9, 1861. There, just east of Jackson Street, it was unloaded with great trouble and—probably—a lot of manpower. As there was hardly any track available to run it on, it was stored for the winter, to be fired up again only in the spring of 1862.[2]

The *Wm. Crooks* was of the then common American 4-4-0 wheel arrangement, with two outside 12-by-22-inch cylinders, 62-inch drivers, 110-pound boiler pressure, and a total weight of just over 55,000 pounds, of which almost 40,000 rested on the drivers, resulting in a tractive effort of only 4,700 pounds.[3] It should be stressed here that while the formula for computing the tractive force of an engine may have been generally known, in actual practice this theoretical figure was hardly ever reached. Track conditions, quality of fuel used, weather, and state of maintenance of the engine were all important factors to be reckoned with. Altogether, the *Wm. Crooks* was an ordinary, but somewhat small engine for the period.

In those years engines with cylinders of 15-inch bore by 22-inch stroke were already common, and the *Wm. Crooks* was lighter and more feeble than its contemporaries. The engine was much damaged in the fire that destroyed the St. Paul shops on June 1, 1867, and for a time it was considered destroyed, but in the end it was rebuilt and back in service in 1869.[4] Since then it enjoyed a special position as the pioneer engine in the state and was always used for special occasions. James Hill preferred to use it for inspections, and as such it withstood the ravages of time and remained in service until 1897. In 1908 it was still around, having been refurbished by the Great Northern Railway at its Jackson Street shops in St. Paul, and was used for promotional purposes. In 1925 it was restored once again to resemble the original more closely (though still not quite). It was donated to the Minnesota Historical Society in 1962 and is now happily preserved for posterity at the Duluth Railroad Museum.

The *Wm. Crooks* was built by Smith & Jackson, a firm officially known as the New Jersey Locomotive & Machine Company of Paterson, New Jersey, founded by James Jackson and Samuel Smith.[5] Neighbors in industrial Paterson were the Rogers Locomotive Works, of 1837, and Danforth, Cooke & Company, of 1853. In 1851 Smith and Jackson took over the famous machine shop of William Swinburne, and under the technical guidance of such luminaries as Zerah Colburn and John Brandt, the firm became known for a simple, straightforward engine, of which the *Wm. Crooks* is a good example. Altogether Smith & Jackson built some 330 engines, until the firm came under new management and was renamed the Grant Locomotive Works in 1867.[6] Under that name it became for a time one of the leading American manufacturers, but the Saint Paul & Pacific never was a customer with the new outfit.

The *Wm. Crooks* was built with a straight boiler with two large domes, one over the firebox and one over the front of the boiler, to provide the necessary steam space to avoid priming, which was caused chiefly by dirty feedwater. A round sand dome was positioned between the steam domes. An early photograph of the engine at Elk River shows it in that condition, with Francis Delano, later superintendent of the Saint Paul & Pacific, at the throttle.[7] Boilers wore out quickly, and the *Wm. Crooks* must have been rebuilt, possibly after the 1867 fire, with a new boiler, this time of the wagon-top model, and in this guise it is preserved. There are other, less noticeable differences between the original and the engine as it is now.[8]

As most engines of the time, the number 1 was a wood-burner, and as wood was still plentiful and cheap in Minnesota, it remained so during the existence of the Saint Paul & Pacific. The railroad never used anything other than cordwood for locomotive fuel. At that time Eastern roads, running through areas that were already denuded of timber, were slowly switching to the more expensive coal. Coal smoke was a nuisance, but in calorific value coal was a much superior fuel. As soon as James Hill was in charge of the Saint Paul & Pacific (or Saint Paul, Minneapolis & Manitoba as it was known by then), he started the changeover to coal. The last engines ordered by the Saint Paul & Pacific from Baldwin were delivered as coal-burners, as "we are about to commence use of coal on the division where these engines will be used and have laid in a supply," as Hill stated at that time.[9]

How an impecunious company such as the Minnesota & Pacific—without a single mile of road in service—managed to pay for their first engines is something of an enigma. The typical cost of an engine such as the *Wm. Crooks*, before the Civil War drove up prices, must have been just under $10,000. Shipping to St. Paul would have

Saint Paul & Pacific No. 16, built by Danforth in 1870 and named *Kerkhoven* after the Amsterdam bankers who sluiced Dutch millions through to Minnesota. (Author's Collection, Great Northern Railway)

meant another $800–900. Most builders at the time sold on credit; they also regularly accepted railroad shares and bonds in part payment, but at a discount, depending on the credit of the road. In this case, Smith & Jackson must have had good faith in the future of the Minnesota & Pacific. But in 1863 the firm was in financial trouble, partly because it had extended too much credit to railroads, and it survived only with help from Wall Street financiers, the Grant family, who later substituted their own name for those of Smith & Jackson.

Another favorite way of paying for rolling stock and rails was by giving over any state bonds, issued in support of a fledgling railroad, to the contractors and suppliers of materials. States generally had a better credit rating than new railroads in virgin territory, and their bonds were therefore accepted with less of a discount. Minnesota state bonds, however, as promised by the legislature, could not have been very suitable for the purpose of paying the builders, as they were very much depreciated by that time. Moreover, most had already been given out to the contractor of the road, Selah Chamberlain, in lieu of cash payments.

Before its demise the Minnesota & Pacific had even ordered a second engine with Smith & Jackson. The Minnesota & Pacific number 2 (later Saint Paul & Pacific number 2)—the *Edmund Rice,* named after one of the incorporators of the line—was also finished in 1861 and was delivered in September; there was no work for it to do in St. Paul. The *Edmund Rice* was also of the 4-4-0 wheel arrangement, but with bigger 14-by-22-inch cylinders, 56-inch drivers, and a weight of 48,000 pounds. Judging from the dimensions, it was probably meant for freight traffic. The *Edmund Rice*—by then Saint Paul, Minneapolis & Manitoba number 2 and having lost its name—survived until 1887, when it was scrapped in St. Paul.[10]

With these two engines, the Saint Paul & Pacific opened its first stretch of line between St. Paul and St. Anthony on July 2, 1862, the first train in the state of Minnesota. The *Wm. Crooks* had the honor of hauling the inaugural train on that day, with engineer W. C. Gardner at the throttle, George Winslow as fireman, and J. B. Rice as conductor.[11] After this, however, it is not easy to follow the history of the Saint Paul & Pacific Railroad locomotives. There is a lot of uncertainty about the earlier engines,

Advertisements for the Baldwin Locomotive Works of Philadelphia and the Rogers Locomotive & Machine Works of Paterson, New Jersey, two of the regular suppliers of locomotives to the Saint Paul & Pacific. (From Poor, *Directory of Railway Officials; American Railroad Journal,* 1868)

apart from the *Wm. Crooks* and the *Edmund Rice,* which are fairly well documented.

With the Branch line to Anoka rapidly coming into use, it was mandatory to have more than two engines, but the Civil War must have meant higher prices and possibly even problems in finding new machines at all. Number 3, named *Minnesota,* was allegedly built in September 1863 by Norris of Philadelphia. Norris Locomotive Works, then under Richard Norris & Son, was by then in decline, after having been the foremost American locomotive builder for the past decades. In 1865, despite Civil War orders, they would close the Philadelphia plant temporarily, then two years later they were to close for good.[12] The *Minnesota* was a smaller-wheeled version of the *Wm. Crooks,* with the same cylinder size and 56-inch driving wheels. Its weight was 50,000 pounds. It was apparently worn out or in bad shape by the time of the Hill takeover and was scrapped before June 1879, never getting a Manitoba number.

Two bigger engines built by Norris in 1865 (they must have been among the very last built by this once famous firm) were bought by the Saint Paul & Pacific. Numbers 6 and 7, the *St. Paul* and the *St. Cloud,* had 16-by-22-inch cylinders, 60-inch drivers, and an engine weight of 60,000 pounds. They lasted until November 1888. Payment for these engines must have been long deferred, as the financial records of the Saint Paul Company mention a payment of $8,750 to Richard Norris & Son in October 1868, charged to equipment.[13] Can this possibly have been the last installment of the price of the *St. Paul* and the *St. Cloud*? The equipment history record also mentions this same outlay in October 1868, gives no names or engine numbers, but lists the purchase of an engine from Norris & Son for $8,750 between the *Benson,* delivered by Mason in July 1868, and the *Jud Rice* of May 1869. *Poor's Manual* mentions a locomotive

stock of seven engines on June 1, 1867, so it may be assumed that both the *St. Paul* and the *St. Cloud* had indeed been delivered, but presumably not fully paid for until more than a year later.[14]

As a kind of stopgap, a used engine was acquired in January 1865, apparently as new engines could not be delivered in time. This was the number 4, the *Itasca,* a 4-4-0 taken over from the Dayton & Union Railroad, a little line grown out of another Southwestern Ohio railroad, the Greenville & Miami, in 1862 and later part of the Baltimore & Ohio. The *Itasca* was built by John Souther of Boston, Massachusetts, and probably for the Greenville & Miami, which had opened for business in 1852, as Souther had all but given up locomotive construction by 1860.[15] It was a fairly small engine, with 14-by-20-inch cylinders and 56-inch drivers. Total weight was 50,000 pounds. It is probable that this engine, being of a nonstandard type, was used mostly on construction trains and such. Existing records show that it spent a lot of time in the shops for all kind of repairs. In March 1867 it needed a lot of heavy work to the tender. Boiler repairs came in June of the same year, and so on. The Manitoba must have been happy to get rid of this antique in 1882. It was sold to the contracting firm of Langdon, Shepard & Company, who were then building the Dakota extension of the Manitoba, for $3,000, not a bad deal.[16]

The prospect of the extension of the Branch line to East St. Cloud, which opened in September 1866, and to Sauk Rapids in July of the next year, and the completion of the bridge across the Mississippi between St. Anthony and Minneapolis (opened on June 10, 1867) made the acquisition of more engines mandatory. Money was tight, however, and prices still high after the end of the Civil War. Moreover, the traditional suppliers of the Saint Paul & Pacific, Smith & Jackson and Norris & Son, had given up the locomotive business, so the company had to look elsewhere. The Danforth Locomotive & Machine Company (successors to the old Danforth, Cooke & Company, also of Paterson, New Jersey) obliged by supplying one engine in 1866, number 5, the *Anoka*.[17] Again a 4-4-0, it was bigger than its predecessors, with 16-by-22-inch cylinders, 60-inch drivers, and a weight of 64,000 pounds. The *Anoka* was a nonstandard type and different from all other engines supplied later by Danforth. Could it be that it was ordered by some other railroad and that the Saint Paul & Pacific picked it up on the cheap? As Great Northern number 4, after being rebuilt with smaller drivers in 1891 to make it more suitable for switching, it survived until sold in 1902.

These seven engines had to supply all motive power on the Branch line and on the first stretches of the Main line. Wayzata, twenty-five miles from St. Anthony, was reached in August 1867, and Delano, forty miles away, in October of the next year. New engines were urgently needed, and this time the company turned to the Mason Machine Works of Taunton, Massachusetts, for their needs.[18] Mason was renowned for producing beautiful, well-balanced engines, and the Saint Paul & Pacific number 8, the *Geo. L. Becker*, must have been no exception. It was Mason works number 270, built in September 1867, with 14-by-22-inch cylinders, 63-inch driving wheels, and total weight of 57,600 pounds, of which 35,000 pounds rested on the drivers. Again, the *Becker* was a one-off engine, and survived until it was scrapped in 1893. The *Becker* arrived by the barge *John Lawler* in October 1867, and the company paid G. S. Strasberger, agent for the Milwaukee & Saint Paul Railroad, a sum of $875 for freight charges from Taunton to St. Paul.[19]

Next came two more Mason engines: works numbers 279 and 283, Saint Paul & Pacific numbers 9 and 10, the *F. R. Delano* and the *Jared Benson*, named for the road's

superintendent and a director. The *Delano* arrived in May 1868 and had 15-by-24-inch cylinders, 60-inch drivers, and a weight of 62,750 pounds, of which 40,350 pounds were available for adhesion. For the *Delano*, the Saint Paul & Pacific paid $12,000 to Mason, plus $625 for rail freight to La Crosse, plus $100 to the Northwestern Union Packet Company to get it to St. Paul by water.[20] The *Benson* came in July of the same year, was somewhat smaller, and cost only $11,500, plus the same $625 in rail freight, but this time $150 was needed to get it by river from La Crosse to St. Paul. Can low water have been the reason for this sudden increase? The *Delano*, after having been rebuilt with smaller (49-inch) drivers in 1891, was sold to a lumber company in British Columbia in 1898. The *Benson* survived to acquire the Great Northern Railway number 5, in 1899, but was scrapped in 1901.

An engine of the same dimensions as the *Delano* was built by Mason, works number 310, in June 1869. Named *Jud Rice* (number 11) by the Saint Paul & Pacific, it cost no less than $14,00 (a $2,000 increase in only one year, due to postwar inflation), plus freight.[21] It survived long enough to acquire Great Northern number 6, in 1899, but was sold in 1902.

All these different engines, with hardly any of the same dimensions and built by five different works, must have been a nightmare for the shops to keep in running order. Apparently, the Saint Paul & Pacific management recognized the problem. In an effort to keep down the number of spare parts and when finances permitted the company started to order new engines in small batches from the same supplier.

In October 1869, with the Branch in full operation and the Main line finished as far as Willmar, new engines were again urgently needed. Business was good and there must have been some money in the till, so this time the Saint Paul & Pacific ordered three identical engines from Danforth. Numbers

12–14, the *Wayzata, Willmar,* and *Litchfield* arrived on the premises between August and October 1869. No record of their actual arrival has been found, so it is not known if they came by barge or by rail. The line of the Minnesota Valley/Saint Paul & Sioux City Railroad, controlled by the Chicago North Western, had been open by way of Mendota since December 1867, and this line was sometimes used for heavy shipments. On the other hand, the contacts were close between the Milwaukee and the Saint Paul & Pacific, and the Milwaukee did a lot of heavy repair for the Saint Paul, supplied parts from their own stores, and generally was the preferred carrier from Chicago, even when this still necessitated transfer to barges for the last leg of the journey. The three new Danforth engines had 15-by-22-inch cylinders, 60-inch driving wheels, and

a total weight of 64,500 pounds, of which 41,800 pounds was available for adhesion. They were all rebuilt with smaller wheels in 1891–1892 and survived to be renumbered as Great Northern numbers 7–9. They were scrapped or sold off in 1901–1902.

After this laudable attempt at some measure of standardization, the Saint Paul & Pacific's next engine—in August 1870—was again a Danforth product, but it was different from the earlier engines. Number 15, named *H. Trott,* for the colorful land commissioner of the company, had 16-by-24-inch cylinders and 60-inch wheels; other dimensions are not known. Despite its nonstandard cylinders, the *Trott* survived to become Great Northern number 10 in 1899 and was sold for scrap only in 1902.

Traffic was still growing and as funds permitted more engines were ordered. Danforth

Saint Paul & Pacific No. 38, the *G. W. Turner,* built by Rogers in 1878. (ALCO Historic Photos)

supplied one more engine, again slightly different from all earlier machines built by them. Number 16, the *Kerkhoven,* was delivered in August 1870. It had 16-by-24-inch cylinders, 63-inch driving wheels, 140-pounds-per-square-inch boiler pressure, and a total weight of 66,000 pounds, with 43,700 pounds available for adhesion, making for a tractive effort of 11,610 pounds. The *Kerkhoven* survived until 1916 as Great Northern number 240 and, being named for the Amsterdam stockbrokers of that name, remained the only engine to visibly reflect the large Dutch interest in the Saint Paul & Pacific. There never was a *Kloos,* a *Lippmann,* or a *Carp.*

At the same time that Danforth was building the *Kerkhoven,* the Saint Paul & Pacific company had turned to a new supplier, the Pittsburgh Locomotive and Car Works, of Pittsburgh, Pennsylvania. This firm was a newcomer in the locomotive-building field, having been organized only in 1865 by Andrew Carnegie with a few other businessmen.[22] As a new entrant in this highly competitive industry, they may have been compelled to offer better credit terms or lower prices to attract business. In July–August 1870, Pittsburgh delivered three engines, Saint Paul & Pacific numbers 17–19, the *Chippewa,* the *Hancock,* and the *C. N. Parker, Jr.,* works numbers 75–77. They had 16-by-24-inch cylinders, 63-inch drivers, and 140 pounds of pressure; they weighed 63,140 pounds, of which 43,700 pounds were on the drivers, which resulted in 11,400 pounds tractive effort. The *Chippewa* was sold as Great Northern (second) number 244 to the Northern Dakota Railway in 1908, while the other two were scrapped only in 1926 and 1923, respectively.

As the Main line was scheduled for opening all the way to Breckenridge (207 miles from St. Anthony) in October 1871, these nineteen engines did not suffice for the expected traffic. Always on the lookout for a bargain, the Saint Paul & Pacific managed to

lay hands on three engines currently being built by Baldwin for the Northern Pacific Railway. As there were still, at the time, close corporate links between the Northern Pacific and the Saint Paul & Pacific, it may be possible that the latter obliged by taking these three machines that were apparently superfluous to the needs of the other company. However it may be, in November–December 1871, Baldwin Locomotive Works of Philadelphia delivered Saint Paul & Pacific numbers 20–23. The Baldwin Works were commonly known under that name, but officially, after the death of Matthias W. Baldwin in 1866, the name was M. Baird & Company.[23] Curiously enough, only one of these four engines ever received a name: number 22 was the *J. H. Randall,* the others remained simply numbers 20, 21, and 23. Baldwin works numbers were 2619, 2621, 2638, and 2639. All four had 15-by-24-inch cylinders, 60-inch drivers, and a total weight of 68,800 pounds with 43,000 pounds resting on the drivers, which made them by far the heaviest engines on the line. They lasted until 1900–1910 as Great Northern numbers 243, (first) 244, and 246. The old *Randall,* by then Great Northern 245, suffered an ignominious end: it was sold to the Minnesota State Fair Association and in 1921 was destroyed in a spectacular, staged, head-on collision. The Saint Paul company paid $10,250 for each of these machines in December 1871, so prices seem to have gone down again after 1869. No transportation costs are given, but they all arrived by way of the Milwaukee road, which by then had opened its right bank line along the Mississippi all the way to St. Paul.[24]

With these twenty-three engines the Saint Paul & Pacific Railroad was to operate its traffic for some years.[25] The 1873 crisis and the subsequent default of the company meant that new purchases were out of the question, and only in 1875 was the road's receiver authorized by the court to buy three more engines from Pittsburgh, Saint

Paul & Pacific numbers 24–26, works numbers 320, 322, 323, very similar to the earlier Pittsburgh engines. They arrived in St. Paul in December 1875. Only by then the price had dropped to $8,500 apiece, which must have been most welcome in view of the strained finances of the railroad company.[26] They were long-lived machines; number 25 was scrapped in 1898, number 24 was changed into a weed-burner in 1902, but number 26 was dismantled only in 1923 as Great Northern number 248.

Toward the end of the receivership of the Saint Paul & Pacific, when negotiations with the Dutch protective committee were well under way, it was deemed necessary and possible to order new engines. Traffic was booming, the St. Vincent extension was finished in 1879, and the other extensions in the Red River valley also had to be operated. So between May and October 1878, the Rogers Locomotive & Machine Company of Paterson, New Jersey, turned out no less than sixteen engines for the Saint Paul & Pacific, the largest order ever placed by the company. Rogers probably had no problems in executing such an order, as the company was second in production only to Baldwin at that time. These Rogers engines had 16-by-24-inch cylinders, 55-inch drivers, 140 pounds of boiler pressure, and a total weight of 66,170 pounds, making a tractive effort of 13,290 pounds.[27] Their arrival in St. Paul must have been most welcome, as business was booming. They all had long and useful lives, most of them being renumbered by the Great Northern, the last (Saint Paul number 39, Great Northern number 265) being scrapped only in 1920. Number 40 (as Great Northern number 266) was destroyed in the staged head-on collision at the Minnesota State Fair on August 17, 1921, together with number 22, the old *J. H. Randall*. Prices had continued to drop since the last order of 1875 and the Saint Paul & Pacific paid only $7,000 apiece for numbers 27–42.[28] Curiously, again only one of these

sixteen engines ever got a name: number 38 became the *G. W. Turner*. The unnamed Saint Paul & Pacific number 42 was Rogers's twenty-five-hundredth engine.

Two more and bigger engines came from Rogers early in 1879. Numbers 43 and 44 had bigger, 17-by-24-inch cylinders, 55-inch drivers, and a total weight of no less than 70,300 pounds, of which 44,800 were available for adhesion, giving a hefty 15,010-pound tractive effort. Both these engines survived into Great Northern days.

Four more engines were ordered from Baldwin in the fall of 1879, Saint Paul & Pacific numbers 47–50, but all were delivered to the Saint Paul, Minneapolis & Manitoba with the same running numbers. Baldwin seems to have had problems with their supply of certain parts and materials, and Hill pressed them to speed up delivery as they were urgently needed on the road.[29] They were somewhat smaller than the preceding Rogers engines, having 16-by-24-inch cylinders and a tractive effort of 11,600 pounds only, despite their total weight of 70,000 pounds. Three of them survived until 1926. Baldwin received only $6,850 apiece for them, a clear indication of the severe competition between engine-makers in the country in those years. These Baldwin engines were delivered in St. Paul in November 1879, but they were preceded by an engine bought by the St. Paul, Minneapolis & Manitoba itself. This was a small 0-4-0 switcher of 24.5 tons weight, delivered in October 1879 and numbered 51 by the Manitoba. It was built by Brooks Locomotive Works of Dunkirk, New York, with works number 354, and it was bought from stock for a sum of $5,250.[30]

The Saint Paul & Pacific numbers 45 and 46 were the only engines of a type other than 4-4-0. They were built by Rogers in April 1879 as 2-6-0s, a wheel arrangement then coming into vogue for freight traffic. These moguls (as the 2-6-0 wheel arrangement was popularly known) must have been strong haulers with 16-by-20-inch cylinders,

An advertisement illustrating the paper wheel, made up of a steel tire with layers of paper or strawboard glued and pressed together. The Allen Paper Car-Wheel Company created the wheel in 1869 and was still very much in business by the late 1880s. (From *The Railroad and Engineering Journal,* 1887)

WM. H. FENNER, JR. President   C H. ANTES, Secretary.   J. C. BEACH, Treasurer.

ALLEN PAPER CAR-WHEEL COMPANY,

General Office, CHICAGO, ILL.
NEW YORK OFFICE, 31 and 33 BROADWAY.

Works: Hudson, N. Y.
No. 1.   No. 2.

Works: Pullman Ill.
No. 9.   No. 11.

Standard Paper Wheel.

Double Plate Spoke.
Cast-Iron Center.

STEEL-TIRED WHEELS,
FOR CAR, LOCOMOTIVE AND TENDER TRUCKS.
Safest, Best and Most Economical Wheels in Use.

small 46-inch driving wheels, a total weight of 67,250 pounds, with 62,000 pounds on the six drivers making for a 13,245-pound tractive effort. The cost of number 46 was only $6,741.29 f.o.b. Chicago. This must have been an excellent deal for the time, as prices were generally increasing sharply during the 1878–1882 boom.[31] These engines were the forerunners of a long and successful line of St. Paul, Minneapolis & Manitoba and Great Northern moguls. The two Saint Paul engines survived until 1902 and 1917, respectively, as Great Northern numbers 12 and 13, after having been rebuilt as 0-6-0 switchers.

At the request of the Hudson Paper Car Wheel Company of Hudson, New York, an experiment was made in October 1879 with their pressed paper wheels for locomotive and tender trucks. A set for one locomotive—total cost $744—was delivered to be tried out. Hill scribbled underneath their letter: "The understanding is that the Hudson Paper Wheel Company put in their wheels on trial to be paid for if they give us satisfaction and if not returned." Paper wheels, made of layers of paper or strawboard glued and pressed together and with a steel tire, were becoming much in demand in these years. Invented by Richard N. Allen in 1869, it took some persuasion to convince railroad superintendents that paper wheels were actually stronger, more resilient, and longer lasting than the more common cast-iron wheels. But by 1870 George Pullman was using them for his sleeping cars, and others soon followed.[32] Use of paper wheels for passenger cars became widespread after 1880, but their use on locomotives and tenders remained limited. The Hudson Paper Wheel Company was one of the original works of the Allen

Paper Car Wheel Company, which had factories at Hudson in New York state, and Pullman and Morris in Illinois.

Repairs and Maintenance

With these fifty engines (or forty-nine, when the sale of the old Norris number 3 is taken into consideration), the Saint Paul & Pacific Railroad ended its corporate existence. Maintenance of these forty-nine machines, of at least twelve classes and manufactured by eight different builders, must have meant a nightmare for the maintenance staff in St. Paul. On the other hand, builders tended to use a lot of standardized fittings on machines of different wheel arrangements and dimensions, which of course tended to simplify maintenance.[33] Early on, the St. Paul shops were under master mechanic C. N. Parker, Jr., who served as such until 1867. Parker was succeeded by John C. Munro, then only twenty-four years old. On September 19, 1876, Munro was discharged for unknown reasons, and in his place came Geo. W. Turner, who stayed on at least until the end of the independent existence of the company. Turner's salary was only $125 a month when he started, but he got a raise to $150 within the next year.[34]

To keep an adequate stock of spare parts for each class of engine was almost impossible; repairs often necessitated laborious fitting and shaping by hand. The Saint Paul & Pacific was certainly not alone in this respect. Even older and much larger roads such as the Big Four and the Union Pacific labored under this lack of standardization.[35] The high frequency of repairs to boilers and running gear called for a well-equipped repair shop and a trained workforce, which must have been hard to achieve for an impecunious and fairly primitive out-of-the-way road such as the Saint Paul & Pacific. In 1876 the payroll of the machine shops listed no less than thirty-five machinists, but of these, fourteen were discharged "for want of

work," five left of their own accord, two were discharged for unknown reasons, and one was transferred, leaving only thirteen in place at the end of that year. Financial stringencies are given as the general reason. But apparently the reduced workforce could not then cope with the repairs, and in 1877 the force was increased again to nineteen machinists, six blacksmiths, seven boilermakers, and a host of laborers, apprentices, wheel pressers, clerks (131 altogether). Most of these men were stationed at St. Paul, with a few in Minneapolis or outlying places.

Examination of the "Branchline vouchers" for 1864–1867 gives a nice indication of how the early machine shops were run.[36] At that time the firm of Wm. B. Litchfield & Company, general contractors, was still responsible for the maintenance of the rolling stock, and the vouchers list items for locomotive repairs, sometimes nicely specified, but more often just saying "general repairs." On June 30, 1864, Litchfield charged a sum of only $29.65 for locomotive repairs, plus $16.80 for brass cocks for engine number 3, but in May 1866 the total bill came to $251.50. And so it goes on: $284.26 for engine number 4 only in February 1867, including a pair of 30-foot tender wheels on an old axle, a lot of oak lumber (for tender frames?), hose strainer, lead putty. This all seems to indicate heavy repairs to the tender of number 4. In that same month, number 2 needed 44 pounds of iron, 12 pounds of boilerplate, and 7 pounds of copper for a whistle, making a sum of $47.90. Number 3 needed 33 pounds of iron and 1 brass pipe for a steam gauge, which ran to $107.74. Number 4 was in the shops again in March 1867, needing a lot of iron, cast steel, packing, and so on, and more than a hundred hours of labor, totaling $110.76. In that same month number 3 got new forward 26-inch truck wheels (at a cost of $55.70), with labor and sundries totaling $100.38. In May 1867 all seven engines spent some time in the shops, for tender axles, truck axles, brake shoes, spring balances, lamp glasses, grate bars, boiler repairs, painting, and a lot more. Rough day-to-day usage of engines and rolling stock on an uneven and unsettled roadbed, with at best semiskilled personnel, must have meant almost continuous repairs and adjustments. On a lighter note, $5 was charged on April 6, 1865, for "celebrating taking of Richmond." Unfortunately no invoices from Litchfield & Company have been found after June 1867, probably because the Saint Paul & Pacific itself then took over the maintenance of the rolling stock. But already in Litchfield's time, the vouchers list a new engine boiler in October 1864, for which a certain Mr. Hurlburt was paid $400. In November 1876 another locomotive boiler arrived by water from La Crosse, weighing 10,000 pounds.

Shop equipment was acquired gradually and from many different suppliers. In October 1864 George Dunbar & Company, Railroad Supplies & Machinery, of Chicago, delivered one locomotive driving-wheel lathe and twenty-foot shears, for $4,500. The vouchers list a lot of other heavy machinery acquired over the months. The Putnam Machine Company supplied one steam engine BX36 complete with boiler and fixtures in February 1868 for $7,710.64.

Despite this equipment, however, the shops apparently could not always cope and the Milwaukee & Saint Paul Railroad continued to execute some machine work for the Saint Paul. This "friendly" road now and then also supplied materials and spare parts, as in July 1864, when the Milwaukee provided the Saint Paul & Pacific with four engine truck axles for $102.50, four 28-inch truck wheels, and four of the same of 26-inch diameter, the lot for some $250, including turning and fitting. In February 1865 they obliged again by supplying 132 copper flue pipes for a sum of $59.60. By 1867 the Saint Paul & Pacific apparently had switched over to using iron flues instead of copper, as invoices have been found for

shipping of "70 boiler flues [gas pipe], 3200 lb," in September 1867.

Gradually the Milwaukee Railroad ended its role as supplier, and, for instance in 1871, wheels, axles, and other parts were purchased from outside manufacturers such as the Cleveland City Forge & Iron Company and May, Swallow & Company. In 1871 Danforth supplied one locomotive cylinder, weighing 1,520 pounds, for $121.60, plus $42 for boring and planing. And the list goes on: tools, nuts, and bolts of all shapes and sizes, springs, iron and steel, boilerplate, paint, lubricating oil, tallow, brass fittings, copper pipe, hundreds of brass axle boxes at 85 cents each, drills, files and emery cloth, coal (from Hill & Acker) for the shop smithies, and so on, thousands of items altogether. After the takeover of the Saint Paul & Pacific by the Canadian American associates, Hill apparently considered the shop equipment to be inadequate for the size of railroad he had in mind. In 1879 he sent a request to the Niles Tool Works of Hamilton, Ohio, for them to give a quote for a lot of heavy workshop equipment, wheel presses, lathes, and such.[37]

General construction of all these engines must have been pretty much standard for the time. The Saint Paul & Pacific, as a small company often hunting for a bargain, was in no position to impose its own standards on the builders. Big railroads such as the Pennsylvania were starting to build up a certain type of engine of its own to reduce the number of spare parts to be kept in stock. But the Saint Paul & Pacific engines clearly reflected the idiosyncrasies of each builder and of the period. The two Smith & Jackson engines seem to have been built with a straight boiler and two steam domes, though they were later rebuilt with wagon-top boilers. First introduced by Rogers in 1850, the wagon-top boiler quickly became a favorite because of its superior steaming qualities, but some builders clung to the straight boiler with two domes.[38] The Danforth and Rogers engines seem to have been delivered with high wagon-top boilers and the Pittsburgh engines with the same type (in all three cases with only one steam dome) but the Baldwins were delivered with straight boilers and two steam domes again. And although all engines were wood-burners, Baldwin and Rogers equipped theirs with sunflower stacks, while Danforth and Pittsburgh built their engines with enormous funnel-shaped bonnet stacks.

Engine brakes were nonexistent, and a hand brake on the tender was deemed sufficient for all purposes. With whistle signals the brakemen on the cars and in the caboose were called upon to operate the car hand brakes. And in case of emergencies the engineer could reverse his engine. Only in the later 1870s were driving-wheel brakes introduced, both steam- and air-operated.[39] The Saint Paul company started introducing the Westinghouse air brake on its passenger

trains in 1878, and in the next year they could report that all passenger cars had been so equipped.[40] It has not been recorded how many engines were fitted with air compressors for this purpose. Freight trains continued to run without an automatic brake for many years to come.

One thing is certain, all engines—and especially the earlier ones—must have looked gorgeous, with Russian iron or planished steel boiler cladding; beautifully designed domes of classical dimensions, covered with polished copper or brass; brass bell stands, whistles, and candlestick flagpoles; elaborate decoration between the driving wheels; a highly varnished wooden cab; and elaborate scrollwork painted on the tender, with bold shaded lettering. Only toward the end of the 1870s did the trend toward a simpler and more severe look become apparent. In the 1880s most engines were just plain black.

Saint Paul, Minneapolis & Manitoba No. 51, built by Brooks in 1879 and the first of a long line of switchers. (Railway & Locomotive Historical Society)

The Crookston station of the Saint Paul & Pacific in 1874. Construction expanded the line to Crookston in late 1873. (Minnesota Historical Society)

Default and Reorganization

By the year 1873 the company seemed to be in fair shape, with traffic picking up and the economy in an upswing, but its real situation was as bad as could be. Even with a small surplus in net earnings, the company could never meet the fixed charges on its enormous debt load. It is highly probable that the interest on the earlier loans had been paid out of the proceeds of the later loans (this would explain the disappearance of so much capital), but this could not go on forever. Fixed charges alone amounted to more than $3 million per annum, a sum impossible to earn out of traffic alone. Crushed by this load and unable to raise more capital in Holland or elsewhere, the company had to default on its interest payments in May 1873, even before the beginning of the general economic crisis in the United States. To make matters worse, the house of Jay Cooke & Company, heavily involved in the Northern Pacific Railroad, had to close its doors on September 18, 1873, thereby precipitating the country into one of its worst crises. All Minnesota was in gloom and the Saint Paul & Pacific went bankrupt.

The Dutch had become more cautious about pumping money into the ailing railroad, for several reasons. First, rumors had been flying about for some years that the company was unstable, financially unsound, and badly managed. The delay in reaching a settlement in the so-called Alabama claims, resulting in a continued tension between Great Britain and the United States, also caused unrest on the financial markets. The Franco-Prussian war of 1870 had caused widespread financial stringency, making Dutch investors wary of any foreign investment.[1]

When the news of the default of the Saint Paul & Pacific Company reached Holland in June 1873, it did not come completely unexpected. Warning voices had already been heard about the inability of a small railroad company in an almost virgin territory to carry such a debt load. The stockbrokers had reserved 20 percent of the last issues to guarantee the interest payments for a time, which is also a sign that the default did not come as a total surprise.

The Dutch Protective Committee

The usual reaction of Dutch brokers, when a lot of capital was threatened by a default of a foreign company or government, was a call for a protective committee. Bondholders were requested to deposit their bonds with the committee, in exchange for certificates, and when a suitable quantity had thus been acquired, the committee asked for authorization to act for all. The

Amsterdam Stock Exchange committee suspended trade in the original bonds, but certificates usually could be traded just as bonds had been before a default, and they took their place in the Amsterdam price lists.

In the case of the Saint Paul & Pacific the protective committee, which was formed on June 20, 1873, consisted of representatives of the stockbroking banking firms of Chemet & Weetjen (in the person of Mr. Lucas H. Weetjen), Kerkhoven & Company, Lippmann, Rosenthal & Company, Tutein Nolthenius & De Haan, and Wurfbain & Company, all of Amsterdam; Voorhoeve & Company, of Rotterdam; and Johan Carp, of Utrecht. It was also usual for a representative of a protective committee, generally a younger man able to withstand the rigors of transatlantic travel, to be sent to the United States to take a look at the property in question. In this case Johan Carp was appointed to go, with the difficult duty of trying to save something from the wreckage.

Johan Carp of Utrecht was thirty-five years old when he was selected to take the boat for America. He was born in Düsseldorf, Germany, in 1838, and moved to the Netherlands, where he entered the Dutch military service and lived in Amersfoort and Arnhem before moving to Utrecht with his wife and children in 1870. He was then a captain in the field artillery, but apparently he quit the military in 1871 and with others set up a beet sugar factory in Utrecht. In 1879 he left Utrecht and settled down in The Hague.[2] He had the advantage of being able to speak English, something rather unusual in an age when educated and cultured Dutchmen would speak French and German, but not necessarily English. English was the language of trade, and it is possible that Carp's sugar business at Utrecht had connections with England. However this may be, Carp arrived in New York on August 19, 1873, and went straight to the office of

John S. Kennedy (more about him later) in New York. Later in August he visited St. Paul and remained there until well into September to take stock of the situation. Although President Becker refused to give him the necessary information about the financial condition of the company, receiver Jesse P. Farley was most helpful in supplying the necessary data.[3]

Having a personal representative on the spot was generally not enough, however. Such a person could hardly stay in America permanently, and moreover a link with the American financial world was considered necessary as well. For this reason Lippmann, Rosenthal & Company contacted the New York firm of Kennedy & Company. On July 31, 1873, they wrote—in French—to introduce Carp to Kennedy:[4]

Mr. Carp wants to stay a few weeks in America in order to progress in studying railroading and particularly, under your direction, Sirs, the St. Paul & Pacific Railroad. We request you, Sirs, to receive Mr. Carp well and give him your assistance and advice in order to attain the purpose of his trip. This trip could at the same time be useful to our Committee if you would like to profit by the presence of Mr. Carp in order to give him the information for us which sometimes is given more easily in conversation than by much lengthy correspondence. As a set off, Mr. Carp, knowing perfectly the state of affairs in your country and the desires of the Holland bondholders, will be at the same time able to give you advice which could be of some influence on the road to be followed by you in this affair.

Lippman, Rosenthal's business associate in New York was John Stewart Kennedy, a Scotsman, born in 1830, who had been representative of British ironmasters in New York before becoming a partner of Morris K. Jesup & Company, important American railroad entrepreneurs, in 1857. Business had been good, and in 1868 Kennedy set up shop for himself in New York as commission house and private banker under the name of J. S. Kennedy & Company. Partners in this firm were his brother-in-law, Henry M. Baker, and Baker's brother-in-law, John S. Barnes. As junior partner Barnes was to do most of the traveling (and was soon to go to Holland). Kennedy had often represented Scottish financial interests in America and had acquired a profound knowledge of American railroad investment as such. He was also representing Robert Benson & Company, the London firm that had been instrumental in first bringing the Saint Paul & Pacific securities onto the European market. How exactly Lippmann Rosenthal came to choose Kennedy as their representative is not quite clear, but it is probable that Benson played the role of intermediary here.[5] However that may be, Kennedy received powers of attorney from the Dutch protective committee, which represented the large majority of all Dutch bondholders.

After the Saint Paul & Pacific defaulted, it was essential for the bondholders to obtain a friendly receivership to protect their interests. The Northern Pacific—already in great financial trouble and itself soon to default—was still holding the majority of Saint Paul & Pacific stock and could make endless trouble for the bondholders. Kennedy and Barnes, acting for Lippmann Rosenthal, therefore applied for a receivership both of the (original) Saint Paul & Pacific Company, which was at the time constructing the extension to St. Vincent, and of the First Division Company, which was running the Branch and the Main lines.

In August 1873 Judge John F. Dillon, federal judge for Minnesota, complied and appointed Jesse P. Farley as receiver for the original Saint Paul & Pacific Company. He was to run the finished part of the railroad (St. Cloud–Melrose)[6] to the best interests of the bondholders and push construction of

the rest of the St. Vincent extension as much as he could. In the meantime a solution to the financial problems was to be worked out by all interested parties, under the leadership of Kennedy & Company. The First Division Company, by far the most important part of the railroad, continued its separate corporate existence for some years under its old directors and with strong Northern Pacific influence, but Farley worked closely together with the old management of the First Division Company—and resided in the company's offices in St. Paul most of the time.

One thing needed to be looked after immediately. The original terms of the land grant connected with the St. Vincent extension had already been extended several times and at this point stipulated that this line should be finished by the end of 1873. Of course, with the present state of the railroad and the general downturn of the economy this was clearly impossible, and so Kennedy, assisted by Johan Kloos, a Dutch engineer in the service of the bondholders, went to Washington to lobby Congress for an extension of time. They were successful, as the deadlines were extended, first into 1877 and finally to January 1, 1879, for the Sauk Centre–Alexandria stretch, and to January 1, 1880, for the last part of the Alexandria–St. Vincent line. The arguments used by Kennedy and Kloos can be seen clearly in a document presented by them to Congress.[7] They stated that the Dutch bondholders, mostly small savers, widows, and retired persons, had bought these St. Vincent extension bonds in good faith and had no influence at all on the bad management of the road. It would not be right to punish them for this lack of good management when they had been led confidently to expect that the land grant would be of considerable value to their investment. Apparently Senate and House bought these arguments and extended the deadlines on June 22, 1874.

Johan H. Kloos was a Dutch civil engineer, with a degree from the prestigious Delft Polytechnic, who was sent out by the Dutch bankers and brokers involved in the Saint Paul & Pacific to keep track of the capital supplied by them. Kloos's position after the default of the company is not quite clear. In 1874 it seems he was working in Farley's office in St. Paul, even acting as his assistant and representative, but there was some misunderstanding about his actual duties. It seems Kennedy thought him only a clerk in Farley's office, and to clear up this misunderstanding, Kloos explained his exact position in a letter to Kennedy: he was appointed by Lippmann Rosenthal, "to assist in all matters relating to the St. Paul & Pacific under your [Kennedy's] guidance."[8]

Kloos was also acting as land commissioner—at Farley's request—as there was no one else available at the time. Trott was land commissioner of the First Division Company only and not responsible for the sale of lands on the St. Vincent extension. Kloos told Kennedy also that he was not on the payroll of the company but was being paid directly by Lippmann Rosenthal, to work together with Leon Willmar in the interests of the Dutch bondholders. He was not their official representative, as Kennedy seems to have been thinking, which would have conflicted with his own position, of course. (Kloos was very active in booming Minnesota land in Holland and Germany.)

About Leon Willmar's position even less is known. He has been referred to as representative of the Dutch bondholders and as a director of the original Saint Paul & Pacific Railroad Company, but it is not clear who paid him. He was a native of Luxembourg, living in London in 1871 at the time of the floating of the St. Vincent extension loan, and acting there for Lippmann Rosenthal.[9] He is said to have later negotiated with Benson and William Moorhead, and to have bought iron rail for the St. Vincent extension line and to have forwarded this to New York.[10] Moorhead was representative of Jay Cooke & Company and of the Northern Pacific Railroad, then still owners of the stock of the Saint Paul & Pacific, and was in London to seek construction capital for his own Northern Pacific. Willmar's name lives on in the town of Willmar, in Kandiyohi County, on the Main line.

To raise sufficient capital to construct the rest of the line Melrose–Alexandria–St. Vincent, receiver Farley was authorized by the court to issue $5 million in receiver's certificates, bearing 10 percent interest and having preference over all earlier bonds, which made them an attractive investment. Despite these advantages, however, the reception of these certificates on the Dutch market—where they were handled by Lippmann Rosenthal—was only lukewarm. They were offered first at a price of 85 percent of par, which meant a real rate of interest of 11.76 percent, but there were few takers. Dutch investors were understandably weary of all Saint Paul securities. Some capital was necessary, however, to continue construction; therefore the last two coupons of the St. Vincent extension loan—each 3.5 percent and guaranteed until July 1874—were converted into the new 10 percent receiver's certificates. And since more than ten thousand bonds of this loan had been deposited with the protective committee, at least $700,000 was raised in this way, enough to continue construction for a time.[11]

Despite all the financial and legal problems, some mileage of the St. Vincent extension had actually been constructed. The railroad bridge at St. Cloud was opened in June 1872, and a stretch of track from St. Cloud to Melrose, thirty-five miles, was opened in November of that year. The line was operated by the First Division Company for a monthly rent of $500.[12] An isolated stretch of some sixty-five miles of the St. Vincent extension was finished between Glyndon and Crookston in November 1873 with the proceeds of the receiver's certificates, but

A view of the Clark Flour Mill at Melrose in 1887 with an unidentified locomotive—probably a Rogers engine—of the Saint Paul, Minneapolis & Manitoba. The mill, owned by E. Clark and W. H. Clark, became an important customer of the Saint Paul & Pacific and its successors. (Minnesota Historical Society)

that was about all, except for a lot of grading and bridge work that was also done on the rest of the line. Glyndon, of course, was on the main line of the Northern Pacific, just east of Fargo/Moorhead, and the line was worked with rolling stock leased from the Northern Pacific. One traveler found this "a rather singular instance of the middle section of a road being finished before either end makes connection."[13] Traffic was slight in the first years, and it was rumored that the real purpose of the construction was to conserve the land grant for that stretch. Farley did indeed claim title for the company to a total of 140 miles of land on the St. Vincent extension, made up of St. Cloud–Melrose, Glyndon–Crookston, and Glyndon–Barnesville.[14]

The last named line, a short piece of the same St. Vincent extension from Glyndon south to what is now Barnesville, was also finished in 1873 and operated now and then. The state of the track was such, however, that all operations were suspended during the winter. There cannot have been much freight offered in winter anyhow, so not many people would have cared about the lack of railroad transportation. Farley himself reported to the railroad commissioner that he closed down all operations until May 1874, and again from November 1874 until May 1875. When running, the road operated at a small profit.[15]

The people of Minnesota grew desperate about the slow progress of railroad construction, and much of the blame was laid at the door of the foreign capitalists, who were said to be interested only in the land, not in the railroad itself. Some people urged the Minnesota legislature to assert the rights of the state to the lands and franchises when the foreign interests were not willing to supply the necessary capital to continue construction. Negative articles in local newspapers and venomous pamphlets were printed full of animosity against "bondholders and moneygrabbers" who were robbing the Union.[16] A bill was introduced in the Minnesota House of Representatives early in 1875 by none other than Francis R. Delano, the former superintendent of the Saint Paul & Pacific and co-owner of the grain elevators along its line. He proposed to have all lands, privileges, and franchises of the Saint Paul & Pacific forfeited to the state, because of the default of the company on the interest payment of its last loan—the 1871 St. Vincent extension loan, for which the guarantee had run out.[17]

Cooler heads prevailed, fortunately, and the bill was laid aside. Delano himself came in for some criticism from the side of the Granger Movement. His company at that point owned most of the grain elevators along the line, and he was accused of charging too high prices and of having practically a monopoly. He was also supposed to be trying to get hold of the St. Vincent extension lines himself, at the expense of the bondholders. Minnesota governor Horace Austin, in a message to the legislature in January 1874, considered the state under some obligation to the lenders of the capital—mostly persons of small means, as was indeed the case. The state should "see to it that they are fully secured in all their rights."[18] Kennedy, as agent for the Dutch bondholders, also gave some hope of a speedy finish to the construction of the lines:

> as soon as the St. Paul & Pacific Railroad company can be reorganized by foreclosure and sale under the mortgage, the purchasers, should they be the bondholders, will undoubtedly proceed, without delay, with the work of construction, *if they are satisfied of a friendly, liberal and just disposition towards them.*[19]

The annual report over 1875–1876 of the Minnesota railroad commissioner advocated caution:

> It would be thought that after encumbering the road and land grant with a debt of fifteen million dollars, and grading the entire line—with bridges framed and ties provided, and one hundred and forty miles of road in detached pieces actually constructed—that the parties in interest would not allow the property, year after year, to lie unproductive and go to waste, ties rotting and embankments crumbling and washing away. Yet for about four years it has been in this condition. It seems reasonable to hope that the bondholders, who supplied about nine millions of dollars for construction of the road—more than enough to have completed the entire line, if properly used—would take hold and complete the road, and render productive the capital now invested, if they had legal possession of the property. This they have been in the courts seeking to acquire for three years or longer. I judge that the only alternative is to remove all hindrances, and facilitate these parties in getting possession; or, to take steps to declare a forfeiture of the rights and franchises to the unbuilt lines and unearned lands, and seek other and new parties, who can give assurance of ability to speedily complete the road. Such parties, I fear, could not be found.[20]

Something was indeed happening. Johan Carp had been in New York and St. Paul again and had talked with everyone concerned. A tripartite agreement was worked out in August 1875 between George Becker, representing the Saint Paul & Pacific First Division; Johan Carp, for the Dutch protective committee; and Edwin C. Litchfield, of Brooklyn, for himself and his brother E. Darwin Litchfield of London, owners of the common stock of the First Division Company after the Northern Pacific had to return the stock to them. A very elaborate plan foresaw a scaling down of the bonded debt to bring down the fixed charges. Foreclosure proceedings were to be postponed indefinitely.[21] One condition to the fulfillment of this agreement was that a majority of the Dutch bondholders would accept it, and this did not happen. The Dutch protective committee did, of course, advocate accepting of the tripartite agreement, but apparently the majority of the bondholders found the financial consequences of the proposals unattractive. Not enough of them came forward, so the agreement lapsed.

Despite this setback, the Litchfield agreement, as it was commonly called, was partially executed. A new board of directors was appointed, who were friendly to the bondholders, and Geo. Becker stepped down. The new president was John S. Barnes, with W. H. Scott and H. M. Baker—all Kennedy appointees—as directors. Another director was Anthony G. Dulman, a New York banker and partner of the firm of Dulman & Scharff. He was of Dutch extraction and acted in many capacities for Dutch investors, to protect their investments in America. Apart from his directorate in the Saint Paul & Pacific, he also had a seat on the boards of (among others) the Illinois Central; the Chicago & North Western; the Chicago, Rock Island & Pacific; the Missouri, Kansas & Texas; the New York, Pennsylvania & Ohio; and the Cleveland, Columbus, Cincinnati & Indianapolis. He was trustee of one of the many mortgages of the Denver Pacific, another Dutch-owned railroad. In short he was one of the key figures in the protection of Dutch interests in American railroads during the 1860s and 1870s.[22] The rest of the Saint Paul & Pacific board was made up of Becker and the two Litchfields, but the Kennedy Dutch crowd clearly was in charge from then on.

Samuel Tilden, who had been trustee of five of the mortgage loans of the Saint Paul & Pacific laid down his trusteeships when he started his (unsuccessful) campaign for the presidency of the United States in 1876. The new board appointed Kennedy in his place. On October 7, 1876, the trustees took legal possession of the First Division Company for the bondholders and appointed

Farley general manager.[23] With most of the other key players living in faraway New York or Amsterdam, Farley was the man in power in St. Paul. Carp, again in St. Paul in the fall of 1876, seemed to think highly of Farley and to have great faith in him: "It is agreeable to me to be able to state here that the interests of the bondholders in every respect are taken care of and defended by Mr. Farley with so much devotion, zeal and knowledge as cannot be sufficiently appreciated."[24]

Farley, greatly assisted by Johan Kloos, had indeed made great progress, especially in the land department. Up to January 1, 1877, the Main line had brought in revenues from land sales of $2,780,646 and the Branch had brought in $397,724. Just under a million acres were unsold, without counting the lands along the St. Vincent extension, which were still being disputed by the Northern Pacific interests and others. Bishop John Ireland had been most active in the sale of lands "for the purpose of collecting people of the same faith in settlements," and he had organized an office for this in the depot at St. Paul. Other clergymen were working along the same lines, and sales of land could confidently be expected to rise.[25]

Farley had also built a short, eleven-mile extension of the line from Crookston to Fisher's Landing on the Red River, to connect with the steamboats there. Rails had been taken from the unused portion of the line north of Crookston, but the other expenses had been carried by the Red River Transportation Company (Norman Kittson and James J. Hill), which, of course, profited greatly from this connection. Farley had also managed to raise the rental fee for the St. Cloud–Melrose line to a more reasonable $1,250 per month; after the takeover by the Kennedy Dutch group, he operated the line as part of the Branch, but with a separate account. All short lines made a slight profit.

Johan Carp also foresaw a string of legal problems with the Northern Pacific over the construction of the final stretches of the St. Vincent extension. Until then all traffic to Manitoba and beyond had been going from Duluth over the Northern Pacific to Glyndon, from there over the Saint Paul & Pacific to Fisher's Landing, and from there down the Red River by water. When Glyndon–Melrose was finished the Northern Pacific would lose all traffic, unless the Brainerd branch was finished at the same time. Technicalities of the law were to mean endless litigation with the Northern Pacific, which obviously was not eager to let go of the promising Manitoba traffic.

Carp therefore advocated construction of a thirty-two-mile cutoff from Breckenridge to Barnesville, which would make the existing Saint Paul & Pacific Main line at one stroke both a real main line and one where the Northern Pacific had no influence at all. That company had tried to influence the Minnesota legislature into making such construction illegal, but a law for that purpose had been declared unconstitutional by the Minnesota Supreme Court.[26] Carp estimated the cost of such a cutoff to be $287,698 (735,000 guilders), and he urged that the sum should be raised in Holland, not in America. With this line in place, income from the Manitoba traffic alone could be well in excess of $300,000 per annum. A company was soon set up for this purpose, the Red River & Manitoba Railroad, for which the capital was found in Amsterdam (more about this line later).

In an extensive and elaborate report dated April 1877 to the members of the Dutch protective committee, Johan Carp gave his opinion of the railroad and its future.[27] He was optimistic: traffic was picking up again and the financial situation of the road was definitely improving through higher net earnings and increased land sales. Even the discovery of gold in the Black Hills of Dakota could work out positively for the company, although he acknowledged that taking the Northern Pacific as far as Bismarck, the present railhead, would be the best way to travel to the mining camps there. But even in that case, a lot of that traffic would surely go by way of St. Paul–Breckenridge–Glyndon if the proposed shortcut were to be built. The physical condition of the railroad was also satisfactory, with some steel rails in place and rerolled and straightened iron rails elsewhere.

Johan Carp also worked out a general but very complicated plan for the reorganization of the company, which he appended to his report. All lines, including extensions and Breckenridge–Barnesville, should be consolidated into one new company. The St. Vincent extension should be finished immediately, but the Brainerd branch could better be given up to other interested parties such as the Northern Pacific. A new 6 percent consolidated mortgage loan was to be issued to a total of $3,700,000—to take care, dollar for dollar, of the two still outstanding first lien loans and to make some reservation for future construction at the same time. The other existing first and second lien bonds would be converted into second mortgage bonds, bearing 7 percent, and preferred and common income bonds, also at 7 percent, plus some common stock. Income bonds, whether preferred or common, were only to pay interest when really earned, just as common stock, and only the first and second mortgage bonds were to yield a regular, fixed rate of interest.[28] Altogether this proposal was not very attractive to the bondholders, as the income bonds were to form the bulk of the new securities, making the yield on the bonds and stock unpredictable at best. Despite attempts on the side of the Dutch bankers to make Carp's plan agreeable, no majority of bondholders could be found to accept, and the plan had to be shelved. The stalemate seemed complete.

The Sale of the Saint Paul & Pacific Railroad

When Johan Carp was formulating his plan for reorganization of the Saint Paul & Pacific Railroad, he had already met the man who would turn out to be the savior of the bondholders. James Jerome Hill was a business man in St. Paul and well on his way to a position of some local importance. He was born in 1838 on a farm at Wellington, near Guelph in the Canadian province of Ontario, and had been fairly well educated for a farm boy. In 1856, when he was seventeen years old, he set out from Canada with no particular aim in mind, went to New York and Philadelphia, and traveled as far south as Savannah. He headed north again and by way of Pittsburgh and Chicago finally arrived in St. Paul in the summer of 1856, where he decided to stay for a while. He would remain in St. Paul until his death in 1916.[1]

In the Minnesota capital he started a transportation business—forwarding goods brought in by steamboat—for which he constructed a shed on the St. Paul levee. When the railroad began operations, he decided to cooperate with this new form of transportation. Together with Egbert S. Litchfield, one of the many Litchfields, he set up a "general transportation business" in 1867 under the name of J. J. Hill & Company and contracted with the Saint Paul & Pacific for the transfer of freight at St. Paul.[2] The cooperation with Litchfield ended in 1869, and the company name changed to Hill, Griggs & Company, then later to Hill & Acker.

This firm branched out into other fields as well. They supplied firewood to the railroad company from 1875 onward, and from there it was a small step to becoming a regular fuel company. On May 1, 1877, Hill with six others incorporated the Northwestern Fuel Company to supply St. Paul and vicinity with coal.[3] The Saint Paul & Pacific contracted with the new firm for the delivery of coal for heating its buildings and for the blacksmiths' fires in its machine shops. Together with Norman Kittson, Hill also owned the Red River Transportation Company that operated steamboats on the Red River, a most profitable business. By this time James Hill was well on his way to becoming one of the leading businessmen of St. Paul, well respected in the community but still not much known outside Minnesota.

Hill formed some vague ideas about taking over the Saint Paul & Pacific Railroad early in 1876. He talked things over with his partner, Norman Kittson, who was doubtful about the possible success. But Hill persisted. He approached John Barnes, the new

Portrait of James Jerome Hill, taken in 1872.

(James J. Hill Papers)

Portrait of George
Stephen, circa 1880.
(James J. Hill Papers)

tion business in the Northwest in general. Carp's general opinion in late 1876 was that this man might be of some use to the Dutch.

The problem was how to lay hands on the necessary capital. Hill clearly needed partners with a solid financial backing, and he himself recognized that fact better than anyone. Fortunately for him he was in a position to enlist the help of some influential Canadians—Donald Smith and George Stephen.

Born in Scotland in 1820, Donald Alexander Smith had come to Canada in 1838 in the service of the Hudson's Bay Company.[5] Slowly he had risen through the ranks to the influential position of chief factor of the company in 1869. He had set up a line of communication for the Hudson's Bay Company between Winnipeg/Fort Garry and St. Paul and had appointed Norman Kittson as its local agent in St. Paul. James Hill he had met for the first time in the winter of 1870, when he was heading south from Winnipeg in a dog sleigh and Hill was coming north in a similar vehicle.[6]

George Stephen was a Scotsman, too, and was distantly related to Smith. Born in 1829, he had emigrated to Canada in 1850, where he worked in a dry-goods store of a relative and eventually became one of the leading Montreal businessmen.[7] He was one of the biggest stockholders of the Bank of Montreal and became its president in 1876. He also became interested in other branches of industry and had set up the Canada Rolling Stock Company in 1870. His distant cousin Donald Smith was among the directors. Stephen would later become Lord Mount Stephen. Both men, Smith and Stephen, seemed to be the ideal partners for Hill and Kittson, as they were supposed to be in a position to muster the solid financial backing needed for Hill's plans.

president of the railroad company, during one of his regular visits to St. Paul, with a request to name a price for the bonds of the Dutch protective committee, for which Kennedy and Barnes were the American agents. At first Barnes had little confidence in Hill, who was still fairly unknown and whose worth at the time was estimated only at some $150,000, certainly not enough to think he could buy the millions in bonds needed to get hold of the railroad.[4] Barnes refused to be drawn and maintained that he could not name a price for the Dutch bonds.

Johan Carp had been introduced to Hill by receiver Jesse Farley in December 1876, and he had talked a lot with Hill and Kittson about the possibility of a sale of the Dutch bonds and about the reorganization plans then afoot. Carp recognized that Hill had a profound knowledge of the ins and outs of the railroad company, and of the transporta-

But first, Hill had to convince these hard-headed Scotsmen of the feasibility of his pipe dreams. Smith was an early convert; it took more to convince Stephen. A meeting was arranged in St. Paul between the four partners-to-be, and Hill took the party over the completed line to Breckenridge in August 1877.[8] Stephen had never seen a prairie, and after the recent devastation wreaked by the grasshoppers the area traversed by the railroad cannot have looked very prosperous. Stephen remained unconvinced of the potential profitability of the railroad, until he saw Bishop Ireland's recent settlement at DeGraff. On being told that this was only the first, and many such colonies were to follow, he changed his mind and endorsed the project.

Meanwhile Hill had already opened negotiations with the Dutch. Carp came to St. Paul again in the winter of 1877, and Hill made him an offer for buying part of the property. As expected, Carp refused, for the Dutch wanted to sell everything at the same time. But direct negotiations had been opened, and Kennedy and Barnes slowly warmed to the idea of a takeover by the Stephen group. Stephen, with his banking connections, was the financial figurehead of the associates, whereas Hill was the practical railroad man and tried to stay in the background during any financial talks with European or American partners. Despite his seeming to play second fiddle in financial matters, however, he always remained the driving force of the associates.

James Hill had some useful contacts in St. Paul. Next door to him on 9th and Canada Streets in St. Paul lived a Dutchman named Caspar Klein, who regularly translated articles from Dutch financial weeklies for Hill.[9] More important was that Klein had an uncle in Amsterdam, Mr. Lucas H. Weetjen, who, as partner of the stockbroking firm of Weetjen & Company, was chairman of the Dutch Saint Paul & Pacific Protective Committee. Klein himself was on the payroll of the Saint Paul & Pacific for some time in 1875 at $120 per month, but his "miscellaneous" services are not specified. By 1877 he was living in London, where Hill wrote him personal, friendly letters, and in 1883 he is mentioned as European agent of the Saint Paul, Minneapolis & Manitoba with an office in Lombard Street, London.[10]

Another Dutchman, a certain Mr. De Clercq, who was temporarily in St. Paul, also gave Hill some information, especially about prices of bonds in Holland.[11] This Mr. De Clercq must have been none other than Dr. A. W. de Klerck, a former teacher at the gymnasium at Deventer, who traveled extensively in the United States and was well versed in the financial manipulations of bankers and brokers. He was a formidable opponent of the stockbroking fraternity in Amsterdam, whom he accused of all manner of unfair dealings and frauds. He later wrote a book on the impoverishment of the Netherlands as caused by the import of American railroad securities, although he fails to really make his point there. But his attacks on almost all brokers in Holland

Portrait of Donald Smith, taken in 1896. (James J. Hill Papers)

were vicious.[12] His role in the Saint Paul & Pacific affair remains obscure, but he seems to have come to St. Paul as representative of a (probably very small) number of bondholders who opposed the actions of the protective committee. Hill found him personally antagonistic to Lippmann Rosenthal but managed to squeeze a lot of information out of him.[13]

The Associates Make an Offer

In May 1877 Hill and his associates at last offered to buy all the Dutch bonds for cash, and with prices of between eighty and eleven cents on the dollar for the various different classes of securities.[14] They did not say where they were going to find the cash. The Dutch committee judged the price too low anyhow and refused the offer but, as expected, came up with a counterproposal. Stephen was sent to England to raise the capital needed for an outright purchase of the bonds. He sailed for England late in September of 1877 and conferred with one of the leading London banking firms, Morton, Rose & Company. The Rose of this firm was John Rose, another Scotsman who had gone to Canada and who was personally well acquainted with Stephen and Smith. He had returned to London in 1869.[15] While Stephen was in London, Johan Carp came over to consult with him and to explain that the Dutch had little confidence in James Hill, who had made a "very disagreeable remark" about possible private interests of members of the Dutch committee—meaning, no doubt, Carp himself and his brother-in-law, Johan Knuppe, who was used now and then as an intermediary but whom Hill saw as a busybody who meddled in the Saint Paul & Pacific affairs without proper authorization.[16] (Hill was mistaken here, as Knuppe was on the payroll of the railroad company as draughtsman in the land department and later even as land commissioner of the St. Vincent extension.)[17]

Morton, Rose & Company moved slowly, despite the personal relationship between Rose and Stephen. To get more local information they contacted their American partner George Bliss for advice. Bliss was cautious and asked General Edward F. Winslow to inspect the property in person. Edward F. Winslow was born in Augusta, Maine, in 1837, and among other occupations had been a contractor for building railroads. After his service in the Union Army he entered railroad service, as so many of his former colleagues, and in 1875 was receiver of the bankrupt Burlington, Cedar Rapids & Minnesota Railroad. After the reorganization of this road as the Burlington, Cedar Rapids & Northern he served as vice president and general manager until 1879, before switching over to the Atlantic & Pacific and the Saint Louis & San Francisco Railroads as vice president. In 1881 he also became president of the New York, Ontario & Western. All these railroads had a substantial foreign (British, Dutch, and German) element in their capitalization, and his name and opinion carried weight in European financial circles.[18]

An experienced railroad executive, well known in London and Amsterdam, Winslow saw little potential in the railroad and was pessimistic about the high cost of upgrading the road to an acceptable standard. Nothing was decided, and Stephen returned empty-handed to New York in December 1877. One positive point of his visit, however, was that he had made the time to cross the North Sea to Amsterdam and had spoken with Leo Lippmann and George Rosenthal and other interested bankers. From them he had received the impression that the Dutch were eager to continue negotiations with the associates, cash or not.

In the meantime, in October 1877 while Stephen was away in Europe, Carp had made the expected counterproposal. He estimated the value of the railroad, including the money necessary for finishing it, at

$6,866,759—much lower than Hill's own estimate. Hill accepted Carp's plan and figures and offered a lump sum for all securities together to the Dutch protective committee. Hill tried to leave to the Dutch the disagreeable task of haggling over the price of each individual bond issue. Carp did not fall into the trap, however. He asked Hill to come up with a detailed offer for each class of bond. Hill could do little else than come forward with a price for each bond, which ranged from 70 cents on the dollar for the first issues, to 13.25 cents for the St. Vincent extension bonds. Everything was to be paid in gold.[19]

When the associates' offer became known in Amsterdam, the Dutch protective committee decided to take a neutral stand, possibly as a result of the adverse criticism of de Klerck and others that they had been bullying the bondholders into accepting the earlier proposals. The protective committee thus did not advise its constituent bondholders to vote for or against this new proposal but merely published the offer and left the decision up to the individual owners. Kennedy, however, saw this as a golden opportunity to extract himself from the morass of the Saint Paul & Pacific business, while assuring his Dutch clients of a fair price for their much depreciated bonds. He and Barnes strongly recommended the offer to Lippmann, Rosenthal & Company. Their opinion became known in Holland through the financial press and must have lent some weight to the advocates of accepting, as a majority of the Dutch bondholders came forward to accept.[20]

The associates' problem of where to find the cash remained, however. Stephen, back in Montreal in January 1878, had to admit defeat. The Dutch were disappointed, as they had understood the associates' last offer to be a firm offer, not an option to buy only if the necessary cash could be found (apparently there had been some obscurity in the wording of the offer). The Dutch protective committee urged Kennedy to continue the negotiations. According to Kennedy, the Dutch were so sure of the existence of a firm contract they actually threatened to sue the associates over what they considered a breach of contract.[21]

It did not come to that, however, as the associates—now thoroughly united in their efforts to get the railroad into their own hands—made a new offer in late January 1878. And a most unusual offer it was: no payment in cash but payment in securities of a new railroad company, to be incorporated after the old Saint Paul & Pacific was sold at foreclosure. In accepting such an offer, the Dutch would need to have an almost unlimited confidence in the ability of James Hill and his associates to make the railroad a paying proposition. But if they did not accept, what then? More litigation with Litchfield probably, with the Northern Pacific possibly, and the need to face a hostile Minnesota legislature? Kennedy and Barnes again strongly urged acceptance, although they must have seen the risks as well as the Dutch did.

The protective committee finally accepted, but only after the associates had consented to higher prices for every class of old bond and with the new bonds to bear 7 instead of the proposed 6 percent interest. The associates had also offered a bonus of $250 in new preferred shares for every new $1,000 bond taken, but the protective committee requested a discount of 10 percent for those who did not have the preferred shares. Moreover, $280,000 in cash—instead of the $125,000 offered for the expenses of the protective committee—was required, plus two seats on the board of the new company. Interest on the old bonds was to be paid by the associates from December 22, 1877.

A stiff price for the associates, but they, again urged on by Kennedy, could do little other than accept. Hill managed to get assurances from the Chicago & North Western and the Milwaukee & Saint Paul that they were prepared to take a minority interest in the new company-to-be, if necessary.[22] When the Dutch decided to accept the offer, an almost audible sigh of relief must have circulated in St. Paul. Hill wrote Stephen: "Mess. Kennedy & Co. have just telegraphed that a large majority of all classes of bonds have assented to our proposal so that we have virtually crossed the Rubicon; this is a great relief."[23]

On March 13, 1878, the formal contract was signed by all parties in Kennedy's New York office.[24] To lay hands on the $280,000 for the Dutch protective committee plus some $400,000 more for legal expenses and further construction of the railroad, Stephen managed to get his own Bank of Montreal to advance $700,000 on a collateral of doubtful value, the personal properties of the four associates. He was later accused of obtaining this loan at a very importune moment for the bank and behind the backs of the other shareholders, but things quieted down after some time and the loan was soon repaid. Hill and the others strained their personal credit to the utmost and pledged all their possessions to obtain this loan. But at the time, the credit of the railroad company had improved so much that more capital could be secured if necessary, and to persuade still hesitating bondholders to come forward the associates could even offer payment—or part payment—in cash instead of new bonds.[25]

The Sale of the Railroad

Altogether the associates acquired a majority of most bonds from the Dutch committee:

$625,000 of the $1.2 million first-section loan of 1862 at 75 percent of par;

$760,000 of the $2.8 million consolidated loan of 1864 at 28 percent of par;

$907,000 of the $3 million second-section loan of 1864 at 30 percent of par;

$3.52 million of the $6 million loan of 1868 at 35 percent of par;

$11.4 million of the $15 million St. Vincent extension loan of 1871 at 13.75 percent of par.

And as most bondholders who assented did not want the preferred shares but opted for the 10 percent discount instead, they got prices for their old bonds ranging from over 83 percent of par to just over 14 percent for the St. Vincent extension bonds, far above the current market prices in Amsterdam. Most bondholders also opted for new bonds instead of cash, and J. Pik, one of the leading Dutch writers on financial topics at the time, figured that taking the new bonds would probably be much more advantageous in the long run and only slightly more risky than taking cash. He ranked the security of the new Saint Paul, Minneapolis & Manitoba bonds as being on the same level as North Missouri or Missouri Pacific, not top-notch but solid enough for investment.[26] Total cost to the associates—for these "committee" bonds only—was figured out by Hill at $4,162,180 plus $300,000 for annual interest since January 1878. Of this purchase price, $1,030,847.50 was to be paid in cash, with the rest in new bonds. With the purchase of other outstanding bonds, not held by the Dutch committee, the price to be paid came to a grand total of $4,875,910.[27]

There were more bonds on the market than those held by the committee. Other bondholders (Dutchmen who had not joined the committee, and also a few Englishmen and Americans) had been selling their bonds on the open market in Amsterdam, London, and New York, and the associates had been busy buying as many of these as they could. Kennedy bought many of the bonds; Lippmann Rosenthal sold the associates a number; and others were also active in the matter. Henry P. Upham, a stockbroker and neighbor of Hill in St. Paul, also bought for the associates and was in constant touch with Lippmann Rosenthal and other Dutch firms—among them Oyens & Company (the same Oyens who back in 1866 had visited St. Paul). Upham subscribed to the official Amsterdam *Prijscourant,* the weekly price list, and was well aware of current prices.[28] In the end the associates had some 90 percent of all outstanding bonds in their hands. Because the senior classes of bonds could be exchanged at par for land, these commanded a fairly high price, which was generally well known both in Holland and in America.[29]

Some Dutch bondholders thought the prices offered by the associates to be too low, and they (a small minority) had not assented in the sale to the associates. Some of them, mostly owners of St. Vincent extension bonds, took action through Hagbarth Sahlgaard, cashier of the St. Paul's Savings Bank and vice consul for Sweden and Norway there.[30] Sahlgaard tried court action to get the sale of the railroad to Stephen and partners declared void, but the court threw out his complaint in June 1880. He represented only a small number of bondholders—less than $1,500,000 of the $15,000,000 loan.[31] Barnes was sent to Amsterdam in July 1878 to straighten matters out with the protective committee, and at the same time to buy as many bonds still in the market as he could lay his hands on.[32] Most were indeed bought up, but during all of 1878 Stephen, Hill, and Kennedy in their correspondence continue to mention the buying of outstanding bonds.

The associates, who had never put anything on paper, drew up a formal contract for themselves, signed on March 27, 1878. Each was to have one-fifth of all profits or losses resulting from the new company; one-fifth was left to Stephen to be disposed of "for the purpose of securing the necessary means to carry out and complete our said agreement."[33] A lot of words have been spent in discussing the exact meaning of

FIRST DIVISION ST. PAUL & PACIFIC R.R. 361
(Trustees for Bondholders in possession.)

HORACE THOMPSON, ⎫
EDMUND RICE, ⎬ *Trustees.*
JOHN S. KENNEDY, ⎭
J. P. FARLEY, Gen. Manager.
W. H. FISHER, Asst. Gen. Manager.
J. B. RICE, Asst. Supt.

J. BOTSFORD, Treasurer.
JAMES W. DORAN,
  Gen. Freight and Ticket Agent.
S. S. BREED, Auditor and Secretary.
A. GUTHRIE, Purchasing Agent.
General Offices—St. Paul, Minn.

Pas. A.M.	Mls	*July 26,* 1877. (St. Paul time.)	Mls	Pas. P.M.
†7 30	0	lve.St.Paul¹.arr.	217	6 37
7 59	10	...St. Anthony...	207	6 08
8 10	11	...Minneapolis...	206	6 00
8 40	21	Minnetonka Mills	196	5 28
8 55	25	....Wayzata²...	192	5 16
9 07	28	....Long Lake....	189	5 04
9 27	33	....Maple Plain...	184	4 44
9 32	35	....Armstrong....	182	4 38
9 54	40	.....Delano³.....	177	4 18
10 21	49	.....Waverly.....	168	3 50
10 36	54	..Howard Lake...	163	3 35
10 54	57	...Smith Lake...	160	3 25
11 06	61	.....Cokato......	156	3 07
11 24	67	.....Dassel......	150	2 49
11 44	72	.....Darwin.....	145	2 29
12 02	78	....Litchfield....	139	2 08
12 26	86	...Swede Grove...	131	1 44
12 44	91	.....Atwater.....	126	1 29
1 05	98	...Kandiyohi...	119	1 05
1 23	104	....Willmar....	113	12 47
P.M.		ARRIVE] [LEAVE		NO'N
1 50	104	....Willmar....	113	12 17
2 10	110	....St. John's....	107	11 56
2 37	118	...Kerkhoven....	99	11 30
3 07	127	...De Graff....	90	10 55
3 40	134	.....Benson.....	83	10 32
4 05	141	.....Randall....	76	
4 35	150	....Hancock.....	67	9 24
5 15	159	.....Morris.....	58	8 54
5 45	168	....Donnelly....	49	8 19
6 30	178	.....Herman.....	39	7 44
6 51	185	.....Gorton.....	32	7 18
7 18	194	.....Tintah.....	23	6 51
7 45	201	...Campbell....	16	
8 09	209	.....Doran.....	8	6 01
8 33	217	**Breckenridge..**	0	†5 37
P.M.		ARRIVE] [LEAVE		A.M.

STATIONS	Mls	Pas. A.M.
[LEAVE		
St. Paul¹	0	†9 12
St. Anthony Junc...	10	9 47
Manomin	17	10 08
Anoka	27	10 48
Itaska	34	11 18
Elk River⁴	39	11 43
Big Lake⁵	48	12 16
Becker	56	12 43
Clear Lake	63	1 11
St. Cloud⁶	75	2 15
St. Joseph	82	2 38
Avon	90	3 10
Albany	95	3 30
Oakes	102	3 50
Melrose	108	4 10
[ARRIVE		
[LEAVE		A.M.
Melrose	0	†9 15
Oakes	6	9 35
Albany	12	9 55
Avon	18	10 15
St. Joseph	26	10 48
St. Cloud⁶	33	11 34
Clear Lake	45	12 15
Becker	52	12 43
Big Lake⁵	60	1 15
Elk River⁴	69	1 55
Itaska	74	2 15
Anoka	81	2 48
Manomin	91	3 30
St. Anthony Junc.	98	4 12
St. Paul	108	4 50
[ARRIVE		P.M.

Train leaves St. Paul for Sauk Rapids 9 10 a. m. Returning, leaves Sauk Rapids for St. Paul 10 30 a. m.

Extra Local Trains—Leave St. Paul for St. Anthony and Minneapolis 11 00 a.m., 3 40, 5 50 p.m. Returning, leave Minneapolis for St. Anthony and St. Paul 7 27, 9 33 a.m., 2 00 p.m.

Train leaves St. Paul for Delano, and intermediate stations, 3 40 p.m. Returning, leaves Delano 6 50 a.m.

Leave Minneapolis for St. Anthony Junction 9 34 a.m., 3 55 p.m. Returning, leave St. Anthony Junction 9 50 a.m., 4 15 p.m.

CONNECTIONS.—¹ With railroads diverging. ² With stages for Excelsior. ³ With stage for Watertown and Rockford. ⁴ With stage for Princeton. ⁵ With stage for Monticello. ⁶ With stage line for points in British North America.

ST. PAUL & PACIFIC R. R. 362

J. P. FARLEY, Receiver.
W. H. FISHER, Gen. Supt.

EDWIN P. FARLEY, Gen. Freight
  and Ticket Agent.
General Offices—St. Paul, Minn.

Train leaves **Clyndon¹** 4 20 p.m. for Rolette, 41 miles, and **Fisher's Landing²,** 75 miles, arriving at Fisher's Landing 10 35 p.m. Returning, leaves Fisher's Landing 4 30 a.m., arriving at Clyndon 10 45 a.m.

CONNECTIONS.—¹ With Northern Pacific R. R. ² With boats of Red River Transportation Co.

Timetable of the Saint Paul & Pacific from July 26, 1877. By this time, the railroad reached as far as Breckenridge on the Main line and Melrose on the Branch line, but it still had only one through train and a couple of local trains. (From *Official Railway Guide,* 1877)

this sentence. It was rumored that the one-fifth part was meant for receiver Jesse Farley, but this cannot be true as it was originally meant for someone else (see the next chapter). In the end the one-fifth part of the stock was largely given to Kennedy as reward for his services. In his accepting this share in the spoils, it is doubtful whether Kennedy acted with total honesty toward his Dutch clients. After all, they had paid him for his services in the understanding that he was to do his utmost in their interests. His acting for both seller and buyer could never have been in their interest only, but the Dutch committee seems not to have cared too much about the double role played by Kennedy. They thought they had struck a fair bargain, which indeed it was, considering the market value of the bonds before the associates became interested.[34]

The associates had to act quickly in another matter too: the Litchfield stock. There were rumors that the Litchfields had offered their stock to the Northern Pacific again, which would have meant a definitive end to all of the associates' plans, for then that company would have used the Saint Paul & Pacific as a feeder to their own system and would never have allowed Hill and associates to develop it into an independent competitor.[35] The Northern Pacific, on its feet again after reorganization, had indeed set up a dummy company—the Western Railroad of Minnesota—to build the Brainerd branch, formally given up by the Saint Paul & Pacific following Johan Carp's advice. The line was opened on November 1, 1878, and officially leased by the Northern Pacific in the next year. From Sauk Rapids, the Northern Pacific used the Saint Paul & Pacific's Branch for entry into St. Paul, where ten acres of bottomland were leased for the location of a terminal for an annual rent of $40,000.[36]

In 1877 James Hill had already tried to come to an understanding with Edwin C. Litchfield but had found him intractable. He

gladly left the rest of the negotiations to Stephen, who indeed had carried on most of the earlier financial dealings with Kennedy and the Dutch committee and who was better qualified for this side of the business. Stephen found Litchfield "a wary bird, on whose tail it is not easy to put salt."[37] In October 1878 he put pressure on Litchfield:

> I am now and have always been ready to consider your position in relation to the property, including the power which your possession of the stock has hitherto given you to delay proceedings in foreclosure. But I have been prevented from making any overtures to you for a settlement of your claims, whatever they may be, by my friends, who have always said it was useless and that nothing would satisfy you but to litigate them to the end and our plans are laid accordingly. But while so resolved to prosecute the matter I am quite prepared to make any reasonable concession that will save time and trouble in the accomplishment of our purpose.[38]

Stephen had several later talks with Litchfield, who certainly was not modest in his demands:

> I had a two hours palaver with Litchfield yesterday and an equally long one today. I cannot say I accomplished anything beyond impressing him with the fact that I meant business and was ready to deal with him for the purchase of his stock and bonds and we were ready to . . . at a price everything with their value, which he tells me he estimates at $1,000,000 and says they are worth $3,000,000 to me.[39]

Stephen countered with an offer of $200,000, which he himself thought most handsome, but which was refused indignantly by Litchfield. Stephen then returned to Montreal and matters rested there for a time. Hill was unsure what to do:

All this points to the advantage to us of an early settlement with Litchfield, which I am opposed as you know to paying him a cent if we could help it, still I do not see that we can prudently refuse him a liberal sum in order to get possession of the property to enable us to run it as it should be run.[40]

Hill's attorneys, Reuben B. Galusha and George B. Young, also outlined the necessity to come to terms with Litchfield, and in the end the associates managed to settle with the "old rat," as Stephen called him, for $500,000 on February 6, 1879.[41] Not a bad deal, as long and costly litigation was then avoided. A down payment of $100,000 in cash was required, while the rest of the sum was probably to be paid in bonds of the new company.

One small thing remained: DeGraff & Company claimed that $400,000 were due them for work undertaken on the St. Vincent extension. They had contracted for the work with William G. Moorhead, when the Saint Paul & Pacific was still owned by the Northern Pacific, but they had never been paid. The Northern Pacific had partly settled with them by releasing twenty-seven hundred tons of iron lying at Duluth, but $400,000 was still outstanding.[42] As DeGraff and his partner Crooks had many friends in the Minnesota legislature, it was imperative to buy him off, which was done somehow (apparently with securities of several American railroads and canal companies, obtained from the estate of Wm. Moorhead, plus some land and $30,000 in cash).[43] With the associates in control of both stocks and bonds, the old Saint Paul & Pacific Company could be wound up and the new company incorporated.

The impressive train shed of the Union Depot, circa 1890. The stub tracks of the Manitoba road are on the left, and the through tracks of the Milwaukee, the Minnesota & Northwestern, and other lines are on the right. (Photo by J. R. H. Cruikshank, West Vancouver, B.C., Minnesota Historical Society)

The Saint Paul, Minneapolis & Manitoba Railroad

The associates proceeded to incorporate a new company, the Saint Paul, Minneapolis & Manitoba Railroad Company, on May 23, 1879, more than a year after they had obtained control of the old Saint Paul & Pacific and the First Division Company. Foreclosure sale of the old companies took place in June, and the new company took possession of all assets of the old. In all, there changed hands 565 miles of railroad plus 102 miles still under construction. All the different earlier companies had all been dissolved and brought under one legal entity: the new railroad took over the old Saint Paul & Pacific proper, the First Division Company, the Red River Valley (Crookston–Fisher's Landing), and the Red River & Manitoba.[1] Directors of the new company were George Stephen (president) and Donald A. Smith, both in Montreal; H. R. Bigelow, R. A. Galusha, James J. Hill, Norman W. Kittson, all of St. Paul; and J. S. Barnes of New York. Bigelow and Galusha were Hill's attorneys in St. Paul, and they stayed on the board only for a short time, being replaced in 1880 by Richard B. Angus, another Canadian connected with the bank of Montreal, and O. H. Northcote, of London. Most important, James Hill was director and general manager and the driving force behind the new railroad.

The Saint Paul, Minneapolis & Manitoba was capitalized at $15 million, with a permitted maximum of $20 million. This stock should be considered as pure water, with no actual monetary value, as the real value of the railroad was represented by its bonded debt. The original shareholders, chiefly the associates and their henchmen, never paid a single dollar for their stock. Only subsequent issues of stock were really sold and paid for in cash. A loan of $12,000 per mile to a maximum of $8 million was issued at 7 percent interest, secured by a first mortgage on all lines plus the land grant. The allowed total of $8 million was indeed issued and many if not most of these bonds (at least $3.5 million, but probably much more) ended up in Amsterdam as payment for the old Saint Paul & Pacific bonds. Redemption by drawing started immediately, and by 1885 a sum of $2,650,000 had already been redeemed.[2]

A second loan, again of $8 million maximum but at 6 percent interest, was also issued in 1879 and secured by a second lien on the railroad, but not on the land grant. Bonds of this loan were marketed by Lippmann Rosenthal in Amsterdam at a first price of no less than 105 percent over par, and even at that high price they were eagerly taken up by the Dutch investing public. Prices of these second mortgage bonds always remained well over par on the Amsterdam Exchange, and those of the first mortgage rose even higher and remained

Table 5 Mileage of Saint Paul and Pacific Railroad

	Branch	Main	St. Vincent	Brainerd[a]	Red River
1862	10				
1863	27.5				
1864	40				
1865	50				
1866	76				
1867	76	16			
1868	76	51			
1869	76	111			
1870	76	135			
1871	76	207			
1872	76	207	132.5	4.5	
1873	76	207	132.5	4.5	
1874	76	207	132.5	4.5	
1875	76	207	132.5	4.5	
1876	76	207	132.5	4.5	
1877	76	207	136	4.5	30
1878	75.2	207.1	241.6	60.5	30
1879	75.2	207.1	319.6	60.5	30

Source: *Report of the Railroad Commissioner* for the year ending June 30, 1879, 21.

Note: [a] The Brainerd branch originally did not go any further than Watab, 4.5 miles from Sauk Rapids; the rest of the line was built by the Northern Pacific.

high until redeemed in 1909. The original first mortgage loan of 1866, of which $486,000 was still outstanding, was continued by the new company and duly redeemed at the time of maturing in 1892, but these bonds were not included in the Amsterdam price lists.

As if these two bonded loans were not yet enough to satisfy the needs of the Dutch investing public, the remaining shares of the Saint Paul, Minneapolis & Manitoba, after the associates had been given their portion, were also introduced in Amsterdam in October 1880—this time not by Lippmann Rosenthal but by another solid old-fashioned house, Stadnitski & Van Heukelom, also of Amsterdam. To make it easy for individual owners, the brokers issued certificates for these shares, as was usually done in the case of foreign shares, to make the cashing of dividends easier. First price at introduction was no less than 80 percent of par, very high for new shares, and they soon soared to over par when a first dividend of 3 percent was declared in 1881. A dividend of no less than 9 percent followed in 1882, and 8 percent in the next year, which drove the Amsterdam prices up to an all-time high of 178 over par in 1884. Dutch confidence in the capabilities of James Hill as railroad manager seem to have been unlimited, and all later issues of shares and bonds of the Saint Paul, Minneapolis & Manitoba and of its successor after 1890—the Great Northern

The impressive (second) Union Depot at St. Paul in 1890. (Minnesota Historical Society)

Railway—were heavily subscribed in Amsterdam. The Hill lines always had a substantial Dutch influence in their capitalization, an influence that lasts to this very day. Some dividends were also paid out in scrip, that is, the right to buy new shares or bonds at a low price, generally much lower than the current market price, which tended to enlarge the Dutch holdings even more.

The Red River & Manitoba Railroad Company

The idea for a line between Breckenridge, the terminus of the Main line of the Saint Paul & Pacific, and the village of Barnesville on the St. Vincent extension, seems to have been first mooted back in 1876 by Johan Carp. By building this shortcut, the traffic to the Red River at Fisher's Landing could be routed over the Saint Paul & Pacific for the whole distance, instead of over the Northern Pacific for part of the way. The Main line, until then not

much more than a long finger stretching out west into the vast but empty nowhere, could be made more profitable, and the Northern Pacific influence could be cut out. James Hill, of course, clearly saw the importance of this line, and as part of the impending deal with the Dutch, he agreed to build the line. In turn, the Dutch protective committee undertook to find the needed construction capital.

The Red River & Manitoba Railroad Company was incorporated in August 1877, without Hill's name among the directors, and shares (at $40 each) of the new road had already been offered in Amsterdam in July 1877 at a price of 94.50 guilders, which meant a discount of some 20 percent. Although interest in this line in Holland was never great, enough capital (at least $200,000) was raised this way to finish construction of the line of 33.5 miles.[3] Farley was general manager of this road, and from its opening in October 1877 it was operated in conjunction with the rest of the Saint

James J. Hill's drawing of his dump car design. In 1880 Hill obtained a U.S. patent for his design. (James J. Hill Papers)

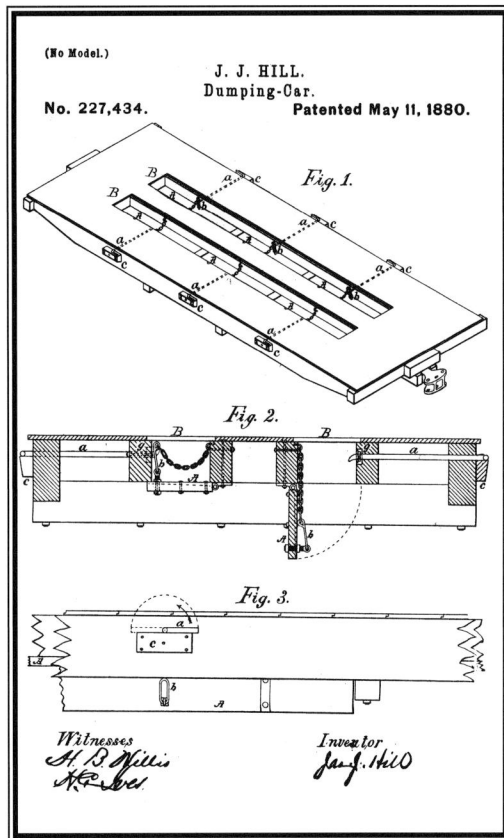

(No Model.)

J. J. HILL.
Dumping-Car.

No. 227,434. Patented May 11, 1880.

Fig. 1.

Fig. 2.

Fig. 3.

Witnesses

Inventor

as enough iron was available, the contractors could lay two miles a day, but there was a hitch: iron was coming through slowly. New flatcars on order from Haskell, Barker & Company of Michigan City, Indiana, had to be loaded with iron at the North Chicago Rolling Mills before being sent on to the North, but by August 1878 only sixty-nine cars had been dispatched. Work had to be stopped in consequence.[5] Only 3,800 tons had been sent off by the other regular supplier, the Cambria Iron Works in Pennsylvania, by September 1, but promises were given to "commence shipping as fast as made." Despite this slow delivery Stephen was unwilling to look anywhere else for iron as long as the Cambria Company could promise 2,000 tons not later than the first week of October. A personal element must have played a role here as well. Apart from his railroad interests, Kennedy was also agent of the Cambria Iron Works and therefore actively soliciting orders. No one seems to have cared much about this double role as long as the iron was coming through.[6]

The continued use of iron at this time instead of the then already proven steel may cause some surprise. Steel was harder and more durable than the soft, brittle iron but it was also much more expensive, and railroad managers were sometimes hesitant to use steel because of the expense involved. In England John Brown of Sheffield, using the newly invented Bessemer process, had rolled the first steel rails in 1860. Others followed. The giant London & North Western Railway switched over to the use of steel rails after a first successful experiment at its Crewe station in 1863. Then the railway set up its own Bessemer steelworks at Crewe in 1865 and started to roll its own rails.[7]

In America the Pennsylvania, Baltimore & Ohio and other major Eastern roads had already imported Bessemer steel rails from England and found them most satisfactory. The first steel rail in America was rolled, as an ex-

Paul & Pacific. A further extension was added to the network when the line from Fisher's Landing was extended some fourteen miles in the direction of Grand Forks, on the western bank of the Red River. Grand Forks itself was to be reached with a bridge across the Red River in January 1880.[4]

Steel versus Iron, and Other Innovations

For Hill in 1878 it was mandatory to finish the St. Vincent extension as soon as possible. The Northern Pacific was on its feet again and aggressively looking for traffic. New contracts were given by Farley in July 1878 to Daniel M. Robbins of St. Paul to finish the stretch from Melrose to Alexandria and from Snake River to the Canadian border, and an all-out effort was made. As long

periment, in 1865 by the North Chicago Rolling Mills, from steel ingots obtained from other American sources. This company would add its own Bessemer converters to produce its own steel only much later, in 1872. The first American company to take up the manufacture of steel rails on a commercial basis was the Cambria Iron Works, the favored supplier of the Saint Paul & Pacific, in 1867. The Cambria Iron Company at Johnston, Pennsylvania, had been founded back in 1853 for the express purpose of rolling rails and had acquired such a good name in this field that they were swamped with orders. Its chief engineer, George Fritz, had successfully adapted the Bessemer process to American circumstances and available raw materials, which made the changeover to steel production financially viable. Initially the American iron and steel industry had great trouble competing with cheap imports from Britain, Germany, and Belgium, but this changed in 1861, when the high protective Morrill tariff was introduced.[8]

Behind this protective barrier the domestic steel industry really took off. In 1868 it was confidently expected that steel would supplant iron completely as soon as more American rolling mills had adapted their plants to the manufacturing of steel rails, causing the price to drop materially.[9] Yet, ten years later, Hill and associates were still laying the outmoded cheap iron rails even for new construction—a decided throwback to earlier times which were long past. In 1880 already more than 29 percent of all rail mileage in America, including side tracks, had been laid with steel rails, and this percentage was to grow rapidly over the next few years. Soon after, the Manitoba road apparently had also switched over to steel on a large scale, for by 1885 two-thirds of its lines

The steamboat landing and railroad yards at St. Paul in the 1890s, with Union Depot in the background. The line of the Minnesota & Northwestern (later Chicago Great Western) that crosses the river here curves away to the right. The Chicago, Milwaukee & Saint Paul's tracks follow the left bank of the river until it bridges the Mississippi farther to the southwest near Pickerel Lake. (Minnesota Historical Society)

The yards of the Chicago, Milwaukee & Saint Paul at St. Paul in the bend of the river, with the Union Depot and its one train shed in the distance, circa 1890. From the depot the Manitoba's tracks curve away to the right to climb out of the river bottom. The high-level Roberts Street bridge and the low-level Minnesota & Northwestern swing bridge can be seen in the left distance. (Minnesota Historical Society)

had been laid with 56-pound steel rails.[10]

The associates apparently were well aware of the need to decide between steel and iron and had asked Farley's expert opinion. Hill wrote Stephen about the outcome:

While east we talked about the merits of iron and steel for new road and since our return I have discussed the matter with Mr. Farley, who thinks that considering the differences in cast, the light grades and moderate traffic, that iron would be quite good enough. His views confirm what was urged in Montreal in favor of iron under all the circumstances. Of course, were it for an old road with a heavy traffic in tons, the case would be entirely reversed.[11]

This conservative short-sightedness would cost them dear, however, as traffic grew so rapidly that the cheap iron rails had to be replaced with steel ones much sooner than expected.

Another novelty was the use of center-dump cars, invented for the purpose by James Hill himself. At the end of 1878 he

had contacted the firm of Jackson & Woodin with a request that they adapt one of their coal dump cars for dumping gravel on the track. Jackson & Woodin of Berwick, Pennsylvania, was a fast-growing car-maker, who had started making plows but had switched over to mine cars and then freight cars by the mid-1860s.[12] Their answer is not known, but apparently it was in the negative, for Hill perfected his own design and applied for a patent on his invention. The U.S. Patent Office refused this application on March 20, 1880, as a similar dump car had been covered by a patent issued to Thomas R. Hutton in November 1879. Thereupon Hill changed his design somewhat, and a patent (number 227,434) was then granted him on May 11, 1880. Not without some pride Hill wrote to Stephen that his dump cars were at work in ballasting on the St. Vincent extension. An engine was sent out by water to help in construction, but even then Stephen had his doubts about the finishing of the line in time for the deadline of the land grant.[13]

Stephen's fears of being too late for the land grant deadline proved unfounded, and the Canadian border was reached on November 12, 1878. The missing link in the Branch line between Alexandria and Barnesville was completed only a year later. In the meantime, traffic to St. Vincent and beyond into Canada could be routed via the Main line and Breckenridge-Barnesville.[14]

Operations

Some stretches of the road, especially on the Branch, were in bad condition at the time of the takeover, and derailments were frequent. Complaints of shippers and passengers were loud and annoying, and something had to be done. Fast running was strictly forbidden: "I will do what I can toward having the trains run slowly and have them leave the stations on time, so as not to be obliged to run too fast in order to reach the next station on time. This last was the cause of at least one of the freight trains getting off last week, and I think of both." Ten thousand new ties were to be put in the track as soon as the danger of frost was past, and thousands of tons of gravel were ready for use, but until these improvements could be made, slow orders were still necessary. Hill estimated the total cost of relaying the Branch with steel rails at just under $271,000. Redressing the roadbed, new ties, fencing, rebuilding of stations, and such would take another $100,000.[15]

A large 50-by-250-foot warehouse for customs was built at St. Boniface on the Canadian border, and first-class water stations with steam pumps were built at several places for $15,000 apiece, to replace the inadequate old windmills in the existing pumping stations. Other work was done at stations, new side tracks installed, culverts and trestles rebuilt, and numerous small items improved. At the end of 1880 Hill could proudly write to Allen Manvel, then general superintendent of the Rock Island,

that in the past eighteen months, twenty-six thousand tons of steel rail had been laid, with twelve thousand tons on order for next year. After delivery of all equipment ordered, more than two thousand boxcars would be available, with one thousand flatcars, seventy passenger cars, five sleeping cars, and seventy-seven locomotives.[16]

Connection with Canada

Traffic was booming on the lines. A Canadian line from Winnipeg south to the border was opened in December 1878, linked up with the Saint Paul & Pacific at Pembina/St. Boniface. This line was meant as a feeder for the construction of the Canadian Pacific across the Continent and was, of course, pushed strongly by Hill. The work was done by the St. Paul contracting firm of Murphy & Upper. Hill was in constant touch with James Upper and ordered rolling stock (fifteen flatcars at $275 each) for him from Wilcox, Carpenter & Sons, of Adrian, Michigan. The last rail on the Canadian line was laid near Pembina/St. Boniface on December 4, 1878, by twenty Manitoba ladies, as Hill proudly wired to Stephen. The line was leased for the time to the Saint Paul, Manitoba & Minneapolis road, as it would take several more years to connect this isolated Canadian line with an all-Canadian railroad.[17] Only in 1884 was the Canadian Pacific Railway finished north of Lake Superior, and only then could all Canadian traffic be routed over Canadian soil. Of course, this caused a considerable drop in traffic on the Manitoba road, but by then Hill was already building his own Dakota extension to tap new traffic.

A Canadian Winnipeg–Pembina project had been proposed earlier, by Smith and Stephen back in 1871, but the Canadian Dominion government had been afraid of interference with the plans for a Pacific Railway, then under consideration, and the Pembina line had languished. Since the Pacific Railway project had been started in earnest, however, and it was clear that all construction material for the line from Winnipeg to the West would have to go by way of St. Paul–Pembina, the situation was then different. Building an all-Canadian line north of Lake Superior presented so many geographical and technical obstacles that the decision was taken to start with the stretch west of Winnipeg. Having a rail link with the outside world was mandatory, and accordingly the Winnipeg–Pembina line was built by the Canadian Pacific Railway—at least officially, it was worked first by the contractors and then by the Saint Paul, Minneapolis & Manitoba for a number of years.[18] All iron and other construction material for this vast project had to be carried over the line of the Saint Paul & Pacific and the Saint Paul, Minneapolis & Manitoba.

In view of the importance of this Canadian traffic it was logical for James Hill to become involved in the consortium set up for the purpose of building the Canadian Pacific Railway, again together with Stephen and Smith. Only in May 1883, after the all-Canadian route north of Lake Superior was finally chosen and under construction, making a conflict of interests unavoidable, did Hill retire from the Canadian Pacific board.[19] Hill naturally wanted as much traffic for western Canada as possible routed over his lines, while the railway board and the Canadian government wanted all to go over their own national line. At about the same time and for the same reasons Stephen and Angus withdrew from the board of the Saint Paul, Minneapolis & Manitoba. By then Hill had already decided to push his Manitoba road west into the Dakotas and so became a fierce competitor to both the Northern Pacific and the Canadian Pacific.

Staff and Employees

New management also brought new staff. For the time being Farley remained general

manager or receiver of the several railroads until the foreclosure sales were finished in 1879. After that, a receiver was no longer necessary, of course, and Farley was formally discharged, much to his disappointment. He had probably counted on a position as general manager or superintendent of the new company, but Hill and his associates were not quite happy with his accomplishments as receiver and general manager. They lamented that he had been scarcely twenty days of every month at his St. Paul job, that he spent the rest of his days on his other railroads and coal interests. Discipline had also been lax in almost every quarter. Some employees owned farms along the line and spent more time on developing their own property than on their duties to the company.[20]

Fisher, Farley's right-hand man, handed in his resignation as general superintendent in April 1879 and was succeeded by E. B. Wakeman. Hill had great confidence in him: "Mr. Wakeman came today and I understand has about closed with Mr. Farley and I sincerely hope a new era will open in the operating department of the St. P. & Pacific." Wakeman was appalled by the operating conditions he found. Hill wrote Stephen:

> Wakeman tells me he never saw so many miles of road being so badly operated in his life. From Breckenridge to St. Vincent the trains are run by a boy at Breckenridge and the conductors do just as they please. In place of hauling from 30 to 35 loaded cars at least as far as Crookston, they take what suits their own convenience and [leave] the balance on some side track to wait for someone else and in that way a large number of cars [are] kept out of use.[21]

Wakeman did not last long in his new capacity, however, and Hill was again looking out for a general superintendent in 1880. He offered the position (at $12,000 per year) first to Charles C. Wheeler, assistant general su-

The steamboat landing at St. Paul, with the Union Depot—now with two train sheds—in the background, circa 1900. The steamers *Lora* and *J. J. Hill* are at the landing. (Photo by C. P. Gibson, Minnesota Historical Society)

perintendent of the Chicago & North Western, then in 1881 to Allen Manvel, who was serving in the same position on the Chicago, Rock Island & Pacific.[22] Manvel accepted and came to St. Paul. First he was general superintendent; then after Hill retired as general manager in 1883 he became president of the road, Hill's successor as general manager until 1889, and then director and president of the Santa Fe. Wakeman, although no longer in charge, continued to serve as assistant general superintendent of the then very much enlarged Manitoba road.[23]

There were changes in most areas of management. Hermann Trott resigned his job as land commissioner in 1879 to become a member of the executive committee of the Minnesota State Forestry Association, of which Geo. L. Becker was president.[24] D. A. McKinlay succeeded him as land commissioner. Knuppe's position is not clear, but he was already farming near Crookston at the time and must have resigned as well. And so it went in almost every department. Harvey Middleton (born 1852) entered service as master mechanic early in 1882, having served on the Philadelphia & Erie and as division master mechanic on the Louisville & Nashville before moving to St. Paul. Charles A. F. Morris, who had served the Saint Paul & Pacific as chief engineer for many years, moved to Portland, Oregon, as chief engineer of the Oregon & California Railroad. He was succeeded as chief engineer by

Charles C. Smith, who had already located part of the old Minnesota & Pacific back in 1857. After his work on the Minnesota & Pacific, Smith had been in the service of the Lake Shore & Michigan Southern and other railroads until being appointed engineer of the Saint Paul, Minneapolis & Manitoba, in December 1881.[25] New brooms made a clean sweep, and Hill himself saw into the smallest detail and the farthest corner. He turned out to be a railroading man of supreme ability.

General Improvements: Depots, Stockyards, Finances

During the general upswing of traffic on the railroad, the old passenger depot in St. Paul was still serving its purpose. But it must have been at the end of its useful existence, and in 1879 it was described as shabby and absolutely inadequate for a city with a population of forty thousand.[26] In Minneapolis (grown to forty-eight thousand), the situation was not very much better. The phenomenon of a union station, used by several railroads collectively, was already known by then, for back in 1853 all railroads entering Indianapolis had joined forces to erect a union station in that city, and other cities had followed suit. In St. Paul the same idea was mooted, and in 1879 a Saint Paul Union Depot Company was incorporated, with Hill the leading advocate and with all railroads entering St. Paul participating.[27]

The capital of the new company was first set at $250,000, but this soon turned out to be not enough; already more than $320,000 had been spent in 1880, of which some $57,000 was spent on the actual building.[28] Hill had some misgivings, however, about the project, as the Saint Paul & Pacific had to provide most of the land needed, which had been acquired and improved over the years at great cost to the company. He wrote Stephen: "My own idea

is to give them [the Union Depot Company] any lands we can spare without any injury to our own permanent business at such prices as will be fair value to them and satisfactory to us." In the end Hill offered the Union Depot Company about one-third of the Saint Paul & Pacific holdings for $250,000, which left the railroad company itself "about 20 acres for freight purposes in a piece 2000 ft long." Of the original eight platform tracks under the overall roof, the two northernmost were owned by the Saint Paul, Minneapolis & Manitoba, thus assuring the company of the best position in the new depot.[29]

The grand depot—part terminus, part through station—was thus built on land owned by the Saint Paul, Minneapolis & Manitoba on the site of the first depot of the Saint Paul & Pacific of 1862. Because of the soft, uneven subsoil it soon began to crack and had to be patched up extensively. Not for long, however, as it burned on July 11, 1884, and had to be rebuilt completely—and on a grander scale, with an impressive clock tower and larger wings.[30] This depot was to serve St. Paul well into the twentieth century, until it too burned on October 3, 1913. The present, fancy, neoclassical structure (now converted into offices and restaurants) was opened in 1920 to replace it. Mark Twain described the first Union Depot: "There is an unusually fine railway station; so large is it in fact, that it seemed somewhat overdone, in the matter of size, at first; but at the end of a few months it was perceived that the mistake was distinctly the other way. The error is to be corrected."[31] About 150 trains arrived daily in the Union Depot in the first years, with the same number of departures.

Another of James Hill's projects was the creation of the Union Stockyards of St. Paul in 1880. All railroads entering the city were connected with this enterprise, which soon outgrew its stockyard business and was transformed in 1883 into the Minnesota Transfer

Railway Company, with the Northern Pacific; the Omaha (Chicago & North Western); the Chicago, Milwaukee & Saint Paul; the Minneapolis & Saint Louis; and the Manitoba all participating. Meant to interconnect the freight operations of all railroads entering St. Paul and Minneapolis, it soon blossomed into a successful kind of belt line and transfer railroad. Herman Haupt, of Civil War fame and at that time in the service of the Northern Pacific, became its first president.[32]

In Minneapolis, which had already outgrown its neighbor St. Paul in population, a large new depot was being constructed as well, but this time not shared but wholly owned by the Saint Paul, Minneapolis & Manitoba. Built at a cost of over $500,000, it had five tracks under its overall roof and was reached from St. Anthony over the beautiful stone arch bridge across the Mississippi River.[33] The new Union Depot, as it was generally known, was also used by other railroads entering Minneapolis.

Traffic on the Manitoba was booming in the first years of its corporate existence. The flow of emigrants into Minnesota, the Dakotas, and Manitoba had started again on a larger scale than ever, after the effects of the general economic crisis wore off. Once the grasshopper invasions had for some mysterious reason come to an end, there was no reason not to try one's luck on the fertile Western soil. Reports about the "bonanza farms" in the Red River valley seeped into Europe and attracted thousands. Molyneux St. John, the Manitoba's agent in London, traveled throughout England and lectured in the smallest places about Minnesota. He wrote: "A trip from Liverpool to the Red River Valley in Minnesota . . . is of a pious nature, either the Holy Land or some biblical subjects. The panoramist says this conciliates the rural parsons and ministers and secures the schoolrooms in the small villages."[34] Thousands of pamphlets in English, German, Swedish, Norwegian, and other languages were printed and distributed to lure ever more emigrants to the lands of the Manitoba. Of the total land grant, amounting to circa 3,848,000 acres, just over 1 million acres had been sold by mid-1880, and sales were picking up again after the slump of the 1870s, with 268,741 acres sold in fiscal year 1879–1880 alone.[35]

In the report of the directors of 1879–1880, it was stated that total earnings of the company from all sources had been $2,933,108, an increase over the previous year of more than a million dollars. Superfluous personnel had been discharged, and the monthly payroll had been reduced from some $350,000 in August to just over $250,000 in October 1879.[36] Steel rail had been laid on 101 miles, hundreds of tons of old, bent, iron rails had been returned to the Cambria Works to be reheated and straightened, sixty-five locomotives were in service, with sixty-nine passenger and mail cars, over fourteen hundred freight cars, and thirty of Hill's own dump cars. Net profits over that fiscal year came to an astonishing $555,795, which is hard to believe but true.

In the next few years the grades on the Main line (apart from the stiff climb out of St. Paul's Union Station), never very severe and which originally averaged only about 1.13 percent, were reduced to a 0.6 percent average. The same engines could then haul more tons and longer trains. Still later, the average grade was even further reduced to 0.3 percent, almost level.[37]

Relations with the Northern Pacific

The Northern Pacific, reorganized after its default and under new management, seemed to become a dangerous competitor again. It had to relinquish its stock in the Saint Paul & Pacific and could not hope to acquire it again once the associates had bought the stock from the Litchfields. A direct connection with St. Paul, shorter than the roundabout route provided by the Saint Paul & Duluth (the former Lake Superior & Mississippi) was sorely needed. Duluth was a good harbour for shipments of grain, but only when there was no ice on Lake Superior. In winter an all-rail connection was needed.

The Northern Pacific had two options: either use the Saint Paul, Minneapolis & Manitoba's line from Sauk Rapids in connection with its own Brainerd–Sauk Rapids branch line, or build a new line from Minneapolis to Sauk Rapids. The town of Minneapolis strongly pushed for the latter option, but for the time being the Northern Pacific favored joint ownership of the Branch line plus access to St. Paul, Minneapolis, and St. Cloud. Hill thought this was going too far and wanted to give them only running rights on the Branch, with all local business to be done by the Saint Paul & Pacific only. After arbitration by neutral parties, a contract was signed late in 1878 between the Northern Pacific and the Saint Paul & Pacific (later continued by the Manitoba) for use of the latter's tracks between Sauk Rapids and St. Paul/Minneapolis and terminal facilities at St. Paul—all at a fair price, of course. All future differences arising between the two companies about the actual connections, traffic arrangements, and rates were to be decided by referees.[38]

The first Northern Pacific train from St. Paul to Bismarck, North Dakota, by way of Brainerd had already run earlier, in March 1878, when negotiations were pending. Much later the Northern Pacific found the running rights arrangement unsatisfactory and decided to build its own line from Minneapolis to Sauk Rapids. The running rights over the Manitoba then lapsed. In June 1878 the Northern Pacific's chief engineer, the former Confederate general Thomas L. Rosser, had been busy surveying a line from Fargo to Pembina on the west bank of the Red River, but as the Saint Paul & Pacific's line on the east bank was then nearing completion and was better located, the Northern Pacific never built its own line.[39]

The Farley Suit

One hard nut remained for the associates to crack. Jesse Farley, who had done his best as receiver and general manager of the railroad, was discharged after the incorporation of the Saint Paul, Minneapolis & Manitoba. James Hill, the new general manager, had become exasperated with Farley's slow ways and frequent absences from St. Paul and had decided the company had no place for him. Farley himself seems to have had hopes of some position on the new railroad and was greatly disappointed by his dismissal. On June 13, 1879, he brought suit against the associates in the district court of Ramsey County, claiming he was entitled to a share in the profits made by the associates in taking over the old Saint Paul from the Dutch. He said he was the first to suggest buying the Dutch bonds and so getting the railroad in his possession and that he had brought in Hill and Kittson. The understanding had been that he, while being receiver, should run the railroad in such a way that the price of its bonds would depreciate so much that his associates could lay hands on the road as cheaply as possible. That this would have been outright breach of confidence—because, as court-appointed receiver, he was supposed to act in the best interests of those same bondholders—he seems to have forgotten.

Hill, Kittson, and their associates of course denied the existence of any oral or written contract with Farley, and the latter could not show any evidence, either, and brought only one witness, his assistant Fisher, to declare that he had heard something that could be construed as a kind of an understanding between Hill and Farley. No written contract could be produced, and the courts threw out Farley's claim. But he fought on, all the way to the U.S. Supreme

Court, which august body, in October 1893, finally upheld the decisions of the lower courts against Farley.[40] He died the next year, a bitter and disappointed man.

For the later historian, the printed transcripts of the Farley suits, covering hundreds of pages, are a great boon, as they give particulars about the early history of the Saint Paul & Pacific that are to be found nowhere else. They should be used with caution, however, as the testimonies of Hill and Stephen were intended to clear their characters and do not always give a historically correct picture. The testimony of Johan Carp, more or less neutral in the conflict, squares absolutely with his written report of 1877, however, and has been used extensively for this story.

An unexpected sequel to the Farley suit was a letter from Johan Carp to James Hill dated February 28, 1894, in which Carp reminds Hill that during the original negotiations of October 1877, when it seemed that several big Dutch bondholders were reluctant to come forward to join the protective committee, Hill had offered Carp $200,000 in stock in the new company if he could persuade those bondholders to agree. Carp did so successfully, which meant that a majority of the Dutch were ready to exchange their bonds, but Hill had never handed over the promised stock. Carp told Hill in his letter that he did not want to press him to fulfill his obligation, but that he only wanted his name cleared. During the Farley suit testimonies, apparently, Hill had made some remarks that placed Carp and Knuppe in a bad light—as people who were working not only in the interests of their constituents, the protective committee, but also in their own interest—hence Carp's letter.[41]

Carp's brother-in-law, Johan Knuppe, then general agent of the Netherlands–American Land Company of St. Paul, supported Carp in a letter to Hill dated May 23, 1894, in which he reminds Hill of the existence of an offer of this sum, written in

Hill's own hand and dated October 18, 1877. For the sake of convenience, he gave Hill a copy of his original letter.[42] From the text of this offer it is not clear for whom the $200,000 was intended, and it only states that the sum can be used to bring the reluctant bondholders forward, but apparently Carp considered this as meant for himself to dispose of as he thought best.

A much later letter from Knuppe to Hill, August 26, 1912, clears up the whole thing.[43] The $200,000 in stock was to be divided by Carp, one-half going to those bondholders that he had to convince, and the other half was for Knuppe as payment in lieu of a promise Carp had made to him and could not fulfill with the railroad in receivership. Nothing would have been for Carp himself, who had, according to Knuppe, "a morbid sense of honor" and who, moreover, was very wealthy already and did not need more. Knuppe at that time was the only sufferer of the nonfulfillment of Hill's promise, but he conceded that all this happened a long time ago and that the legal part of the promise was dead, but that the moral part still lived. He was leaving Minnesota for good and was going to settle in Brandon, Manitoba, as agent of the land company, and just wanted to remind Hill of the affair. He left everything to him and ended his letter:

> And if you are unwilling or unable to look at the matter as I do, then I shall always try to look only with admiration at your wonderful achievements, will try to have no further ill feelings against anybody and to wish that you may enjoy many years of your well earned rest. Farewell.
>
> NB I keep no copy of this letter, and leave St. Paul this afternoon.

In this same letter of 1912 Knuppe also nicely solves the mystery of the missing fifth part of the stock of the new company (mentioned in the preceding chapter). It

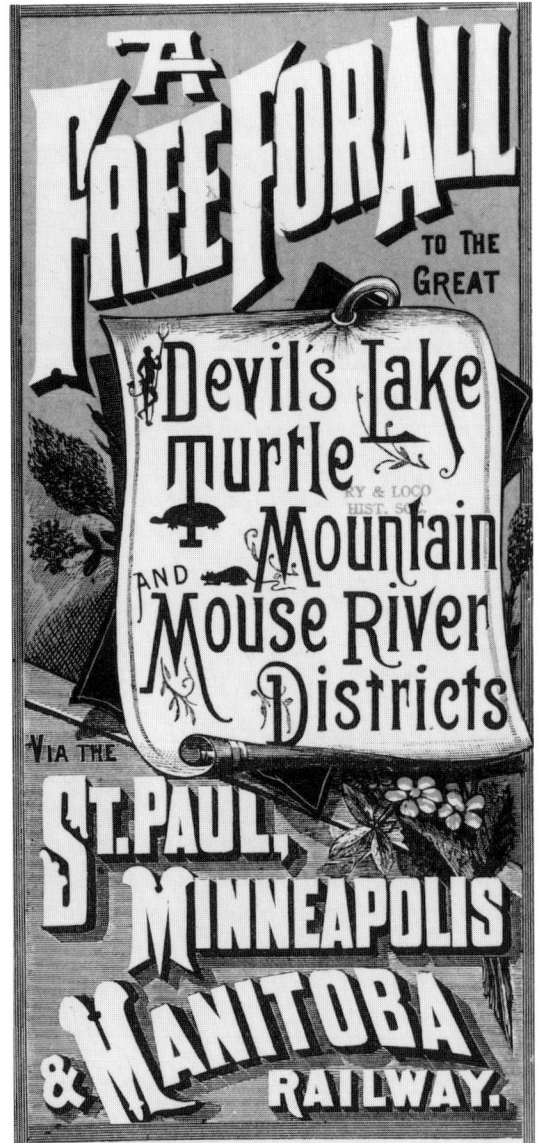

Two covers from timetables of the Saint Paul, Minneapolis & Manitoba in 1885. (Railway & Locomotive Historical Society)

was not Kennedy who was meant originally as the beneficiary, but Johan Carp! In his letter to Hill, Knuppe refers to a letter from Norman Kittson to Carp dated May 26, 1877, marked "private and confidential," which ended as follows:

> The stock will be divided into tenths, of which four tenths will go to our Canadian friends, and four tenths to ourselves, leaving two tenths to be disposed of hereafter. If the proposed arrangement is carried out and we get the bonds, and after the Committee is discharged and your duties therewith at an end, should you wish to join with us in the new enterprise it will give us great pleasure to have you do so.

Carp never answered this letter, as Knuppe thought he should have done, but later in 1877 told Hill that he was not interested in participating himself.[44]

Apart from Carp and Knuppe, many others held a grudge against the associates. Some of the mudslinging in the courts, of course, did damage the reputations of those involved. Gustavus Myers raked up the old story again in 1909, not openly siding with Farley but insinuating that Hill could never have gathered his great fortune by legal means alone and that at least part of Farley's accusations must have been true. Stephen's integrity was attacked in the parliament of Canada in 1884, when a fellow member accused him of having driven down the price of the "Dutch" bonds in collusion with the receiver, "and having used the receiver as his tool, he forgot the old adage that there should be honour among thieves."[45] The matter was patched up, as usual, but Stephen's reputation was tarnished somewhat. Unaffected, at least outwardly, by these proceedings, Hill, Stephen, and Smith went on to greater things, fortunes, and even ennoblement in the case of the latter two. Only Kittson, already old and worn-out in the 1870s, retired from active life after the Saint Paul &

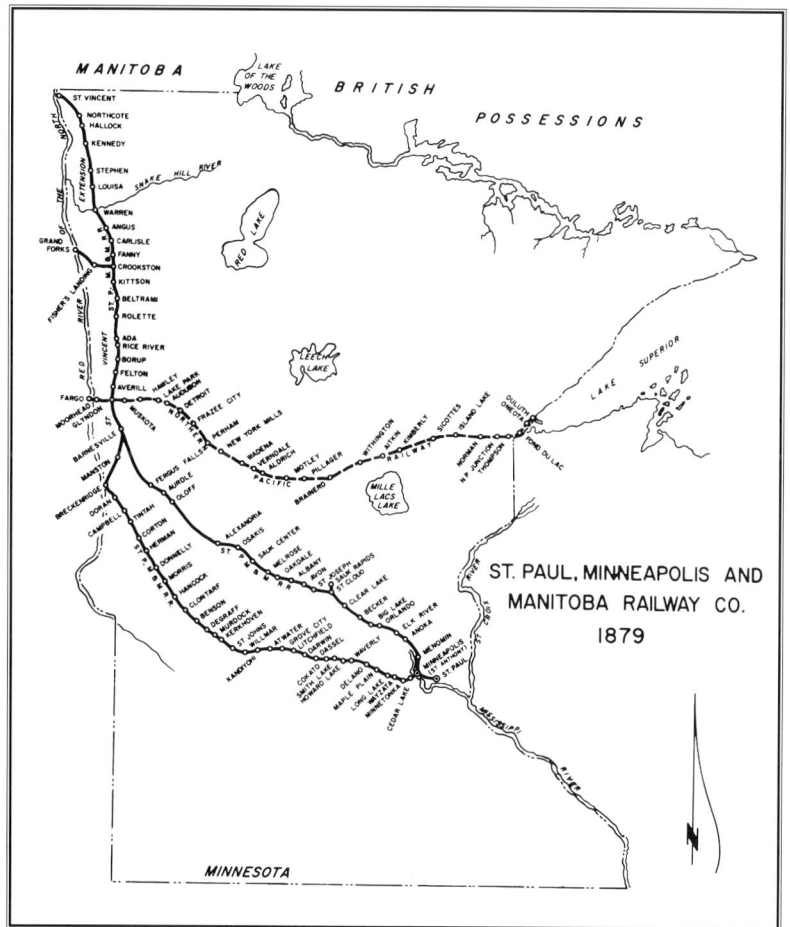

Pacific affair and died soon after.

Hill was universally praised for his ability as a master railroader. Investors in America and Europe were most pleased with the financial performance of his railroads and were eager to continue to invest in his companies. In his 1885 report Henry Minot nicely summed up the feelings of New York's Wall Street, London's Lombard Street, and Amsterdam's Damrak: "The President and General Manager deserve great credit for the thoroughness and good sense with which they have brought the property from its low state in 1880 into good condition and efficiency." And two years later, the *Railroad Gazette* went even farther in its praise, saying "J.J. Hill *is* the company to all intents and purposes. . . . His success may be estimated by the statement that he is now worth from $16,000,000 to $20,000,000, and some of his associates nearly as much."[46] A far cry from his lowly position ten years before.

The extent of the Saint Paul, Minneapolis & Manitoba Railroad shortly after its incorporation. (From Hidy, Hidy, Scott, and Hofsommer, *The Great Northern Railway*, courtesy Harvard Business School Press)

JIM HILL IN CROOKSTON
SEPT. 17 '08

James J. Hill and his wife, Mary, descending from their special train at Crookston, on the original Saint Paul & Pacific line, in 1908. Well into the twentieth century, James J. Hill remained the driving force behind the Great Northern Railway. He toured his domain extensively and took great interest in the improvement of agriculture and stock raising. (James J. Hill Papers)

In its first appearance, the Saint Paul & Pacific was not very different from other Midwestern railroads of the era. It followed the usual pattern of being promoted by local or regional businessmen and boosters. When the money ran out, as it soon did, the railroad resorted to Eastern railroaders and capitalists, and when these did not come forward with enough construction capital, the road tried to float bond loans on foreign capital markets. Again, nothing out of the ordinary, as most American railroad companies did the same. Owing to the Civil War, however, the European capital markets were disturbed and not very eager to sink money into an unknown railroad in faraway Minnesota.

The London Exchange, then the world's leading financial market, was rumored to be biased in favor of the Southern cause because of its cotton interests, but this is probably not the real reason behind the London brokers' refusal to handle the Saint Paul & Pacific securities. The London market was clogged with American railroad bonds at the time, and new securities of doubtful value were not exactly welcome. This is the reason that the first European contact of the people behind the Saint Paul road—Londoner Robert Benson—looked to the Amsterdam market, which was then just getting interested in American railroad paper.

Amsterdam, with a lot of enthusiasm, jumped into the fray and was soon established as the leading financier of the Saint Paul & Pacific railroad. This was distinctly unusual at the time, when most American railroads had a lot of foreign—British, German, French, or Dutch—capital in their financial structure, but scarcely ever so overwhelmingly from one country alone. Dutch interest in the Saint Paul & Pacific was financial in the first place. Its securities were bought with expectations of regular payments of the stipulated interest. The emigration schemes for bringing Dutch farmers to Minnesota came as a result of the financial involvement in the railroad, not the other way around.

After the default of the company, during the long and agonizingly slow process of reorganization, it was remarkable that the leading railroads entering St. Paul from the South or the East were not interested in taking over the ailing Saint Paul & Pacific. After all it would have formed an excellent extension into the Northwest for such roads as the Chicago & North Western, the Chicago, Burlington & Quincy, or the Chicago, Milwaukee & Saint Paul. Apparently these companies' conservative management, impressed by the general crisis and many bankruptcies of neighboring railroads, viewed the shaky Saint Paul road more as a liability than an asset and refused to be drawn into what they considered a financial morass.

When James Hill was thinking about the purchase of the Saint Paul & Pacific bonds from the Dutch, he approached the North Western and the Milwaukee for support, and they cautiously declared their willingness to help him out, if need be. In the end nothing came of this, and Hill managed quite well on his own, thereby avoiding any outside control over his road. All three roads later did extend their lines into the

Construction of the Saint Paul, Minneapolis & Manitoba's western extension across the endless prairies of North Dakota in the 1880s. (James J. Hill Papers)

Northwest, but at a time when the Saint Paul, Minneapolis & Manitoba and its successor, the Great Northern, were already well established as the major carriers in the area. The Milwaukee in the twentieth century did finally reach the Pacific (and bankrupted itself in the process), whereas the others never did get any further than Wyoming or Montana.

The only railroad that was really interested in the Saint Paul & Pacific was the Northern Pacific, which found itself stuck in Duluth, a good port for timber, grain, and ores, at least during the summer months, but not really the terminus the railroad needed. The Saint Paul & Pacific seemed the ideal short connection with the railroad hubs of St. Paul, Chicago, and the rest of the

world. Indeed, the Northern Pacific had already tried to gain control of its smaller neighbor, but its own bankruptcy and managerial woes prevented it from keeping a firm hold. It had to let the Saint Paul road drift loose. Then when the Northern Pacific itself was on its feet again, it found to its dismay that the Saint Paul & Pacific was in the hands of a strong-willed railroader, who had absolutely no intentions of being bought off or simply chased away.

One point worth remarking is that the Dutch never contemplated taking over the operation of the railroad themselves. True, they had not invested their money in order to run a railroad in America, but in some other cases, they were forced to do so to save their investment from complete loss.

One victim of the 1873 crisis, the narrow-gauge Cairo & Saint Louis, was largely owned by Dutch investors led by the well-known Amsterdam house of Wertheim & Gompertz. After its reorganization as the Saint Louis & Cairo in 1881, the little road was operated by executives both American and Dutch, appointed by A. C. Wertheim, whose firm held the majority of shares and all the bonds. Five years later, after the road was in the black again, it was leased to the Mobile & Ohio and direct Dutch control ended. When the Denver Pacific (Denver–Cheyenne) and its subsidiary the Denver & Boulder Valley defaulted in 1877, the court gave both roads over to the Dutch majority bondholders, who again included A. C. Wertheim. In this case the Dutch ran both roads only for a short time, as all Dutch bonds were sold to Jay Gould in 1879. Again, Wertheim and his compatriots were willing to operate a foreign railroad themselves until a good deal could be made, rather than clearing out as soon as possible.

Why Lippmann Rosenthal and the other houses involved in the Saint Paul & Pacific crash were not inclined to run the road themselves is not quite clear. It may have been too early for that; the Dutchmen may have needed more time to get used to the idea. After all the Saint Paul & Pacific was one of the very first large-scale Dutch investments in American railroads, and the bankers involved had little experience with this kind of transaction. Initially, Lippmann Rosenthal did not even have a clerk in their office who was fluent enough in English to write business letters in that language. How would they then set about sending trusted people to run a railroad for them in America? Whatever their considerations may have been, they chose to sell out.

The Dutch would have been willing to negotiate a deal with any interested party, as long as they could unload their millions of bonds at a reasonable price. They had no particular preference for James J. Hill and his associates, but he appeared to be the only seriously interested party. Indeed, during the first years after the default of their company, the Dutch had little confidence in Hill, who was then a relatively unknown businessman from outside St. Paul. But after Hill found partners in the Canadian financiers Smith and Stephen, things definitely changed. It now became clear that Hill was by far their best option for a sale of their bonds, and Johan Carp and Lippmann Rosenthal, urged on by Kennedy in New York, gradually came to see Hill in a more favorable light.

Indeed, Hill played his cards masterfully. He succeeded not only in getting the Dutch bonds at a fairly low price but also in instilling in the Dutch bankers so much confidence in his capabilities as a railroader that they were willing to sell their bonds on credit, even to invest millions more in his new railroad—the Saint Paul, Minneapolis & Manitoba. Both parties thought they had a fair deal, as indeed they had, and neither party regretted the risks it took. And the risks were awe-inspiring, for Hill as much as for the Dutch. They were as if condemned to each other. Hill needed millions in credit to buy the bonds and then recondition the dilapidated railroad; the Dutch were only to get their money back if Hill succeeded in rebuilding the road and running it as intended. In this he succeeded above reproach, and the Manitoba in the hands of Hill became a model for other railroads in the land. He turned out to be one of the greatest masters of railroading for more than thirty years. In the end he effectively controlled both his old rival, the Northern Pacific, and the Chicago, Burlington & Quincy.

Hill was a hard taskmaster, and his subordinates were sometimes driven to despair by his boundless energy, his drive for economy, and his eye for the smallest detail. He was feared, at best respected, but not really loved, although his staff generally did find

Jim Hill (center, with hand in pocket) with a group of old-timers in front of the restored *Wm. Crooks* at the Union Depot in St. Paul in 1908. (James J. Hill Papers)

him a reasonable and respectable boss. His reputation was tarnished right from the start by his treatment of receiver Jesse Farley, which was shabby, possibly dishonest to some extent. But if Farley was right in his claims, then his own dishonesty would have far surpassed that of Hill. As court-appointed receiver he would have run the railroad against the orders of the court and against the interests of the bondholders, who had placed their trust in him.

The Dutch and other foreign bondholders and shareholders cared little about

Hill's reputation. As long as he managed his road well and paid regular interest on its bonds, they had little to complain about. And when the dividends turned out higher than ever expected, the investors had reason only to congratulate themselves on their good fortune in having sold their almost worthless bonds to him, at a time when no one seemed to understand the latent potential of the Saint Paul & Pacific. Over the years, before 1914, no less than twenty-three different securities—both bonds and shares—of the Great Northern and its subsidiaries and predecessors were listed on the Amsterdam Exchange. Only the Southern Pacific and the Union Pacific were more popular in Holland.

◆ ◆ ◆

To better illustrate the new course of the railroad, in 1890 it was renamed Great Northern Railway. Hill built swiftly and soundly across Montana, Idaho, and Washington. His Great Northern reached the Pacific Ocean at Seattle in 1893. The successor of the old Saint Paul & Pacific had finally reached the goal expressed in the corporate name of its pioneering predecessor. Hill found an easier grade across the mountains (and consequently a cheaper route) than the Northern Pacific, and his railroad soon overshadowed its old rival in most respects. Mileage of the Saint Paul, Minneapolis & Manitoba/Great Northern combination, including subsidiaries, grew from just under one thousand miles in 1882 to some twenty-eight hundred miles ten years later, and it was to grow still further in subsequent years. And this railroad company, one of the most successful of all railroads in America, had begun in 1862 as a tiny, ten-mile line between St. Paul and St. Anthony, part of that first Minnesota railroad. This Saint Paul & Pacific Railroad Company had truly been "a railroad empire in the making."

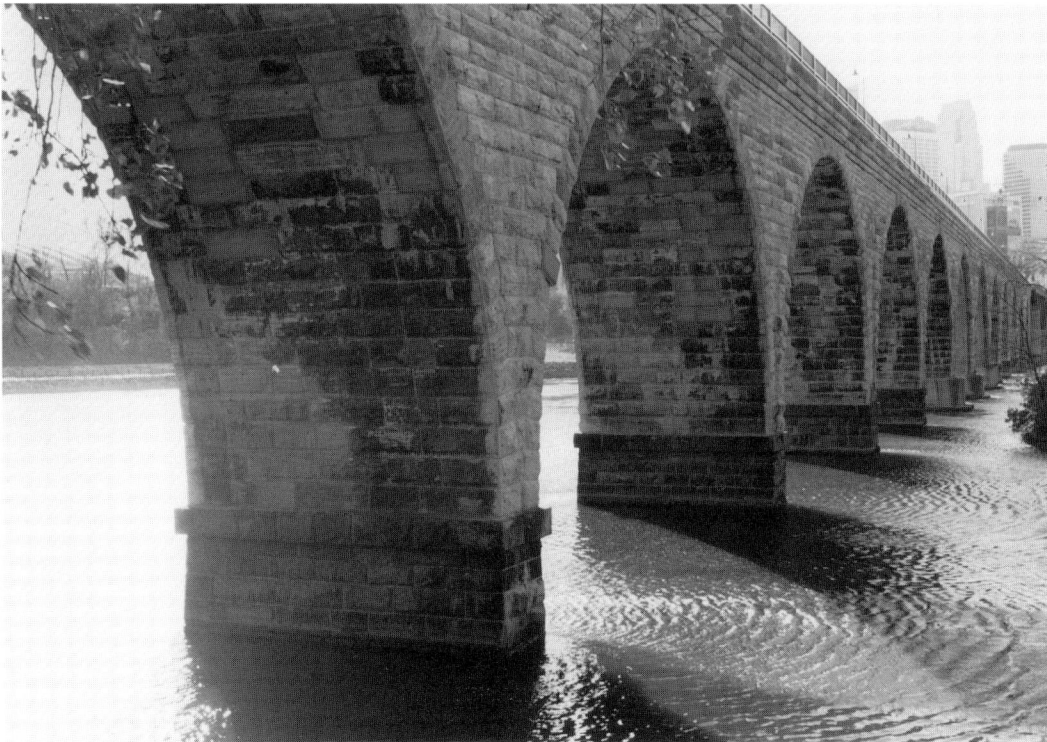

The stone arch bridge that carried the Saint Paul, Minneapolis & Manitoba tracks across the Mississippi River at Minneapolis to reach the new Union Station. The bridge now supports a public footpath. (Photo by Jannie W. Veenendaal)

Notes

Introduction

1. For the Illinois Central land grant, see Howard G. Brownson, *History of the Illinois Central to 1870,* 17–39. For the land grant policy in general, see Lloyd J. Mercer, *Railroads and Land Grant Policy: A Study in Government Intervention.* For investors, see Augustus J. Veenendaal, Jr., *Slow Train to Paradise: How Dutch Investment Helped Build American Railroads,* 180, 225.

2. Veenendaal, *Slow Train to Paradise,* 130–39. See also Ralph W. Hidy, Muriel E. Hidy, and Roy V. Scott, *The Great Northern Railway: A History.*

3. Arthur M. Johnson and Barry M. Supple, *Boston Capitalists and Western Railroads: A Study in the Nineteenth-Century Railroad Investment Process.* About Forbes, see John L. Larson, *Bonds of Enterprise: John Murray Forbes and Western Development in America's Railway Age.*

4. Brownson, *History of the Illinois Central;* Veenendaal, *Slow Train to Paradise,* 58–61.

5. Thomas C. Cochran, *Railroad Leaders, 1845–1890: The Business Mind in Action,* 425.

6. Mira Wilkins, *The History of Foreign Investment in the United States to 1914,* 76, 198.

1: Early Minnesota

1. Louis Joliet (1645–1700), a Canadian-born Frenchman, originally pursued a religious career but later returned to the world and was sent out with Father Marquette to explore the course of the Mississippi River. They reached present-day Memphis, Tennessee, in 1673 and then returned to Canada. Joliet ended his career as professor of hydrography at the Jesuit College of Quebec. Jacques Marquette (1637–1675), French Jesuit missionary in Quebec since 1666, established several missions on the shores of Lake Michigan and was sent out with Joliet to travel down the Wisconsin and Mississippi Rivers in 1673. He died on the shores of Lake Michigan. Daniel Greysolon, sieur Duluth (circa 1636–1710), French nobleman and soldier, arrived in Canada about 1675 and went in 1678 on a journey of exploration to the Lake Superior area. He died in Montreal. *Dictionnaire de Biographie Française* (Paris: Librairie Letonzey et Ané, 1970), 2:88–90.

2. Louis Hennepin (1640–1705), a Franciscan priest, born in Ath, Belgium, was in North America and French Canada from 1676 to 1682. Back in Europe, he obtained leave to settle in the Dutch Republic to publish his travel journals. He died in Utrecht (*Biographie Nationale de Belgique* [Bruxelles: Bruylart, Christophe et Cie., 1886–1887], 9:77–81). For the French discoveries in the American Northwest, see William W. Folwell, *A History of Minnesota,* 1:1–52.

3. About the history of Canada, see Donald Creighton, *A History of Canada: Dominion of the North,* or Desmond Morton, *A Short History of Canada.*

4. E. E. Rich, *The Fur Trade and the Northwest to 1857,* 7; Alvin C. Gluek, *Minnesota and the Manifest Destiny of the Canadian Northwest,* 3.

5. Paul C. Phillips, *The Fur Trade,* 1:269–70, 431–47; Rich, *The Fur Trade,* 186–88.

6. Hiram M. Chittenden, *The American Fur Trade of the Far West,* 1:313–45, 380–81.

7. Folwell, *History of Minnesota,* 1:69–70.

8. Wilkins, *Foreign Investment,* 29–37; P. J. van Winter, *Het aandeel van den Amsterdamschen handel aan den opbouw van het Amerikaansche gemeenebest,* 2:386–88; Veenendaal, *Slow Train to Paradise,* 8–9; Folwell, *History of Minnesota,* 1:78

9. Creighton, *History of Canada,* 201–02.

10. Lucile M. Kane, June D. Holmquist, and Carolyn Gilman, eds., *The Northern Expeditions of Stephen H. Long: The Journals of 1817 and 1823 and Related Documents,* 16–17; John E. Parsons, *West on the Forty-Ninth Parallel: Red River to the Rockies, 1872–1876,* 5–6; C. C. Andrews, *Minnesota and Dacotah: In Letters Descriptive of a Tour Through the North-West in the Autumn of 1856,* 104.

11. Kane, Holmquist, and Gilman, *Northern*

Expeditions, 20; Parsons, *West on the Forty-Ninth Parallel,* 24, 31.

12. About the American expeditions into Minnesota, see Folwell, *History of Minnesota,* 1:89–130.

13. Lucile M. Kane, *The Waterfall That Built a City: The Falls of St. Anthony in Minneapolis,* 9–10.

14. Folwell, *History of Minnesota,* 1:160.

15. Thomas Douglas, fifth earl of Selkirk (1771–1820), a close friend of the famous writer Sir Walter Scott, established his first colony in North America on Prince Edward's Island in 1803 and started the Red River colony in 1811. *Dictionary of National Biography* (London: Smith, Elder, 1888), 15:350–53. For the fate of his settlements, see Gluek, *Minnesota,* 26–29; Creighton, *History of Canada,* 273.

16. For a history of St. Paul, see J. Fletcher Williams, *A History of the City of St. Paul, and of the County of Ramsey, Minnesota;* also Kane, *Waterfall,* 13.

17. J. W. McClung, *Minnesota as it is in 1870: Its General Resources and Attractions,* 25.

18. For the legal history of Minnesota, see William Anderson and Albert J. Lobb, *A History of the Constitution of Minnesota.* For St. Paul in 1849, see Folwell, *History of Minnesota,* 1:248.

19. Folwell, *History of Minnesota,* 1:304.

20. C. M. Oehler, *The Great Sioux Uprising.*

21. McClung, *Minnesota as it is,* 247, 24–25.

22. James H. Baker, "History of Transportation in Minnesota," 20. Clarence W. Rife, "Norman W. Kittson: A Fur Trader at Pembina."

23. For the Red River cart, see Williams, *City of St. Paul,* 303–06; Lass, *Minnesota: A History,* 71. For the traffic, see McClung, *Minnesota as it is,* 127.

24. Williams, *City of St. Paul,* 295; John H. Stevens, *Personal Recollections of Minnesota and its People and Early History of Minneapolis,* 112–13.

25. Arthur J. Larsen, "Roads and the Settlement of Minnesota," 230–31; Baker, "History of Transportation," 18; Williams, *City of St. Paul,* 300–301.

26. Theodore C. Blegen and Philip D. Jordan, *With Various Voices: Recordings of North Star Life,* 226–28, after a story by Walter S. Pardee in the possession of the Minnesota Historical Society.

27. Josiah B. Chaney, "Early Bridges and Changes of the Land and Water Surface in the City of St. Paul," 132–34; Williams, *City of St. Paul,* 437. A second Wabasha Street bridge was built on the original piers in the early twentieth century, and this one lasted until 1996. A completely new bridge opened in 1998.

28. Kane, *Waterfall,* 14–32.

29. From the Minnesota newspaper *Express,* 24 December 1853, quoted in ibid., 38.

30. Ibid., 40; Stevens, *Personal Recollections,* 255–63.

31. Williams, *City of St. Paul,* 357.

32. Louis C. Hunter, *Steamboats on the Western Rivers: An Economic and Technological History,* 22.

33. Ibid., 45.

34. There is an excellent treatise on steamboat technology in ibid., 61–180.

35. For the *Moselle* accident, see ibid., 285–86; for the *John Rumsey,* see Williams, *City of St. Paul,* 416.

36. Frank J. Fugina, *Lore and Lure of the Upper Mississippi River,* 132; Hunter, *Steamboats,* 231.

37. For a history of the different lines to St. Paul, see Hunter, *Steamboats,* 630–35.

38. Figures are from ibid., 45, 635.

39. Stevens, *Personal Recollections,* 113.

40. Morton, *Short History of Canada,* 46.

41. John M. Gibbon, *The Romantic History of the Canadian Pacific, the Northwest Passage of Today,* 127–28.

42. The story of steamboating on the Red River is largely taken from Marion H. Herriot, "Steamboat Transportation on the Red River."

43. Walter Havighurst, *Voices on the River: The Story of the Mississippi Waterways,* 118–20.

2: The First Railroads

1. *DeBow's Review* 24 (May 1858), 394, in Eugene Alvarez, *Travel on Southern Antebellum Railroads, 1828–1860,* 13.

2. A survey of gauges in use and lines constructed can be found in George R. Taylor and Irene Neu, *The American Railroad Network, 1861–1900,* 35–41.

3. For a survey of land grants, see Mercer, *Railroads and Land Grant Policy.*

4. William W. Folwell, "The Five Million Loan," 189.

5. James E. Vance, *The North American Railroad: Its Origin, Evolution, and Geography,* 210.

6. Sydney A. Patchin, "The Development of Banking in Minnesota," 114–66; list of banks in Williams, *City of St. Paul*, 411–12.

7. Henry J. Winser, *The Great Northwest: A Guide-Book and Intinerary for the Use of Travellers over the Lines of the Northern Pacific Railroad*, 18–20.

8. McClung, *Minnesota as it is*, 248–50.

9. Kane, *Waterfall*, 100–113; Blegen and Jordan, *With Various Voices*, 161–68.

3: The Minnesota & Pacific Railroad Company

1. Rasmus S. Saby, "Railroad Legislation in Minnesota, 1849 to 1875," 11.

2. "Minnesota & Pacific Railroad Statement" (undated), in J. J. Hill Library (HE.2791 G75).

3. *Saint Paul, Minneapolis & Manitoba Railway Cy. Records and Indentures*, J. J. Hill Library (HE.2791 G79). See also Saby, "Railroad Legislation," for particulars of the different charters of all railroad companies chartered in Minnesota.

4. Warren Upham and Rose B. Dunlap, *Minnesota Biographies*, 632; Williams, *City of St. Paul*, 255–56.

5. Williams, *City of St. Paul*, 216–19; Upham and Dunlap, *Minnesota Biographies*, 624.

6. Warren Upham, *Minnesota Geographic Names: Their Origin and Historic Significance*, 587.

7. David Chauncey Shepard, was born in Geneseo, New York, in 1828 and came to St. Paul in 1857. He set up as an engineer, and after his term of office with the Saint Paul & Pacific, he founded a railroad contracting firm in 1871, together with Robert B. Langdon and A. H. Linton. This firm built parts of the Saint Paul & Pacific, and much later also many of the Western lines of the Great Northern and of the Saint Paul, Minneapolis & Manitoba in the Dakotas and Montana. Shepard retired in 1894. Upham and Dunlap, *Minnesota Biographies*, 698; Frank P. Donovan, Jr., *Gateway to the Northwest: The Story of the Minnesota Transfer Railway*, 25; Duncan J. Kerr, *The Story of the Great Northern Railway and James J. Hill*, 14.

8. William Crooks was born in New York City in 1832, graduated as army engineer from West Point Military Academy, and became assistant to John B. Jervis (1795–1885), the famous engineer who laid out many of the early railroads in New York and the inventor of the four-wheel locomotive truck. Crooks remained active in railroad construction but had no connection with the Saint Paul & Pacific or its successors. He died in Portland, Oregon, in 1907, where he had moved for health reasons. *Collections of the Minnesota Historical Society* 12 (1908), 794.

9. Leonard B. Irwin, *Pacific Railways and Nationalism in the Canadian-American Northwest, 1845–1873*, 128–35; as public relations officer of the Saint Paul & Pacific, see Lars Ljungmark, *For Sale—Minnesota: Organized Promotion of Scandinavian Immigration, 1866–1873*, 88.

10. William Crooks, "The First Railroad in Minnesota."

11. Printed report of the chief engineer to the president of the Minnesota & Pacific, presented January 12, 1858, in J. J. Hill Library (HE.2791 G74).

12. About Matthew Fontaine Maury (1806–1873) and his scientific accomplishments, see Benjamin W. Labaree, William M. Fowler, Jr., Edward W. Sloan, John B. Hattendorf, Jeffrey J. Safford, and Andrew W. German, *America and the Sea: A Maritime History*, 332–34.

13. Irwin, *Pacific Railways and Nationalism*, 14–18.

14. August Derleth, *The Milwaukee Road: Its First Hundred Years*, 42.

15. For details of the contracts between Chamberlain and the Minnesota & Pacific, see Simeon P. Folsom, *Statement of the Inception of the Minnesota & Pacific*, J. J. Hill Library (HE.2791 G745).

16. Crooks, "First Railroad in Minnesota."

17. Folwell, "Five Million Loan," 203–04.

18. Saby, "Railroad Legislation," 51–52.

19. J. Edgar Thomson (d. 1874), native of Pennsylvania, made his career as engineer of railroads in the South until 1847, when he became chief engineer of the Pennsylvania Railroad. In 1852 he took over the presidency of the company and remained in that function until his death. He was considered one of the foremost railroad men in America in his time. James A. Ward, *J. Edgar Thomson: Master of the Pennsylvania*.

20. The story of the negotiations with Thomson can be found in Crooks, "First Railroad in Minnesota." Thomson was later personally interested in Minnesota railroads such as the Lake Superior & Mississippi River. In 1868 he came to

Minnesota with a large group of Eastern financiers. Ward, *Thomson,* 164–67.

21. John H. Randall, "The Beginning of Railroad Building in Minnesota," 217; Williams, *City of St. Paul,* 403. No Dayton & Cincinnati Railroad is listed in William D. Edson, *Railroad Names: A Directory of Common Carrier Railroads Operating in the United States, 1826–1982.*

22. Williams, *City of St. Paul,* 403–04.

23. In their meeting of July 25, 1864, the directors of the Saint Paul & Pacific Railroad decided to buy back 65,950 acres of land between St. Paul and St. Anthony from Drake for $84,000, mostly to be paid for in bonds. MHS, GN Records, Minutes of meetings of directors Saint Paul & Pacific Railroad (132.D10.8F).

24. John C. Luecke, *The Great Northern in Minnesota: The Foundations of an Empire,* 4.

4: The Saint Paul & Pacific Railroad Company

1. George Loomis Becker (1829–1904), native of New York State, studied law at the University of Michigan and came to St. Paul in 1849. He later entered local politics and was state senator from 1868 to 1871. He died in St. Paul. Williams, *City of St. Paul,* 250–52; Upham and Dunlap, *Minnesota Biographies,* 43.

2. Saby, "Railroad Legislation," 54–55.

3. From *Saint Paul Daily Press* of May 23, 1863, and *Saint Paul Pioneer Press* of July 23, 1863, quoted in Luecke, *The Great Northern in Minnesota,* 5–6.

4. Randall, "Beginning of Railroad Building," 217, 219; Chaney, "Early Bridges," 137–38; *American Railroad Journal* (1868): 641.

5. MHS, GN Records, Miscellaneous financial records St. Paul office, 1862–1864, entry for June 30, 1862 (132.J12.6).

6. McClung, *Minnesota as it is,* 188.

7. Randall, "Beginning of Railroad Building," 217.

8. Details on the buildings along the St. Paul riverfront can be found in Folsom, *Statement.* Simeon P. Folsom was right-of-way agent of the Saint Paul & Pacific from 1862 to 1876 and as such was in a good position to know these facts.

9. Some of the corporate records were preserved somehow, possibly because they were lo-cated elsewhere at the time of the fire, but in its annual report to the Minnesota railroad commissioner for 1878, the company states that all statistics and books were lost. MHS, GN Records (132.D10.7B).

10. Williams, *City of St. Paul,* 428.

11. From *Saint Paul Daily Pioneer,* March 25, 1869, cited in Luecke, *The Great Northern in Minnesota,* 16.

12. There were at least four brothers Litchfield involved in the Saint Paul & Pacific business: Electus Backus Litchfield (1813–1889), the eldest brother, a New York railroad contractor; E. Darwin Litchfield, a banker and railroad promoter who operated from London; Edward (Edwin) C. Litchfield (d. 1885), a New York lawyer and railroad promoter; and Egbert S. Litchfield, a half-brother and the first partner of James J. Hill in St. Paul. Electus's son, William B. Litchfield, acted as general superintendent of the Saint Paul & Pacific in 1864 and was a director of the company in 1866. William's son, Electus D. Litchfield, was architect of the St. Paul Public Library and the J. J. Hill Reference Library in 1915–1917. It is probable that the firm of Danas & Litchfield, 18 William Street, New York, agents for American and foreign railroad iron, rolling stock, and supplies, had some connection to the same Litchfield family. They advertised regularly in the *American Railroad Journal* of 1869.

13. Minutes of board meeting of April 1, 1863. MHS, GN Records, Board minutes (132.D10.8F).

14. Williams, *City of St. Paul,* 404.

15. The official invitation to board the first train on the Branch line on January 18, 1864, signed by W. B. Litchfield, general superintendent, can be found in MHS, GN Records, Histories and related papers (132.D19.8F).

16. Figures from McClung, *Minnesota as it is.*

17. Randall, "Beginning of Railroad Building," 219–20. Partners in this construction firm were Andrew and Charles A. DeGraff and William Crooks. Andrew DeGraff, of old Dutch stock, was born in Amsterdam, New York, in 1811 and came to Minnesota in 1857, where he built many railroads. He died in St. Paul in 1894. His son Charles A. DeGraff was born in New York City in 1843 and came with his father to Minnesota and was engaged with him in the contracting business. He later farmed near Janesville and died in

St. Paul in 1887. Upham and Dunlap, *Minnesota Biographies,* 171.

18. Details taken from the *Report of the Board of Minnesota Railroad Commissioners,* 1875, in MHS.

19. MHS, GN Records, Voucher abstracts, 1868, Main line (132.J8.4).

20. MHS, GN Records, Purchase books, 1871–1880 (138.J16.6F–7B).

21. Dates of line openings are taken from Folsom, *Statement.*

22. Monthly construction estimates, Main line, May–October 1871, in MHS, GN Records (132.D11.1B). All figures given and signed by Charles W. Morris, by then chief engineer of the railroad.

23. McClung, *Minnesota as it is,* 233–34.

24. Xeroxed copy of the first time card of 1872 in MHS, GN Records, Histories and related papers (132.D19.8F). The original has not been found.

25. Contracts with Smith & Simmons, September 21, 1863; with Burbank, October 16, 1866; with Davidson, April 20, 1868. MHS, GN Records, Contracts 1862–1876 (132.D11.1B).

26. *Report of an instrumental survey for a railroad line of the Saint Paul & Pacific Railroad to the Missouri River and return,* made by James D. Skinner, C.E., May–July 1871, by order of Geo. L. Becker, in MHS, GN Records, Histories and related papers (132.D19.8F).

27. MHS, GN Records, Payrolls 1869–1871 (132.D11.2F).

28. Derleth, *Milwaukee Road,* 283.

29. About the Sioux War, see Oehler, *The Great Sioux Uprising;* also Folwell, *History of Minnesota,* 2:109–264.

30. Ann Regan, "The Irish," 136.

5: Finances

1. Even in 1890 this same amount of old 8 percent Saint Paul & Pacific bonds was still outstanding, according to an undated (1891) brochure named *Laws Constituting the Charter of the Saint Paul, Minneapolis & Manitoba Railway Company and Record of its Organization,* found in the J. W. Barriger Library in St. Louis. A survey of all loans issued by the Saint Paul & Pacific may be found in *Saint Paul, Minneapolis & Manitoba Railway Cy. Records and Indentures* of 1886.

2. Russell Sage (1816–1906) was a congressman and railroad financier, later close friend and collaborator of Jay Gould. Paul Sarnoff, *Russell Sage: The Money King.* Samuel J. Tilden (1814–1886) was a New York lawyer, specializing in railroad matters, and politician. He was Governor of New York 1874–1876, and in 1876 the unsuccessful candidate for the Democratic Party in the hotly contested and much disputed presidential elections. *Dictionary of American Biography* (London and New York: Oxford University Press, Charles Scribner's Sons, 1936), 18: 537–41.

3. Sarnoff, *Russell Sage,* 94–98; Derleth, *Milwaukee Road,* 84.

4. Gustavus Myers, *History of the Great American Fortunes,* 3:11–62.

5. Sarnoff, *Russell Sage,* 124.

6. Baker, "History of Transportation," 26.

7. Adler, *British Investment,* 147. For a general survey of Dutch financial interest in American railroads, see Veenendaal, *Slow Train to Paradise,* in which chapter 12 deals with the Saint Paul & Pacific, and Appendixes A and B list the different securities held in Holland.

8. Saby, "Railroad Legislation," 55–56.

9. Charles E. Russell, *Stories of the Great Railroads,* 16–17.

10. Saby, "Railroad Legislation," 56. Details of the incorporation of the new First Division Company in *Saint Paul, Minneapolis & Manitoba Railway Cy. Records and Indentures,* 99–110.

11. For all Saint Paul & Pacific loans, see Veenendaal, *Slow Train to Paradise,* ch. 12.

12. MHS, GN Records, Branch line vouchers, March 2, 1868 (132.D10.9B).

13. Quoted from McClung, *Minnesota as it is,* 251.

14. Stewart H. Holbrook, *James Hill: A Great Life in Brief,* 43.

15. Adler, *British Investment,* 205, gives 74 percent of par as first price in London, but there is no indication at all that Benson actually sold the St. Vincent Extension bonds in England.

16. Lippmann, Rosenthal, & Company never made their commission public, but the figure of 10 percent was mentioned in the contemporary newspapers.

17. Martinus Cohen Stuart, *Zes maanden in Amerika,* 289–90.

18. *Report of Railroad Commissioners,* for the

year ending August 31, 1874, lxx–lxxi.

19. Early issues of the *American Railroad Journal*, J. J. Hill Library, St. Paul.

20. For a history of the Northern Pacific Railroad, see Louis T. Renz, *The History of the Northern Pacific Railroad*, and Eugene V. Smalley, *History of the Northern Pacific Railroad*.

21. Smalley, *Northern Pacific*, 148–49.

22. Ibid., 296–99.

6: Dutch Interests in Minnesota

1. For early Dutch-American financial and commercial relations, see Van Winter, *Het aandeel*. For foreign (including Dutch) investment in America, see Wilkins, *Foreign Investment*. For Dutch investment in American railroads, see Veenendaal, *Slow Train to Paradise*. For the Holland Land Company, see Paul D. Evans, *The Holland Land Company*, and Augustus J. Veenendaal, Jr., "'Dutch' Towns in the United States."

2. Evans, *The Holland Land Company*.

3. Veenendaal, *Slow Train to Paradise*, 171.

4. About Dutch investment funds in general, see W. H. Berghuis, *Ontstaan en ontwikkeling van de Nederlandse beleggingsfondsen tot 1914*. For the Dutch investment funds specializing in American railroad securities, see Veenendaal, *Slow Train to Paradise*, 155–63.

5. About the character of the Dutch investing public, see Veenendaal, "An Example of 'Other People's Money,'" esp. 151–52, 157.

6. W. v. O. B., *Nieuwe finantieele beschouwingen: een handleiding bij geldbelegging in fondsen bij den aanvang van het jaar 1869*, 28.

7. Muriel E. Hidy, "A Dutch Investor in Minnesota, 1866: The Diary of Claude August Crommelin." About H. J. de Marez Oyens (1843–1911), see Veenendaal, *Slow Train to Paradise*, 75–76. Crommelin died young, but de Marez Oyens had a long and distinguished career in Dutch American railroad finance.

8. J. H. Kloos's first book (in Dutch) was *Minnesota in zijne hulpbronnen, vruchtbaarheid en ontwikkeling geschetst voor landverhuizers en kapitalisten* of 1867. Next came his *Report Relative to the Resources, Population and Products of the Country along the Brainerd and St. Vincent Extensions of the Saint Paul & Pacific Railroad*, prepared for the company at the express wish of President Becker and published in 1871. In the same year he also

published in German "Geologische Notizen aus Minnesota."

9. J. Knuppe, *Land en dollars in Minnesota en de Dakota's: Inlichtingen voor landverhuizers*.

10. J. J. Pas, *Benton county in den staat Minnesota, als geschikte plaats voor eene kolonie van Nederlandsche landbouwers*. About Dutch emigration to the United States in general, see Van Hinte, *Netherlanders in America*, and Lucas, *Dutch Immigrant Memoirs*.

11. The Dutch name of the association was Vereeniging tot ondersteuning der emigratie van minvermogenden naar den Noordamerikaanschen Staat Minnesota, or the Association for support of the emigration of the indigent to Minnesota.

12. The full title was *Landverhuizer. Maandblad ter bevordering der emigratie naar den Noord-Amerikaanschen Staat Minnesota* (The Emigrant: Monthly for the propagation of emigration to Minnesota).

13. S. R. J. van Schevichaven, *De Noord-Amerikaansche staat Minnesota*, published in 1872.

14. Williams, *City of St. Paul*, 468.

15. Martinus Cohen Stuart, *Zes maanden in Amerika*, 281–84.

7: Traffic and Operations

1. "Articles of agreement made and entered into this sixth day of February 1866 by and between the First Division of the Saint Paul & Pacific RR and J. J. Hill of St. Paul, MN," for the lease of part of the railroad land between the Mississippi River and the railroad tracks for building a transfer shed. The other contract for the handling of freight at St. Paul was signed January 15, 1867. Both in J. J. Hill Papers, GC, box 3.

2. MHS, GN Records, Station records, 1863–1879 (138.J16.8F–1B).

3. All figures taken from *Report of Railroad Commissioners*, 1872–1873, 37–64.

4. The figures for business between Minneapolis and St. Paul, easily the most important for passengers, was prorated each month.

5. J. H. Beadle, *The Undeveloped West: Or, Five Years in the Territories*, 717–18.

6. Folwell, *History of Minnesota*, 3:93–111.

7. Kane, *Waterfall*, 102–03.

8. Luecke, *The Great Northern in Minnesota*, 13.

9. MHS, GN Records, Purchase books,

1871–1880 (138.J16.6F–7B).

10. MHS, GN Records, Contracts, 1862–1876 (132.D11.1B).

11. Memorandum of contract with North Chicago Rolling Mill Company, December 19, 1878, and March 14, 1879, in J. J. Hill Papers, GC, box 11, F19.

12. Figures are taken from consecutive volumes of Henry V. Poor, *Manual of the Railroads of the United States* (hereafter quoted as *Poor's Manual*).

13. *Poor's Manual, 1874–1875*, 671, gives twenty locomotives for the Main line plus eight for the Branch, which is clearly too high. In his next issue for 1875–1876, Poor gives the correct numbers, seventeen for the Main line and six for the Branch.

14. MHS, GN Records, Equipment history records (138.J13.8F).

15. For construction details of the current freight cars, see John H. White, Jr., *The American Railroad Freight Car from the Wood-Car Era to the Coming of Steel*, especially 192–242.

16. All purchases for whatever purpose were split between the Branch and Main lines, although this does not necessarily mean that an item was used on only one line. Cars must have been switched around as necessary, but for accounting purposes the division between Branch and Main lines was retained to the end. MHS, GN Records, Purchase books, 1871–1880 (138.J16.6F–7B).

17. John H. White, Jr., *The American Railroad Passenger Car*, 2:648, 654.

18. From the *Saint Paul Daily Pioneer*, November 7, 1866, as quoted in Luecke, *The Great Northern in Minnesota*, 175.

19. White, *American Railroad Passenger Car*, 2:651–52, 654, 206.

20. Talbott and Hobart, *Biographical Directory*, 30.

21. Liston E. Leyendecker, *Palace Car Prince: A Biography of George Mortimer Pullman*, 81.

22. [Henry D. Minot], *The Saint Paul, Minneapolis & Manitoba Railway Company as an Investment Property*.

23. Luecke, *The Great Northern in Minnesota*, 181.

24. The Baker system used brine instead of water to prevent freezing of the piping when not in use. For more particulars of the car-heating systems of the times, see White, *American Railroad Passenger Car*, 2:379–91.

25. For the several lighting systems in use, see White, *American Railroad Passenger Car*, 2:413–22.

26. Charles F. Adams, Jr., *Notes on Railroad Accidents*, 51–53. For the technical details of the Miller system, see White, *American Railroad Passenger Car*, 2:563–66.

27. Augustus J. Veenendaal, Jr., *De IJzeren Weg in een land vol water: beknopte geschiedenis van de spoorwegen in Nederland, 1834–1958*, 51. In 1883 the Dutch government made the air brake mandatory for all passenger trains running faster than sixty kilometers per hour. For details on the development of train brakes, see White, *American Railroad Passenger Car*, 2:544–57.

28. MHS, GN Records, Payroll 1877 (132.D11.2F).

29. Henrietta M. Larson, *The Wheat Market and the Farmer in Minnesota, 1858–1900*, 123.

30. Ibid., 80.

31. Ibid., 89–91, 143.

32. John F. Stover, *American Railroads*, 127–30; Eliot Jones, *Principles of Railway Transportation*, 186–91; Alfred D. Chandler, Jr., *The Railroads: The Nation's First Big Business*, 188–89.

33. Saby, "Railroad Legislation," 153.

34. Alonzo Jay Edgerton was born in Rome, New York, in 1827 and came to Minnesota in 1855. He served in the Civil War and reached the rank of brigadier general before being demobilized. He was Minnesota state senator in 1859 and 1877–1878. Upham and Dunlap, *Minnesota Biographies*, 200.

35. MHS, GN Records, Branch line vouchers (132.D10.9B), and Purchase books, 1871–1880 (138.J16.6F–7B).

36. Irwin, *Pacific Railways and Nationalism*, 115.

37. Correspondence between Trott and Becker, dated 1864 and later, in MHS, GN Records, Land Department circulars 1863–1879 (132.D19.10F).

38. Copies of these brochures are in the John W. Barriger Library in St. Louis and in MHS, GN Records, Land Department circulars.

39. Ljungmark, *For Sale—Minnesota*, 74.

40. Hans Mattson (1832–1893) was born in Sweden, emigrated to the United States in 1851, and arrived in Minnesota in 1853. During the Civil War he was colonel of the Third Minnesota Infantry and afterward state immigration agent in Chicago and editor of the *Svenska*

Amerikanaren there, and in 1867 and again in 1870 he was secretary of the Minnesota State Board of Immigration. After his stay with the Saint Paul & Pacific his career included a stint as U.S. consul at Calcutta, two terms as secretary of state of Minnesota, and a directorship of the Dutch-owned Maxwell Land Grant Company of New Mexico. Ljungmark, *For Sale—Minnesota*, 267–68.

41. John G. Rice, "The Swedes," 258; Ljungmark, *For Sale—Minnesota*, 87–131.

42. About John Ireland's immigration schemes, see James P. Shannon, *Catholic Colonization on the Western Frontier*, 44–88, and Regan, "The Irish," 138.

43. Details from several editions of the railroad's *Guide to the Lands of the First Division of the Saint Paul and Pacific Railroad Company*.

44. Shannon, *Catholic Colonization*, 96–98, 199–204.

45. Figures from *Poor's Manual, 1871–1872*, 482.

46. Figures taken from *Poor's Manual, 1878*, 786–87.

47. Figures taken from *Poor's Manual, 1880*, 826–31.

8: Management and Staff

1. Chandler, *The Railroads*, 97–108. Daniel Craig McCallum (1815–1878) was general superintendent of the New York & Lake Erie Railroad from 1854 to 1857. He became director of the U.S. Military Railroads in 1862, brigadier in 1864, and major general in 1865. James A. Ward, "Daniel Craig McCallum." See also Walter Licht, *Working for the Railroad: The Organization of Work in the Nineteenth Century*, 15–16.

2. Upham and Dunlap, *Minnesota Biographies*, 172. Edmund Quincy Sewall was born in 1828 in Newburyport, Massachusetts, and served as engineer on many railroads. Before he came to St. Paul he was general superintendent of the New Orleans, Jackson & Great Northern. After his years on the Saint Paul & Pacific he served as treasurer and superintendent of the Saint Paul & Duluth before moving to the Chicago, Milwaukee & Saint Paul as comptroller. Talbott and Hobart, *Biographical Directory*, 217.

3. Justus B. Rice was born in Woodstock, Vermont, in 1833 and was probably related to Edmund Rice, also born in the same area. "Jud" Rice

was a passenger conductor on the Michigan Central before coming to St. Paul in 1856. From 1868 to 1880 he was the assistant superintendent of the Saint Paul & Pacific. In 1880 he became superintendent of the Saint Cloud & Fergus Falls Division of the Saint Paul, Minneapolis & Manitoba. Upham and Dunlap, *Minnesota Biographies*, 638; Talbott and Hobart, *Biographical Directory*, 202.

4. Jesse P. Farley was born in Tennessee in 1813 and moved to Dubuque, Iowa, and into the railroad business. He died in Dubuque in 1894. Upham and Dunlap, *Minnesota Biographies*, 216.

5. William H. Fisher was born in New Jersey in 1844, was from early on involved in the railroad business, and came to St. Paul in 1873. He was later president and general manager of the Saint Paul & Duluth Railroad. Upham and Dunlap, *Minnesota Biographies*, 224.

6. E. B. Wakeman was appointed general superintendent of the Saint Paul, Minneapolis & Manitoba and ended his career as general superintendent of the Great Northern Railway.

7. Charles A. F. Morris was born in Ireland in 1827 and emigrated to America in 1849. In 1854 he came to St. Paul and served first in the Saint Paul & Pacific, then later as engineer for the Northern Pacific. He died in Excelsior, Minnesota, in 1903. Upham and Dunlap, *Minnesota Biographies*, 317. Charles C. Smith served on the Lake Shore & Michigan Southern and the Indianapolis, Bloomington & Western Railroads before returning to St. Paul in 1881. Talbott and Hobart, *Biographical Directory*, 223.

8. John H. Randall was born in Ithaca, New York, in 1829, moved to Winona, Minnesota, in 1859, and later settled in St. Paul. He served as ticket agent of the Saint Paul & Pacific until becoming railroad commissioner in 1875. He died in St. Paul in 1891. Upham and Dunlap, *Minnesota Biographies*, 626.

9. Walter S. Alexander was born in Burlington, New York, in 1838 and moved to St. Paul in the 1860s. He was freight agent of the Saint Paul & Pacific and the Saint Paul, Minneapolis & Manitoba for many years after 1878 and was president of the Eastern Minnesota Railway in 1890. Upham and Dunlap, *Minnesota Biographies*, 8.

10. A. L. Mohler began his railroad career in 1869 on the Chicago and North Western. He moved to the Rockford, Rock Island & Saint Louis and later to the Burlington, Cedar Rapids & West-

ern before joining the Manitoba road. Talbott and Hobart, *Biographical Directory,* 167.

11. Hermann Trott was born in Hanover, Germany, in 1830, got a degree in engineering there, and came to Minnesota in 1856, settling in St. Paul in 1858. He was land commissioner of the Saint Paul & Pacific until 1879 and afterward served the Northern Pacific in the same capacity. He died in St. Paul in 1903. Upham and Dunlap, *Minnesota Biographies.* 794.

12. Veenendaal, *Slow Train to Paradise,* 132.

13. Knuppe, *Land en dollars.*

14. MHS, GN Records, Payrolls, 1869–1871, 1876–1877 (132.D11.2F).

15. Harvey Middleton, born in Philadelphia in 1852, worked for the Philadelphia & Erie and the Louisville & Nashville, before being appointed master mechanic of the Saint Paul, Minneapolis & Manitoba in February 1882. Talbott and Hobart, *Biographical Directory,* 164.

16. MHS, GN Records, Personnel records, Mechanical engineering department, 1873–1877 (132.D11.1B).

17. Ibid.

18. Ducker, *Men of the Steel Rails,* 59–63.

19. Survey of wages paid in the railroad industry in Licht, *Working for the Railroad,* 126 (average daily wages of railroad labor compared to nonrailroad, 128).

20. McClung, *Minnesota as it is,* 188.

21. MHS, GN Records, Personnel.

22. Licht, *Working for the Railroad,* 126 (machinists' wages elsewhere), 166.

23. Ducker, *Men of the Steel Rails,* 57–59.

24. Shelton Stromquist, *A Generation of Boomers: The Pattern of Railroad Labor Conflict in Nineteenth-Century America;* H. Roger Grant, *Brownie the Boomer: The Life of Charles P. Brown, an American Railroader;* Licht, *Working for the Railroad,* 74–76.

25. Talbott and Hobart, *Biographical Directory,* 26.

26. Ibid., 98 (Guthrie), 124 (Jenks).

27. Luecke, *The Great Northern in Minnesota,* 181.

28. Regan, "The Irish," 136.

29. Licht, *Working for the Railroad,* 49–50.

30. H. Roger Grant, *Living in the Depot: The Two-Story Railroad Station,* especially 16–17.

31. Licht, *Working for the Railroad,* 44.

32. Chandler, *The Railroads,* 136–37; Stromquist, *A Generation of Boomers,* 175–77;

Robert V. Bruce, *1877: Year of Violence,* 221–25, 283–84.

33. Licht, *Working for the Railroad,* 175–79, 207–13.

34. Ibid., 35. In 1880, 354 railroad companies (52 percent) employed less than one hundred workers; 185 companies (27 percent) had between one hundred and five hundred employees; 60 railroads (9 percent) had between five hundred and one thousand; and 84 firms (12 percent) employed more than one thousand.

9: Accidents

1. The printed *Annual Reports of the Minnesota Railroad Commissioner* are an excellent source for accidents and can be found through the Minnesota Historical Society. The fiscal year ended June 30. Cited hereafter as *Report RR Commissioner* with the year.

2. *Report RR Commissioner, 1875–1876,* 139.

3. Beadle, *The Undeveloped West,* 724.

4. *Report RR Commissioner* for the year ending August 31, 1872, 24.

5. Thomas Prosser & Son, New York, were the sole importers of Krupp steel wheels, tires, springs, boilerplates, and such. *American Railroad Journal,* 1869.

6. Veenendaal, *Slow Train to Paradise,* 132.

7. *St. Paul Pioneer Press,* July 23, 1863, as quoted in Luecke, *The Great Northern in Minnesota,* 5.

8. MHS, GN Records, Branch line vouchers (132.D10.9B).

9. *Report RR Commissioner, 1871–1872,* 156.

10. Robert L. Frey, ed., *Railroads in the Nineteenth Century,* 76–78.

11. *Report RR Commissioner, 1872–1873,* 43.

12. MHS, GN Records, Annual reports to railroad commissioner, 1875–1879 (132.D10.7B).

13. MHS, GN Records, Purchase books, 1871–1880 (138.J16.6F–7B).

14. *Report RR Commissioner, 1871–1872,* 156.

15. *Report RR Commissioner, 1877–1878,* 61.

16. MHS, GN Records, Annual reports to railroad commissioner, 1875–1879 (132.D10.7B).

17. Williams, *City of St. Paul,* 452; MHS, GN Records, Purchase books 1871–1880 (138.J16.6F–7B).

18. MHS, GN Records, Annual reports to railroad commissioner, 1875–1879 (132.D10.7B).

19. Ibid.

20. James J. Hill, General correspondence, Box 11, F13.

21. James J. Hill, Diaries (transcripts), J. J. Hill Library.

10: Locomotives

1. MHS, GN Records, Equipment history records from 1880 (138.J13.8F).

2. George B. Abdill, *Rails West,* 10; Folsom, *Statement.*

3. Norman C. Keyes and Kenneth R. Middleton, "The Great Northern Railway Company: All-Time Locomotive Roster, 1861–1970," 40. Folsom, *Statement,* gives 56-inch diameter for the drivers.

4. John H. White, Jr., *American Locomotives: An Engineering History, 1830–1880,* 75, 358–59; Luecke, *The Great Northern in Minnesota,* 21.

5. The Smith & Jackson works number of the *Wm. Crooks* is not known.

6. White, *American Locomotives,* 358; John H. White, Jr., *A Short History of American Locomotive Builders in the Steam Era,* 69

7. A reproduction of this photograph may be found in Abdill, *Rails West,* 10.

8. A photograph of the preserved engine may be seen in Reed Kinert, *Early American Steam Locomotives: The First Seven Decades, 1830–1900,* 92.

9. White, *American Locomotives,* 83–90; Hill to Burnham, Parry, Williams & Company, October 15, 1879, in Hill Papers, Letterpress books, RR series, vol. R1 (quotation).

10. Keyes and Middleton, "Great Northern . . . Locomotive Roster," 41.

11. Folsom, *Statement.*

12. White, *American Locomotive Builders,* 73.

13. MHS, GN Records, Voucher abstracts 1868 (132.J8.4).

14. MHS, GN Records, Equipment history records (138.J13.8F); *Poor's Manual, 1869–1870,* 369.

15. Edson, *Railroad Names,* 41; White, *American Locomotive Builders,* 93.

16. MHS, GN Records, Equipment history records (138.J13.8F).

17. White, *American Locomotive Builders,* 38.

18. Ibid., 63.

19. MHS, GN Records, Branch line vouchers, 1864–1867 (132.D10.9B).

20. MHS, GN Records, Equipment history records (138.J13.8F).

21. Ibid.

22. White, *American Locomotive Builders,* 75.

23. John K. Brown, *Baldwin Locomotive Works, 1831–1915,* 97.

24. MHS, GN Records, Equipment history records (138.J13.8F).

25. *Poor's Manual, 1871–1872* gives sixteen locomotives, which is clearly too low. The issue for 1872–1873 gives a total of twenty-one, and the one for 1873–1874 has a total of thirty, a figure that includes the (leased) engines for the Melrose/St. Vincent extension. New locomotives of the Saint Paul & Pacific were only to arrive on the premises in 1875.

26. MHS, GN Records, Equipment history records (138.J13.8F).

27. White, *American Locomotive Builders,* 87. Entries for July 23, August 12, October 2, 1878, in the purchase books of the Saint Paul & Pacific in the Great Northern records in the MHS give a driving-wheel diameter of 57 $^5/_8$ inches for numbers 35, 37, 39.

28. MHS, GN Records, Equipment history records (138.J13.8F).

29. Hill to Burnham, Parry, Williams & Company, September 10, October 15, 1879. Hill Papers, Letterpress books, RR series, vol. R1.

30. The switcher was offered to Farley in a letter from Brooks of May 5, 1879, as being in stock and ready for shipment. Hill Papers, GC, box 41.

31. White, *American Locomotives,* 23.

32. Hudson Paper Car Wheel Company to J. J. Hill, October 15, 1879, in Hill Papers, GC, box 41 (quotation); White, *American Railroad Passenger Car,* 2:534–38.

33. White, *American Locomotives,* 25.

34. Data on the staff and workforce of the Saint Paul & Pacific are to be found in MHS, Great Northern records: for shop employees, engineers, and firemen, see Personnel records (132.D11.1B), and for the whole workforce, see Payrolls 1869–1871, 1876–1877, 1878–1879 (132.D11.2F, 3B, 4F).

35. Brown, *Baldwin Locomotive Works,* 68, 77.

36. MHS, GN Records, Branch line vouchers 1864–1867 (132.D10.9B). These only cover the Branch line, not the expenses charged to the Main line, then still under construction.

37. Hill to Niles Tool Works, July 29, 1879, in

Hill Papers, Letterpress books, RR series, vol. R1.

38. White, *American Locomotives,* 95–96.

39. Ibid., 184.

40. Annual reports to the railroad commissioner of Minnesota, 1874–1879, in MHS, GN Records (132.D10.7B).

11: Default and Reorganization

1. Senate Papers, 43d Congress, April 1874, in J. W. Barriger Library, St. Louis.

2. Information obtained from the Municipal Archives of Utrecht. From 1895 he was the first partner in the Utrecht sugar factory, then named Carp & Company, but apparently he did little actual work there, as from 1879 he was living in The Hague, the Dutch center of government, and without any stated profession, probably as a man of independent means. The sugar business was closed down in 1907.

3. Many details have been taken from the so-called *Farley Suit Transcripts,* the printed court records of the subsequent suit of Farley versus Hill and Associates. A copy of these transcripts is available in the J. J. Hill Library (HE.2791 G79 F3). No records of the Dutch protective committee itself have been found in the archives of the Amsterdam Stock Exchange.

4. Lippman, Rosenthal to Kennedy, July 31, 1873, signed by J. Premsela and George Rosenthal (original in French, an English translation scribbled underneath), MHS, GN Records, New York office files (132.D10.5B).

5. For Kennedy's career, see Saul Engelbourg and Leonard Bushkoff, *The Man Who Found the Money: John Stewart Kennedy and the Financing of Western Railroads;* for Barnes, ibid., 16; for Benson, 45–46.

6. The railroad bridge across the Mississippi at St. Cloud was opened for traffic in June 1872.

7. Folwell, *History of Minnesota,* 3:448; Petition to the Honorable Members of the Senate and House of Representatives, in MHS, GN Records, Printed legal documents, 1871–1880 (132.D11.1B).

8. Kloos to Kennedy, February 9, 1874, in MHS, GN Records, New York office files, folder 14 (132.D10.5B).

9. Upham and Dunlap, *Minnesota Geographic Names,* 272, calls him a native of Belgium, which is not impossible, as part of Luxembourg forms a province of Belgium. His son, Paul Willmar, is reported to have fought for Emperor Maximilian of Mexico, whose wife was a Belgian princess. Later Paul farmed near the town of Willmar and returned to Belgium in 1881.

10. Testimony of George Stephen, *Farley Suit Transcripts,* 1279.

11. Veenendaal, *Slow Train to Paradise,* 134.

12. *Poor's Manual, 1876–1877,* 551.

13. Beadle, *The Undeveloped West,* 727.

14. Folwell, *History of Minnesota,* 3:447.

15. *Report RR Commissioner* for the year ending June 30, 1875.

16. See, for instance, *The Anti-Monopolist,* St. Paul, October 4, 1877, which contains the Greenback Cathechism (quoted from Blegen and Jordan, *With Various Voices,* 321–24). This cathechism was a long list of complaints and wishes of the so-called Greenback Party, which in the 1860s and 1870s was in favor of "easy" money—the issuance of paper dollars or greenbacks—which would possibly cause inflation, which in turn could help debtors among agrarians and artisans, the core of the constituency of the party. They objected to the partial resumption of specie payment by the U.S. government in 1875, and were successful three years later when further cancellation of greenbacks was stopped.

17. Folwell, *History of Minnesota,* 3:449. A printed pamphlet containing Delano's remarks concerning "A bill declaring all the lands, property, privileges, rights and franchises pertaining to the uncompleted parts of the lines of the Saint Paul & Pacific Railroad Company forfeited to the State of Minnesota" is to be found in the Hill Papers, Special file no. 1, Early railroad papers.

18. Deposition of Johan Carp, *Farley Suit Transcripts,* 469 (accusations against Delano's monopoly, 480); Folwell, *History of Minnesota,* 3:449 (quotation).

19. Deposition of Kennedy, *Farley Suit Transcripts,* February 3, 1875 (emphasis in original), quoted in Engelbourg and Bushkoff, *The Man Who Found the Money,* 48–49.

20. *Report RR Commissioner* for the year ending June 30, 1876, 2.

21. Folwell, *History of Minnesota,* 3:450.

22. About Dulman, see Veenendaal, *Slow Train to Paradise,* 100–101.

23. A copy of the official notice of trustees,

October 9, 1876, signed by them and by all officers and station agents of the First Division of the Saint Paul & Pacific Company is to be found in Hill Papers, GC, box 6, F11.

24. Deposition of Johan Carp, in *Farley Suit Transcripts,* 438.

25. Ibid., 491.

26. Ibid., 496–503.

27. Carp's original Dutch report has not been found in the archives of the Amsterdam Stock Exchange, but an English translation is in MHS, GN Records (132.D11.1B).

28. Carp's plan, dated April 1877, is in *Farley Suit Transcripts,* 505–28. The original has not been found.

12: The Sale of the Saint Paul & Pacific Railroad

1. About James J. Hill many books have been written. Albro Martin, *James J. Hill and the Opening of the Northwest,* and Michael P. Malone, *James J. Hill: Empire Builder of the Northwest,* are the most recent. Joseph G. Pyle, *The Life of James J. Hill,* is still useful for printing a lot of documents and figures, but more laudatory than factual.

2. Articles of agreement between Egbert S. Litchfield and J. J. Hill, September 16, 1867, about setting up of transportation business, and Memorandum of agreement between J. J. Hill & Company and the Saint Paul & Pacific Railroad Company about transfer of freight at the St. Paul depot, September 16, 1867, both in Hill Papers, GC, box 3, F.

3. Articles of incorporation of the Northwestern Fuel Company in Hill Papers, GC, box 7, F12.

4. Clarence W. Rife, "Norman W. Kittson: A Fur Trader at Pembina"; Engelbourg and Bushkoff, *The Man Who Found the Money,* 56–57.

5. Smith later had a most distinguished career in the Canadian government service and Canadian Pacific Railway. As a reward for his services, he was raised to the British peerage as Lord Strathcona and Mount Royal. He died in 1914. Beckles Willson, *The Life of Lord Strathcona and Mount Royal.*

6. Ibid., 1:368.

7. Heather Gilbert, *Awakening Continent: The Life of Lord Mount Stephen.*

8. Ibid., 1:39–40; Willson, *Lord Strathcona,* 2:62–63. About the way Hill enlisted Canadian

help, see Dolores Greenberg, "A Study of Capital Alliances: The St. Paul & Pacific," and W. Kaye Lamb, *History of the Canadian Pacific Railway,* 54–63.

9. Deposition by J. J. Hill in *Farley Suit Transcripts,* 25.

10. MHS, GN Records, Purchase books, 1871–1880 (138.J16.6F–7B); Knuppe, *Land en dollars,* 36. Hill to Klein (then living at 110 Cannon Street, London) on May 12, 1877: "best love to Mrs. Klein and the children." Hill Papers, Letterpress books, Personal and private papers, vol. 1.

11. Deposition of J. J. Hill, *Farley Suit Transcripts,* 761.

12. A. W. De Klerck's book is titled *De verarming van Nederland met betrekking tot den aanvoer van Amerikaansche spoorwegaandeelen* and was published in 1886. For more about him, see Veenendaal, *Slow Train to Paradise,* 48.

13. In the Hill Papers, GC, box 10, F20, there is a postcard written from Amsterdam by A. W. De Klerck to F. R. Delano on February 19, 1878, with the following text: "Dear Sir, The partners of the Canadian combination are Geo. Stephen, pres. Bank of Montreal, dir. Hudson Bay Co.; Donald A. Smith, dir. Hudson Bay Co.; N. W. Kittson, pres. Red River Steam Nav. Co., gen. agent Hudson Bay Co.; James J. Hill, dir. Red River Steam Nav. Co. Be so kind and communicate this with Mr. Trott, if he does not know it." What De Klerck thought to accomplish with this information is not clear, as everybody in St. Paul must have known these facts by then. For Hill's opinion of De Klerck, see his testimony in *Farley Suit Transcripts,* 573.

14. The letter from Hill and Kittson to Carp that contains the official proposal, dated St. Paul, May 26, 1877, gives all the different prices offered for the bonds of the Dutch protective committee. Hill Papers, GC, box 7, F14.

15. On the firm of Morton, Rose & Company, see Dolores Greenberg, *Financiers and Railroads, 1869–1889: A Study of Morton, Bliss & Company,* 148–57. Also Gilbert, *Awakening Continent,* 1:40–42.

16. Carp to Barnes, Utrecht, October 13, 1877, in MHS, GN Records, New York office files (132.D10.6F).

17. MHS, GN Records, Purchase books 1871–1880 (138.J16.6F–7B), and *Poor's Manual, 1879,* 794.

18. Talbott and Hobart, *Biographical Directory,*

268; Veenendaal, *Slow Train to Paradise,* 86, 136.

19. Dutch sources quoted in Veenendaal, *Slow Train to Paradise,* 135–36.

20. Engelbourg and Bushkoff, *The Man Who Found the Money,* 60–61.

21. Testimony of John S. Kennedy, in *Farley Suit Transcripts,* 1050.

22. Hill to Kennedy, January 26, 1878, and undated note by Hill, in Hill Papers, GC, box 10, F18–19. Also Hill to Kittson, February 13, 1878, in Letterpress books, Personal and private papers, vol. 1.

23. Hill to Stephen, February 23, 1878, in Hill Papers, Letterpress books, Personal and private papers, vol. 1.

24. A signed copy of the contract is in Hill Papers, GC, box 10, F22.

25. Greenberg, *Financiers and Railroads,* 156; James J. Hill, *Highways of Progress,* 148; J. Pik, *De Amerikaansche spoorwegwaarden: bijdrage tot de kennis der te Amsterdam verhandelde fondsen,* 146.

26. Pik, *De Amerikaansche spoorwegwaarden,* 146, 151.

27. "Memorandum of distribution of bonds of the $8,000,000 issue of the Saint Paul, Minneapolis & Manitoba Ry. Co.," December 15, 1879, with calculations by Hill himself, in Hill Papers, GC, box 12; Financial statement written by Hill, circa April 1, 1878, in ibid., box 10, F21.

28. Testimony of Hill and Upham, in *Farley Suit Transcripts,* 573, 1069.

29. Testimony of Hill, in *Farley Suit Transcripts,* 30.

30. Hagbarth Sahlgaard was born in Kongsberg, Norway, in 1844 and died in St. Paul 1892. He had been living in St. Paul since 1866. Upham and Dunlap, *Minnesota Biographies,* 665.

31. Copy of the Dutch financial weekly *De Nieuwe Financier en Kapitalist* of Sunday, August 1, 1880, with the outcome of the Sahlgaard suit, in Hill Papers, GC, box 12, F13.

32. Stephen to Hill, Montreal, July 10, 1878, in ibid., box 11, F1. Only a small number of bonds were still held in Holland by parties outside the protective committee.

33. Text of the agreement in Pyle, *Life of James J. Hill,* vol. 1, appendix V.B. See also Gilbert, *Awakening Continent,* 1:44–45, and Engelbourg and Bushkoff, *The Man Who Found the Money,* 71–73.

34. The rhyme about James Hill later coined by disappointed Montana homesteaders must not have applied to the Dutch: "Twixt Hell and Hill there's just one letter: / Were Hill in Hell, we'd feel much better." Quoted from Jonathan Raban, *Bad Land: An American Romance,* 255.

35. Gilbert, *Awakening Continent,* 46–49.

36. Smalley, *History of the Northern Pacific Railroad,* 296–99; *Annual Reports to the Stockholders of the Northern Pacific,* for 1877, 6–7, and for 1879, 17–18.

37. Stephen to Hill, Montreal, September 25, 1878, Hill Papers, GC, box 11, F8.

38. Stephen to Edwin C. Litchfield, October 8, 1878 (copy), ibid., F9.

39. Stephen to Hill, New York, October 17, 1878, ibid, F11.

40. Hill to Stephen, St. Paul, December 26, 1878, ibid., F13.

41. Copy of the agreement between the associates, Edwin C. Litchfield, and E. Darwin Litchfield for $500,000, ibid., F18.

42. Memorial of DeGraff & Company to the legislature of Minnesota, February 25, 1878, in Hill Papers, Special file no. 1, Miscellany Saint Paul & Pacific.

43. Copy of letter from R. L. Ashhurst to J. C. Pullitt, Philadelphia, March 1, 1878, in Hill Papers, GC, box 10, F21.

13: The Saint Paul, Minneapolis & Manitoba Railroad

1. Folwell, *History of Minnesota,* 3:462; James J. Hill, "My Story of the Great Northern," in Blegen and Jordan, *With Various Voices,* 177–80.

2. For stocks, see Brooks Adams, *Railways as Public Agents: A Study in Sovereignty. With an Historical Financial Analysis of the Great Northern Railway System,* 74–78. For loans, see J. D. Santilhano, *Amerikaansche spoorwegen: Overzicht van de in Nederland verhandeld wordende Amerikaansche Spoorwegfondsen,* 471.

3. Pik, *De Amerikaansche spoorwegwaarden,* 144; Veenendaal, *Slow Train to Paradise,* 137; Carp to Barnes, Utrecht, July 30, 1877, in Hill Papers, GC, box 7, F28.

4. Luecke, *The Great Northern in Minnesota,* 42.

5. Contract between Farley and Robbins, July 2, 1878, in Hill Papers, GC, box 11, F1. Hill to Haskell, Barker & Company, July 18, 1878, and

text of telegram from Hill to Kennedy, August 26, 1878, both in Hill Papers, Letterpress books, RR series, vol. R1.

6. Hill to Stephen, September 2, 8, 1878, in Hill Papers, GC, box 11, F5 (quotation). Text of telegram from Stephen to Kennedy, August 14, 1878, in Hill Papers, Letterpress books, Personal and private papers, vol. 1. For Kennedy, see Engelbourg and Bushkoff, *The Man Who Found the Money,* 50–51.

7. Walter K. V. Gale, *Iron and Steel,* 73; Brian Reed, *Crewe Locomotive Works and Its Men.*

8. James M. Swank, *History of the Manufacture of Iron in All Ages, and Particularly in the United States from Colonial Times to 1891,* 221, 410–13, 393.

9. Henry M. Flint, *The Railroads of the United States: Their History and Statistics,* 412–25. The total American production of steel rails had risen from a modest 2,550 tons in 1867 to almost a million tons in 1880. In the same year the production of iron rails was less than half, and it had almost completely ended by 1883. Swank, *Manufacture of Iron,* 415, 440.

10. Swank, *Manufacture of Iron,* 441; [Minot], *The Saint Paul, Minneapolis & Manitoba.*

11. Hill to Stephen, April 5, 1878, in Hill Papers, Letterpress books, Personal and private papers, vol. 1.

12. Hill to the Jackson & Woodin Manufacturing Company, Pennsylvania, December 26, 1878, in Hill Papers, Letterpress books, Personal and private papers, vol. 1. For Jackson & Woodin history, see White, *American Railroad Freight Car,* 141.

13. Patent applications and so on by Hill, in Hill Papers, GC, box 12, F4, F7; copy of Hutton's patent in box 11; Hill to Stephen, September 13, 1878, in box 11, F6; Stephen to Hill, Montreal, October 1, 1878, box 11, F7.

14. List of opening dates of the Branch line in *Report RR Commissioner* for the year ending June 30, 1879, 124.

15. Hill to Stephen, December 26, 1878, in Hill Papers, Letterpress books, Personal and private papers, vol. 1 (quotation); Hill to Stephen, June 30, 1879, in ibid., RR series, vol. R1.

16. Hill to Manvell, December 28, 1880, in Hill Papers, Letterpress books, Personal and private papers, vol. 1.

17. Hill to Jas. Upper, August 29, 1878, and Text of telegram, Hill to Stephen, December 4,

1878 (both in ibid.); Kerr, *Story of the Great Northern,* 12.

18. Willson, *Lord Strathcona,* 1:463; Harold A. Innis, *A History of the Canadian Pacific Railway,* 89. Agreement between the Dominion of Canada and the Saint Paul, Minneapolis & Manitoba about operation and rates of the Pembina branch (owned by the government of Canada and operated by the Canadian Pacific Railway), 1880, in Hill Papers, GC, box 12, F1.

19. Gibbon, *History of the Canadian Pacific,* 248–49; William J. Wilgus, *The Railway Interrelations of the United States and Canada,* 129.

20. Hill to Stephen, March 12, 1879, in Hill Papers, Letterbooks 1879, 255.

21. Hill to Stephen, March 19, April 12, 1879, in Hill Papers, Letterpress books, Personal and private papers, vol. 1.

22. Hill to Wheeler, November 23, 1880, and Hill to Manvell, March 15, 1881, ibid. Charles C. Wheeler served on many railroads and was assistant superintendent of the Chicago & North Western from 1880 to 1881. He was general manager of the Atchison, Topeka & Santa Fe from 1881 to 1883, before returning to the Chicago & North Western as general superintendent in 1883. Alan Manvell was born in 1837 and served the Chicago, Rock Island & Pacific from 1859 in several capacities. Talbott and Hobart, *Biographical Directory,* 158, 259.

23. For Manvel, see Keith L. Bryant, Jr., *History of the Atchison, Topeka & Santa Fe Railway,* 151. For Wakeman, see *Poor's Directory of Railway Officials, 1888,* 81.

24. Trott to Hill, April 12, 1879, in Hill Papers, GC, box 11, F21.

25. Talbott and Hobart, *Biographical Directory,* 164, 169, 223.

26. Story from *Springfield (Mass.) Weekly Republican,* September 23, 1880, reprinted in Blegen and Jordan, *With Various Voices,* 235.

27. Taylor and Neu, *American Railroad Network,* 38; *Report RR Commissioner* for the year ending June 30, 1879, 21. Participants in the Union Depot Company, apart from the Manitoba road, were the Chicago, Milwaukee & Saint Paul; the Northern Pacific; the Saint Paul & Duluth; the Saint Paul & Sioux City; the Chicago, Saint Paul & Minneapolis (that is, West Wisconsin); and the Saint Paul, Stillwater & Taylors Falls.

28. Notices of the Saint Paul Union Depot

Company, 1880, in Hill Papers, GC, box 12, F16. The Milwaukee and the Saint Paul, Minneapolis & Manitoba were the largest shareholders.

29. Hill to Stephen, January 28, March 19, 1879, in Hill Papers, Letterpress books, Personal and private papers, vol. 1; [Minot], *The Saint Paul, Minneapolis & Manitoba.*

30. Chaney, "Early Bridges," 137.

31. Mark Twain, *Life on the Mississippi,* quoted from Winser, *The Great Northwest,* 23–24.

32. Donovan, *Gateway to the Northwest.*

33. [Minot], *The Saint Paul, Minneapolis & Manitoba;* Winser, *The Great Northwest,* 27.

34. Molyneux St. John to R. B. Angus, Liverpool, May 21, 1880, in Hill Papers, GC, box 12, F8.

35. Saint Paul, Minneapolis & Manitoba, Report of the directors for the year ending June 30, 1880, in J. J. Hill Library (HE.2791 G78).

36. Hill to Kennedy, November 16, 1879, in Hill Papers, Letterpress books, Personal and private papers, vol. 1.

37. Kerr, *Story of the Great Northern,* 16.

38. Hill wanted a fair price after all investments made by the Saint Paul & Pacific in the terminal facilities at St. Paul and the road between St. Paul and St. Anthony. Hill to Kennedy, October 30, 1878, in Hill Papers, Letterpress books, Personal and private papers, vol. 1. Draft of the agreement between the Northern Pacific and the Saint Paul & Pacific, July 1878, in Hill Papers, GC, box 11, F1. The final contracts were signed in September 1878.

39. Renz, *History of the Northern Pacific,* 56–57, 59–60.

40. For the Farley suit, see Gilbert, *Awakening Continent,* 1:52–54; Engelbourg and Bushkoff, *The Man Who Found the Money,* 68–69; Folwell, *History of Minnesota,* 3:462–74.

41. J. Carp to J. J. Hill, The Hague, February 28, 1894, in Hill Papers, GC, box 48.

42. J. Knuppe to J. J. Hill, St. Paul, May 23, 1894, in Hill Papers, GC, box 49. The text of Hill's offer of October 18, 1877 is: "Mr. Knuppe informs us that you have cabled him to say that it will be necessary in order to induce several large holders of bonds to come into the proposed arrangement, to give them an amount of the common stock of the new company when organized and that you request that we allow you to dispose of $200,000 of such stock for that purpose. We are willing to have you make this arrangement provided that it is the only change or modification which shall be made in the pending negotiations with the Committee, and provided that Mr. George Stephen, now in London, has not already made this or a similar arrangement, and that this has his approval. Very respectfully, N. W. Kittson, Jas. J. Hill."

43. J. Knuppe to J. J. Hill, St. Paul, August 23, 1912, in Hill Papers, GC, 8/18–9/16/12.

44. Ibid.

45. Myers, *History of the Great American Fortunes,* 672–78; Gilbert, *Awakening Continent,* 1:155 (quotation).

46. [Minot], *The Saint Paul, Minneapolis & Manitoba,* 24; *Railway Gazette,* vol. 31, April 15, 1887, 255.

Bibliography

For this study two archival collections have been used extensively, the J. J. Hill Papers and the Saint Paul & Pacific archives. The Hill Papers are located in the James Jerome Hill Reference Library in St. Paul, Minnesota. Although James J. Hill became involved with the Saint Paul & Pacific Railroad only after its default, he collected for his own use many papers and documents dating from the earlier period. His private correspondence—preserved in the Hill Library and catalogued as General Correspondence (referred to in this study as GC)—also has been found to be a fertile source for his own views and actions. His outgoing correspondence has been preserved in the form of letterpress books, which are unfortunately sometimes hard or even impossible to read. The microfilms made from these letterpress copies are often better, but still difficult to use. They have been used where and when possible.

The second major source were the archives of the Saint Paul & Pacific Railroad Company itself. Although a lot of papers and material must have been lost when the company's offices at St. Paul burned in 1877, some documents evidently were rescued or were kept elsewhere at the time of the fire. The successor company, the Saint Paul, Minneapolis & Manitoba, kept its predecessor's papers among its own records and in turn saw them incorporated into the archives of the Great Northern Railway. These Great Northern archives have been transferred to the Minnesota Historical Society in St. Paul and are referred to in this study as MHS, GN Records.

Details of the financial transactions with the Dutch bondholders originally came from the archives of the Amsterdam Stock Exchange but have here been summarized based on my own earlier book on the subject of Dutch investment in American railroads. Another major source of literature, pamphlets, and such was the John W. Barriger Library, housed in the Mercantile Library of St. Louis. Barriger, during his long life as a railroad executive, brought together an enormous collection of railroadiana, books, trade journals, maps, and photographs, and they have been used extensively for this study.

Books and Articles

Abdill, George B. *A Locomotive Engineer's Album: The Saga of Steam Engines in America.* Seattle: Superior Publishing Company, 1965.

————. *Rails West.* Seattle: Superior Publishing Company, 1960.

Adams, Brooks. *Railways as Public Agents: A Study in Sovereignty. With an Historical Financial Analysis of the Great Northern Railway System,* by Frederick O. Downes. Boston, 1910.

Adams, Charles F., Jr. *Notes on Railroad Accidents.* New York: Putnam, 1879.

Adler, Dorothy R. *British Investment in American Railways, 1834–1898.* Charlottesville: University Press of Virginia, 1970.

Alvarez, Eugene. *Travel on Southern Antebellum Railroads, 1828–1860.* Tuscaloosa: University of Alabama Press, 1974.

Anderson, William, and Albert J. Lobb. *A History of the Constitution of Minnesota.* Research Publications of the University of Minnesota, Studies in the Social Sciences, 15. Minneapolis: University of Minnesota Press, 1921.

Andrews, C. C. *Minnesota and Dacotah: In Letters Descriptive of a Tour Through the North-West in the Autumn of 1856.* Washington, D.C.: Robert Farnham, 1857.

Atkins, Annette. *Harvest of Grief: Grasshopper Plagues and Public Assistance in Minnesota, 1873–1878.* St. Paul: Minnesota Historical Society Press, 1984.

Baker, James H. "History of Transportation in Minnesota." *Collections of the Minnesota Historical Society* 9 (1901): 1–34.

Beadle, J. H. *The Undeveloped West: Or, Five Years in the Territories.* Philadelphia: National Publishing Company, 1873.

Berghuis, W. H. *Ontstaan en ontwikkeling van de Nederlandse beleggingsfondsen tot 1914.* Assen, the Netherlands: Van Gorcum, 1967.

Bishop, Judson W. "History of the St. Paul & Sioux City Railroad, 1864–1881." *Collections of the Minnesota Historical Society* 10, no. 1 (1905): 399–415.

Blegen, Theodore C., and Theodore L. Nydahl. *Minnesota History: A Guide to Reading and Study.* Minneapolis: University of Minnesota Press, 1960.

Blegen, Theodore C., and Philip D. Jordan, eds. *With Various Voices: Recordings of North Star Life.* St. Paul: Itasca Press, 1949.

Brown, John K. *The Baldwin Locomotive Works, 1831–1915.* Baltimore: Johns Hopkins University Press, 1995.

Brownson, Howard G. *History of the Illinois Central Railroad to 1870.* Ph.D. diss., University of Illinois, 1909.

Bruce, Robert V. *1877: Year of Violence.* Indianapolis: Bobbs-Merrill, 1959.

Bryant, Keith L., Jr. *History of the Atchison, Topeka & Santa Fe Railway.* Lincoln: University of Nebraska Press, 1974.

Carey, John W. *The Organization and History of the Chicago, Milwaukee & St. Paul Railway Company.* N.p. [1892].

Casey, Robert J. *Pioneer Railroad: The Story of the Chicago & North Western System.* New York: McGraw-Hill, 1948.

Chandler, Alfred D., Jr. *The Railroads: The Nation's First Big Business.* New York: Harcourt, Brace and World, 1965.

Chaney, Josiah B. "Early Bridges and Changes of the Land and Water Surface in the City of St. Paul." *Collections of the Minnesota Historical Society* 12 (1908): 131–48.

Chicago & Northwestern Railway Company. *Yesterday and Today: A History of the Chicago and North Western Railway System.* 3d ed. Chicago: Winship Co., 1910.

Chittenden, Hiram M. *The American Fur Trade of the Far West.* 2d ed. 2 vols. New York: The Press of the Pioneers, 1935.

Clarke, Tomas C., et al. *The American Railway: Its Construction, Development, Management and Appliances.* New York: Charles Scribner's Sons, 1889.

Cleveland, Frederick A., and Fred W. Powell. *Railroad Promotion and Capitalization in the United States.* New York: Longmans, Green, 1909.

Cochran, Thomas C. *Railroad Leaders, 1845–1890: The Business Mind in Action.* Cambridge: Harvard University Press, 1953.

Cohen Stuart, Martinus. *Zes maanden in Amerika.* 2d ed. Haarlem, the Netherlands: Tjeenk Willink, 1879.

Creighton, Donald. *A History of Canada: Dominion of the North.* Rev. ed. Boston: Houghton Mifflin, 1958.

Crooks, William. "The First Railroad in Minnesota." *Collections of the Minnesota Historical Society* 10, no. 1 (1905): 445–48.

Currie, A. W. *The Grand Trunk Railway of Canada.* Toronto: University of Toronto Press, 1957.

Derleth, August. *The Milwaukee Road: Its First Hundred Years.* New York: Creative Age Press, 1948.

Dinger, J. *Overzicht van alle ter beurze van Amsterdam verhandeld wordende binnen- en buitenlandse effecten.* 5th ed. 2 vols. Amsterdam: J. M. E. and G. H. Meijer, 1873.

Donovan, Frank P., Jr. *Gateway to the Northwest: The Story of the Minnesota Transfer Railway.* Minneapolis: Frank P. Donovan, Jr., 1954.

———. *Mileposts on the Prairie: The Story of the Minneapolis & St. Louis Railway.* New York: Simmons and Boardman, 1950.

Ducker, James H. *Men of the Steel Rails: Workers on the Atchison, Topeka & Santa Fe Railroad, 1869–1900.* Lincoln: University of Nebraska Press, 1983.

Edson, William D. *Railroad Names: A Directory of Common Carrier Railroads Operating in the United States, 1826–1982.* Potomac, Md.: William D. Edson, 1984.

Engelbourg, Saul, and Leonard Bushkoff. *The Man Who Found the Money: John Stewart Kennedy and the Financing of Western Railroads.* East Lansing: Michigan State University Press, 1996.

Evans, Paul D. *The Holland Land Company.* Buffalo: Buffalo Historical Publications, 1924.

Farley Suit Transcripts. J. J. Hill Library. HE.2791 G79 F3.

Flint, Henry M. *The Railroads of the United States: Their History and Statistics.* Philadelphia: John E. Potter, 1868.

Folsom, Simeon P. *Statement of the Inception of the Minnesota and Pacific.* J. J. Hill Library. HE.2791 G745.

Folwell, William W. "The Five Million Loan." *Collections of the Minnesota Historical Society* 15 (1915): 189–214.

———. *A History of Minnesota.* 4 vols. St. Paul: Minnesota Historical Society, 1926.

Foner, Philip S. *The Great Labor Uprising of 1877.* New York: Monad Press, 1977.

Frey, Robert L., ed. *Railroads in the Nineteenth Century.* New York: Facts on File, 1988.

Fugina, Frank J. *Lore and Lure of the Upper Mississippi River.* Winona, Minn.: Frank J. Fugina, 1945.

Gale, Walter K. V. *Iron and Steel.* London: Longmans, Green, 1969.

Gibbon, John M. *The Romantic History of the Canadian Pacific, the Northwest Passage of Today.* New York: Tudor Publishing, 1937.

Gilbert, Heather. *Awakening Continent: The Life of Lord Mount Stephen.* 2 vols. Aberdeen: Aberdeen University Press, 1976–1977.

———. "The Unaccountable Fifth: Solution of a Great Northern Enigma." *Minnesota History* 42 (1970–1971): 175–78.

Gilman, Rhoda R. "Last Days of the Upper Mississippi Fur Trade." *Minnesota History* 42 (1970–1971): 122–40.

Gluek, Alvin C. *Minnesota and the Manifest Destiny of the Canadian Northwest.* Toronto: University of Toronto Press, 1965.

Grant, H. Roger, ed. *Brownie the Boomer: The Life of Charles P. Brown, an American Railroader.* DeKalb: Northern Illinois University Press, 1991.

———. *The Corn Belt Route: A History of the Chicago Great Western Railroad Company.* DeKalb: Northern Illinois University Press, 1984.

———. *Living in the Depot: The Two-Story Railroad Station.* Iowa City: University of Iowa Press, 1993.

———. *The North Western: A History of the Chicago & North Western Railway System.* DeKalb: Northern Illinois University Press, 1997.

Greenberg, Dolores. *Financiers and Railroads, 1869–1889: A Study of Morton, Bliss & Company.* Newark: University of Delaware Press, 1984.

———. "A Study of Capital Alliances: The St. Paul & Pacific." *Canadian Historical Review* 57 (1976): 25–29.

Guide to the Lands of the First Division of the Saint Paul and Pacific Railroad Company. Minnesota Historical Society.

Hammer, Kenneth M. "Genesis of a Miller's Road: The Minneapolis, St. Paul & Saulte Ste. Marie." *Railroad History* 146 (spring 1982): 23–28.

Havighurst, Walter. *Voices on the River: The Story of the Mississippi Waterways.* New York: Macmillan, 1964.

Hayes, William E. *Iron Road to Empire: The History of One Hundred Years of the Progress and Achievements of the Rock Island Lines.* New York: Simmons and Boardman, 1953.

Heilbron, Bertha L. *The Thirty-Second State: A Pictorial History of Minnesota.* St. Paul: Minnesota Historical Society, 1958.

Herriot, Marion H. "Steamboat Transportation on the Red River." *Minnesota History* 21 (1940): 245–71.

Hewitt, George. *Minnesota: Its Advantages to Settlers.* St. Paul: Pioneer Press, 1867.

———. *Minnesota, zijn voordeelen voor landverhuizers en kolonisten.* 2d ed. Heerenveen, the Netherlands: F. Hessel, 1868.

Hidy, Muriel E. "A Dutch Investor in Minnesota, 1866: The Diary of Claude August Crommelin." *Minnesota History* 37 (1960): 152–60.

Hidy, Ralph W., Muriel E. Hidy, Roy V. Scott, and Don L. Hofsommer. *The Great Northern Railway: A History.* Boston: Harvard Business School Press, 1988.

Hill, James J. *Highways of Progress.* New York: Doubleday, Page, 1910.

Hinte, Jacob van. *Netherlanders in America: A Study of Emigration and Settlement in the Nineteenth and Twentieth Centuries in the United States.* Grand Rapids: Baker Book House, 1985.

Holbrook, Stewart H. *James Hill: A Great Life in Brief.* New York: Alfred A. Knopf, 1955.

———. *The Story of the American Railroads.* New York: Bonanza Books, 1947.

Holmquist, June D., ed. *They Chose Minnesota: A Survey of the State's Ethnic Groups.* St. Paul: Minnesota Historical Society, 1981.

Hunter, Louis C. *Steamboats on the Western Rivers: An Economic and Technological History.* Cambridge: Harvard University Press, 1949.

Innis, Harold A. *A History of the Canadian Pacific Railway.* 1923. Reprint, Toronto: University of Toronto Press, 1971.

Irwin, Leonard B. *Pacific Railways and Nationalism in the Canadian-American Northwest, 1845–1873.* New York: Greenwood Press, 1968.

Johnson, Arthur M., and Barry M. Supple. *Boston Capitalists and Western Railroads: A Study in the Nineteenth-Century Railroad Investment Process.* Cambridge: Harvard University Press, 1967.

Jones, Eliot. *Principles of Railway Transportation.* New York: Macmillan, 1927.

Josephson, Matthew. *The Robber Barons.* 1934. Reprint, New York: Harcourt, Brace and World, 1962.

Kane, Lucile M. *The Waterfall That Built a City: The Falls of St. Anthony in Minneapolis.* St. Paul: Minnesota Historical Society, 1966.

Kane, Lucile M., June D. Holmquist, and Carolyn Gilman, eds. *The Northern Expeditions of Stephen H. Long: The Journals of 1817 and 1823 and Related Documents.* St. Paul: Minnesota Historical Society, 1978.

Kerr, Duncan J. *The Story of the Great Northern Railway Company—and James J. Hill.* Princeton: Newcomen Society [Princeton University Press], 1939.

Keyes, Norman C., and Kenneth R. Middleton. "The Great Northern Railway Company: All-Time Locomotive Roster, 1861–1970." *Railroad History* 143 (1980): 20–162.

Kinert, Reed. *Early American Steam Locomotives: The First Seven Decades, 1830–1900.* New York: Bonanza Books, 1962.

Klerck, A. W. de. *De verarming van Nederland met betrekking tot den aanvoer van Amerikaansche spoorwegaandeelen.* Amsterdam: J. Clausen, 1886.

Kloos, J. H. "Geologische Notizen aus Minnesota." *Zeitschrift der Deutschen Geologischen Gesellschaft* (1871).

———. *Minnesota in zijne hulpbronnen, vruchtbaarheid en ontwikkeling geschetst voor landverhuizers en kapitalisten.* 2d ed. Amsterdam: H. de Hoogh, 1867.

———. *Report Relative to the Resources, Population and Products of the Country along the Brainerd and St. Vincent Extensions of the Saint Paul & Pacific Railroad.* St. Paul: Pioneer Printing, 1871.

Knuppe, J. *Land en dollars in Minnesota en de Dakota's: Inlichtingen voor landverhuizers.* Rotterdam: Van Hengel and Eeltjes, 1883.

Labaree, Benjamin W., William M. Fowler, Jr., Edward W. Sloan, John B. Hattendorf, Jeffrey J. Safford, and Andrew W. German. *America and the Sea: A Maritime History.* Mystic, Conn.: The Museum of America and the Sea, 1998.

Lamb, W. Kaye. *History of the Canadian Pacific Railway.* New York: Macmillan, 1977.

Larkin, F. Daniel. "John B. Jervis." In *Railroads in the Nineteenth Century,* ed. Robert L. Frey, 202–07. New York: Facts on File, 1988.

Larsen, Arthur J. "Roads and the Settlement of Minnesota." *Minnesota History* 21 (1940): 225–44.

Larson, Henrietta M. *Jay Cooke: Private Banker.* Cambridge: Harvard University Press, 1936.

———. *The Wheat Market and the Farmer in Minnesota, 1858–1900.* Studies in History, Economics, and Public Law, edited by the Faculty of Political Science of Columbia University, vol. 122, no. 2. New York: Columbia University Press, 1926.

Larson, John L. *Bonds of Enterprise: John Murray Forbes and Western Development in America's Railway Age.* Boston: Graduate School of Business Administration, Harvard University, 1984.

Lass, William E. *Minnesota: A Bicentennial History.* New York and Nashville: W. W. Norton & Company and American Association for State and Local History, 1977.

Leyendecker, Liston E. *Palace Car Prince: A Biography of George Mortimer Pullman.* Niwot: University Press of Colorado, 1992.

Licht, Walter. *Working for the Railroad: The Organization of Work in the Nineteenth Century.* Princeton: Princeton University Press, 1983.

Ljungmark, Lars. *For Sale—Minnesota: Organized Promotion of Scandinavian Immigration, 1866–1873.* Göteborg, Sweden: Akademiförlaget, 1971.

Lucas, Henry S. *Dutch Immigrant Memoirs and Related Writings.* 2 vols. Assen, the Netherlands: Van Gorcum, 1955.

———, ed. "Early Dutch Settlement in Minnesota." *Minnesota History* 28 (1947): 120–31.

Luecke, John C. *The Great Northern in Minnesota: The Foundations of an Empire.* St. Paul: Grenadier Publications, 1997.

Malone, Michael P. *James J. Hill: Empire Builder of the Northwest.* Norman: University of Oklahoma Press, 1996.

Martin, Albro. *James J. Hill and the Opening of the Northwest.* New York: Oxford University Press, 1976.

McClung, J. W. *Minnesota as it is in 1870: Its General Resources and Attractions.* St. Paul: J. W. McClung, 1870.

Mencken, August. *The Railroad Passenger Car: An Illustrated History of the First Hundred Years with Accounts of Contemporary Passengers.* Baltimore: Johns Hopkins University Press, 1957.

Mercer, Lloyd J. *Railroads and Land Grant Policy: A Study in Government Intervention.* New York: Academic Press, 1982.

Mickelson, Sig. *The Northern Pacific Railroad and the Selling of the West.* Sioux Falls: Center for Western Studies, 1993.

[Minot, Henry D.]. *The Saint Paul, Minneapolis and Manitoba Railway Company as an Investment Property.* Boston: Lee, Higginson, 1885.

Morton, Desmond. *A Short History of Canada.* Edmonton, Alberta: Hurtig, 1983.

Mountfield, David. *The Railway Barons.* New York: Norton, 1979.

Myers, Gustavus. *History of the Great American Fortunes.* 3 vols. Chicago: Charles H. Kerr, 1910.

Oberholtzer, E. P. *Jay Cooke: Financier of the Civil War.* 2 vols. Philadelphia: George W. Jacobs, 1907.

Oehler, C. M. *The Great Sioux Uprising.* 1959. Reprint, New York: Da Capo, 1997.

Oliphant, Laurence. *Minnesota and the Far West.* Edinburgh and London: William Blackwood and Sons, 1855.

Oss, S. F. van. *American Railroads as Investments.* London: Effingham Wilson, 1893.

Parsons, John E. *West on the Forty-Ninth Parallel: Red River to the Rockies, 1872–1876.* New York: William Morrow, 1963.

Pas, J. J. *Benton county in den staat Minnesota, als geschikte plaats voor eene kolonie van Nederlandsche landbouwers.* Amsterdam: C. van Helden, 1868.

Patchin, Sydney A. "The Development of Banking in Minnesota." *Minnesota History Bulletin* 2 (1917–1918): 111–68.

Petersen, William J. *Steamboating on the Upper Mississippi.* Iowa City: State Historical Society of Iowa, 1968.

Peterson, Harold F. "Early Minnesota Railroads and the Quest for Settlers." *Minnesota History* 13 (1932): 25–44.

Phillips, Paul C. *The Fur Trade.* 2 vols. Norman: University of Oklahoma Press, 1961.

Pik, J. *De Amerikaansche spoorwegwaarden: bijdrage tot de kennis der te Amsterdam verhandelde fondsen.* Groningen, the Netherlands: Erven B. van der Kamp, 1879.

Poor, Henry V. *Poor's Directory of Railway Officials.* New York, 1888.

———. *Poor's Manual of the Railroads of the United States.* New York, 1870/71–1881.

Porter, Kenneth W. *John Jacob Astor: Business Man.* 2 vols. Cambridge: Harvard University Press, 1931.

Pritchett, John P. *The Red River Valley, 1811–1849: A Regional Study.* New Haven: Yale University Press, 1942.

Prosser, Richard S. *Rails to the North Star.* Minneapolis: Dillon Press, 1966.

Pyle, Joseph G. *The Life of James J. Hill.* 2 vols. Garden City, N.Y.: Doubleday, 1917.

Quiett, Glenn C. *They Built the West: An Epic of Rails and Cities.* 1934. Reprint, New York: Cooper Square, 1965.

Raban, Jonathan. *Bad Land: An American Romance.* New York: Vintage Books, 1997.

Randall, John H. "The Beginning of Railroad Building in Minnesota." *Collections of the Minnesota Historical Society* 15 (1915): 215–20.

Reed, Brian. *Crewe Locomotive Works and Its Men.* Newton Abbot, England: David and Charles, 1982.

Regan, Ann. "The Irish." In *They Chose Minnesota,* ed. June D. Holmquist, 130–52. St. Paul: Minnesota Historical Society, 1981.

Renz, Louis T. *The History of the Northern Pacific Railroad.* Fairfield, Wash.: Ye Galleon Press, 1980.

Report of the Board of Minnesota Railroad Commissioners. Minnesota Historical Society, St. Paul. 1872–1881.

Rice, John G. "The Swedes." In *They Chose Minnesota,* ed. June D. Holmquist, 248–76. St. Paul: Minnesota Historical Society, 1981.

Rich, E. E. *The Fur Trade and the Northwest to*

1857. Toronto: McClelland and Steward, 1967.

———. *The Hudson's Bay Company, 1660–1870.* 3 vols. Toronto: McClelland and Stewart, 1960.

Richardson, Reed. *The Locomotive Engineer, 1863–1963: A Century of Railway Labor Relations and Work Rules.* Ann Arbor: University of Michigan Press, 1963.

Rife, Clarence W. "Norman W. Kittson: A Fur Trader at Pembina." *Minnesota History* 6 (1925): 225–52.

Russell, Charles E. *Stories of the Great Railroads.* Chicago: Charles H. Kerr, 1914.

Saby, Rasmus S. "Railroad Legislation in Minnesota, 1849 to 1875." *Collections of the Minnnesota Historical Society* 15 (1915): 1–188.

Saint Paul, Minneapolis & Manitoba Railway Cy. Records and Indentures. J. J. Hill Library. HE.2791 G79.

Santilhano, J. D. *Amerikaansche spoorwegen: Overzicht van de in Nederland verhandeld wordende Amerikaansche Spoorwegfondsen.* Rotterdam: Nijgh and Van Ditmar, 1884.

Sarnoff, Paul. *Russell Sage: The Money King.* New York: Ivan Obolensky, 1965.

Schevichaven, S. R. J. van. *De Noord-Amerikaansche staat Minnesota.* Amsterdam: C. F. Stemler, 1872.

Schultz, Duane. *Over the Earth I Come: The Great Sioux Uprising of 1862.* New York: St. Martin's Press, 1993.

Shannon, James P. *Catholic Colonization on the Western Frontier.* New Haven: Yale University Press, 1957.

Shippee, Lester B. "The First Railroad between the Mississippi and Lake Superior." *Mississippi Valley Historical Review* 5 (1918–1919): 121–42.

Smalley, Eugene V. *History of the Northern Pacific Railroad.* New York: Putnam, 1883.

Stevens, John H. *Personal Recollections of Minnesota and its People and Early History of Minneapolis.* Minneapolis: N.p., 1890.

Stover, John F. *American Railroads.* Chicago: University of Chicago Press, 1961.

Stromquist, Shelton. *A Generation of Boomers: The Pattern of Railroad Labor Conflict in Nineteenth-Century America.* Urbana and Chicago: University of Illinois Press, 1987.

Swank, James M. *History of the Manufacture of Iron in All Ages, and Particularly in the United States from Colonial Times to 1891.* Philadelphia: American Iron and Steel Association, 1892.

Talbott, E. H., and H. R. Hobart, eds. *The Biographical Directory of the Railway Officials of America.* Chicago and New York: The Railway Age Publishing Company, 1885.

Taylor, George R. *The Transportation Revolution, 1815–1860.* New York: Rinehart, 1951.

Taylor, George R., and Irene Neu. *The American Railroad Network, 1861–1900.* Cambridge: Harvard University Press, 1956.

Upham, Warren. *Minnesota Geographic Names: Their Origin and Historic Significance.* 1920. Reprint, St. Paul: Minnesota Historical Society, 1969.

Upham, Warren, and Rose B. Dunlap. *Minnesota Biographies.* Collections of the Minnesota Historical Society, no. 14. St. Paul: Minnesota Historical Society, 1912.

Vance, James E., Jr. *The North American Railroad: Its Origin, Evolution, and Geography.* Baltimore: Johns Hopkins University Press, 1995.

Veenendaal, Augustus J., Jr. *De IJzeren Weg in een land vol water: beknopte geschiedenis van de spoorwegen in Nederland, 1834–1958.* Amsterdam: De Bataafsche Leeuw, 1998.

———. "'Dutch' Towns in the United States." In *The Low Countries and Beyond,* ed. Robert S. Kirsner, 309–22. Publications of the American Association for Netherlandic Studies, no. 5. Lanham, Md.: University Press of America, 1993.

———. "An Example of 'Other People's Money': Dutch Capital in American Railroads." *Business and Economic History,* 2d ser., 21 (1992): 147–58.

———. *Slow Train to Paradise: How Dutch Investment Helped Build American Railroads.* Stanford: Stanford University Press, 1996.

W. v. O. B. [Oosterwijk Bruyn, W. van]. *Nieuwe finantieele beschouwingen: een handleiding bij geldbelegging in fondsen bij den aanvang van het jaar 1869.* Amsterdam: H. de Hoogh, 1869.

Ward, James A. "Daniel Craig McCallum." In *Railroads in the Nineteenth Century,* ed. Robert L. Frey, 246–48. New York: Facts on File, 1988.

———. *J. Edgar Thomson: Master of the Pennsylvania.* Westport, Conn.: Greenwood Press, 1980.

Weeveringh, J. J. *De Noord-Amerikaansche spoorwegfondsen aan de Amsterdamsche beurs.* 2d ed. Haarlem, the Netherlands: Erven F. Bohn, 1887.

Westermann, J. C. *The Netherlands and the United States: Their Relations in the Beginning of the Nineteenth Century.* The Hague: M. Nijhoff, 1935.

White, John H., Jr. *American Locomotives: An Engineering History, 1830–1880.* Baltimore: Johns Hopkins University Press, 1968.

———. *The American Railroad Freight Car from the Wood-Car Era to the Coming of Steel.* Baltimore: Johns Hopkins University Press, 1993.

———. *The American Railroad Passenger Car.* 2 vols. Baltimore: Johns Hopkins University Press, 1978.

———. *A Short History of American Locomotive Builders in the Steam Era.* Washington, D.C.: Bass, 1982.

Wilgus, William J. *The Railway Interrelations of the United States and Canada.* New Haven: Yale University Press, 1937.

Wilkins, Mira. *The History of Foreign Investment in the United States to 1914.* Cambridge: Harvard University Press, 1989.

Williams, J. Fletcher. *A History of the City of Saint Paul, and of the County of Ramsey, Minnesota.* Collections of the Minnesota Historical Society, no. 4. St. Paul: Minnesota Historical Society, 1876.

Willson, Beckles. *The Life of Lord Strathcona and Mount Royal.* 2 vols. Boston and New York: Houghton Mifflin, 1915.

Winser, Henry J. *The Great Northwest: A Guide-Book and Intinerary for the Use of Travellers over the Lines of the Northern Pacific Railroad.* New York: Putnam's, 1883.

Winter, P. J. van. *Het aandeel van den Amsterdamschen handel aan den opbouw van het Amerikaansche gemeenebest.* 2 vols. The Hague: M. Nijhoff, 1927–1933.

Index